FRUIT AND VEGGIES 101 BUSHES & BERRIES CONTAINER & RAISED BEDS FRUIT GARDENS

GARDENING GUIDE ON HOW TO GROW FRUIT BUSHES & BERRIES USING ORGANIC STRATEGIES FOR CONTAINER & RAISED BEDS GARDENS (PERFECT FOR BEGINNERS)

GREEN ROOTS

Fruit and Veggies 101

BUSHES & BERRIES
CONTAINER & RAISED
BEDS FRUIT GARDENS

GARDENING GUIDE ON HOW TO GROW FRUIT
BUSHES & BERRIES USING ORGANIC STRATEGIES
FOR CONTAINER & RAISED BEDS GARDENS

(Perfect For Beginners)

GREEN ROOTS

CONTENTS

A SPECIAL GIFT TO OUR READERS

Included with your purchase of this book is our list of "27 horticulture Myths Debunked"
This list will provide and aid you as a new (or soon-to-be) gardener by actively informing you of the myths and irrelevant practices to avoid during your gardening journey.

Visit the link below to let us know which email address to deliver to

www.gardengreenroots.com

INTRODUCTION

AN INTRODUCTION TO CONTAINER & RAISED BED FRUIT GARDENING

Gardening is one of the most rewarding and therapeutic activities one can engage in. It not only provides an avenue to connect with nature but also offers a sense of accomplishment when you see your plants bloom and bear fruit. However, not everyone has the luxury of a large garden space. This is where fruit containers and raised bed gardening come into play.

Fruit container gardening is a method of growing fruits in containers instead of planting them in the ground. This practice is ideal for urban dwellers with limited outdoor space, as it allows for the cultivation of a variety of fruits in small spaces like balconies or patios. From strawberries to dwarf varieties of citrus trees, container gardening opens up a world of possibilities to those who thought they couldn't grow their own fruit.

On the other hand, raised bed gardening involves growing plants in soil that is higher than the surrounding soil. Raised beds are generally enclosed with wood, stone, or concrete and can be of any length or width. The key advantage of this method is improved drainage and soil quality, which can lead to higher yields. They're particularly popular for growing vegetables and herbs but are equally effective for fruit-bearing plants.

Both methods offer several benefits, including better control over soil conditions, easier pest and weed management, and higher productivity due to improved growing conditions. Additionally, they make gardening accessible to people with mobility issues, as they reduce the need for bending and kneeling.

This book will guide you through the process of setting up your own fruit container and raised bed garden, from choosing the right containers and soil mix, selecting the best fruit varieties, maintaining your plants, to finally harvesting your own fresh, homegrown fruits. Whether you're a seasoned gardener or a complete beginner, these gardening methods will bring you closer to achieving your dream of growing your own fruit, no matter how limited your space might be.

WHAT IS FRUIT CONTAINER & RAISED BED GARDENING?

Understanding the concept of fruit container and raised bed gardening is crucial for several reasons. Firstly, these methods democratize gardening, making it accessible to a wider range of people. Whether you live in a high-rise apartment or have mobility issues that make traditional gardening difficult, these techniques allow you to cultivate your own fruits.

Secondly, they offer greater control over your gardening environment. In a container or raised bed, you have the ability to customize the soil, control the watering, and even move the plants around for optimal sunlight. This can result in healthier plants and better fruit yields compared to traditional in-ground gardening.

Thirdly, fruit container and raised bed gardening encourage sustainable living practices. By growing your own fruit, you contribute to reducing the demand for commercially grown produce, which often involves long-distance transportation and extensive use of pesticides and fertilizers. This way, you're not only feeding yourself but also helping the environment.

Finally, understanding these gardening methods can bring immense personal satisfaction. There's something uniquely rewarding about eating fruit that you've grown yourself. It can also serve as a relaxing hobby that reduces stress and promotes physical well-being.

Understanding the concept of fruit container and raised bed gardening is not just about learning to grow your own fruit—it's about improving your quality of life, promoting sustainability, and finding joy in the simple act of nurturing a plant from seed to fruit-bearing maturity.

THE SCIENCE BEHIND WHY FRUIT CONTAINER & RAISED BED GARDENING WORKS

Fruit container and raised bed gardening are based on several scientific principles that optimize plant growth, which include the control of soil composition, temperature regulation, efficient water use, and pest management.

Firstly, the soil composition can be precisely controlled in containers and raised beds. The soil is the primary source of nutrients for plants, and different fruits have specific nutrient requirements. In traditional gardening, you are dependent on the natural soil conditions, which may not be ideal for all types of fruit. However, in container and raised bed gardening, you can tailor the soil mix to meet the specific needs of each fruit plant.

This includes adjusting the pH level, nutrient content, and organic matter in the soil, which directly affects the health and productivity of the fruit plant.

Secondly, temperature regulation plays a crucial role in plant growth. Containers and raised beds warm up more quickly than ground soil because they are exposed to more sunlight from all sides. This can extend the growing season, allowing for earlier planting in the spring and longer growth into the fall. Likewise, in colder climates, portable containers can be moved indoors or to warmer locations to protect the plants from frost.

Thirdly, efficient water usage is another advantage of these gardening methods. Both containers and raised beds offer superior drainage compared to in-ground gardens. Overwatering can lead to waterlogged soil and root rot, which can kill plants. However, with improved drainage in containers and raised beds, excess water can easily escape, reducing the risk of overwatering. At the same time, the enclosed nature of containers and raised beds helps retain the necessary moisture, keeping the soil from drying out too quickly.

Lastly, pest management is easier in container and raised bed gardening. Raising the soil level makes it harder for pests to reach the plants. Additionally, containers can be easily moved if a pest problem arises, preventing the spread of pests and diseases.

The science behind fruit container and raised bed gardening involves a combination of soil science, thermodynamics, hydrology, and pest management. These principles work together to create an optimal growing environment, leading to healthier plants and higher fruit yields. This makes these gardening methods not only practical but also efficient and environmentally friendly.

BALANCE & DIVERSITY IN A SUSTAINABLE FRUIT GARDEN

The importance of balance and diversity in a sustainable fruit garden using fruit container and raised bed gardening cannot be overstated. These two principles are crucial to creating a healthy, productive, eco-friendly garden.

Balance in a fruit garden is about ensuring that each element of the garden contributes to the overall health and productivity of the system. In container and raised bed gardening, this means balancing the types of fruit plants you grow and the resources they require. For instance, different fruits have varying nutrient, sunlight, and water needs. By understanding these requirements, you can ensure that your garden has a balanced mix of plants that complement rather than compete with each other. This balance can also extend to the soil composition, as the nutrient needs of one plant can be supplemented by the waste of another.

Diversity, on the other hand, is about having a wide variety of fruit plants in your garden. A diverse garden is more resilient to pests and diseases, as it reduces the likelihood of a single pest or disease wiping out your entire harvest. Each plant species attracts different beneficial insects and repels certain pests, creating a natural form of pest control. Additionally, diversity maximizes the use of space, as different plants have different growth habits and can fill various niches in the garden. For example, some fruit plants may be climbers and can be grown vertically, while others are bushy and provide ground cover.

Furthermore, diversity in a fruit garden not only creates a healthier ecosystem but also leads to a more nutritious and varied harvest. Different fruits provide different types of nutrients, so a diverse garden will provide a more balanced diet. Additionally, if one type of fruit fails to produce in a particular season, you'll still have others to rely on.

In a sustainable fruit garden, balance and diversity work hand in hand. A balanced garden ensures that resources are used efficiently and that plants complement rather than compete with each other. Meanwhile, a diverse garden is more resilient and productive, providing a variety of nutrients and tastes. By applying these principles to container and raised bed gardening, you can create a sustainable fruit garden that's good for you and the environment.

CHAPTER 1
CONTAINER & RAISED BED FRUIT GARDENS (TECHNIQUES)

BENEFITS & DISADVANTAGES OF FRUIT CONTAINER GARDENING

Understanding the benefits and disadvantages of fruit container gardening is crucial for various reasons. Firstly, it helps you decide whether this gardening method aligns with your lifestyle, resources, and gardening goals. For instance, if you live in an apartment with limited space but still want to enjoy home-grown fruits, understanding the space-saving benefit of container gardening could encourage you to try it. Equally, knowing the challenges, such as the frequent watering needs and potential for higher costs, can help you better prepare and plan, ensuring a more successful gardening experience.

Secondly, understanding the pros and cons of container gardening can guide your choice of plants. Not all fruits are suitable for container growth; some may become root-bound or stressed in a pot, leading to poor growth and fruit production. By knowing the limitations of container gardening, you can select dwarf or miniaturized varieties that are bred to thrive in containers.

Lastly, this understanding can influence your care practices. Container-grown plants have different care requirements compared to their in-ground counterparts. For example, they may need more frequent watering and feeding due to the limited soil volume. Awareness of these needs can help you provide optimal care, leading to healthier plants and more bountiful yields.

Understanding the benefits and disadvantages of fruit container gardening is vital to making informed decisions, selecting suitable plants, and providing appropriate care. It equips you with the knowledge needed to overcome challenges and maximize the advantages, ultimately leading to a rewarding gardening experience.

Benefits Of Fruit Container Gardening

Fruit container gardening provides a multitude of benefits that make it an attractive choice for many gardeners. One of the standout advantages is its adaptability. Container gardening lets you grow a wide variety of fruit trees in confined spaces. This makes it perfect for those with small yards, balconies, or even just a sunny windowsill. The portability of containers also means you can move your plants around to maximize sunlight, protect them from harsh weather conditions, or bring them indoors during colder months if they aren't frost-resistant.

Another prominent benefit of container gardening is the level of control it gives over the growing conditions. With traditional gardening, you're primarily dependent on the existing soil composition; however, with container gardening, you can tailor the soil mix to perfectly suit the nutritional needs of each plant. This ability to create an optimal growing environment often leads to healthier plants and potentially more abundant harvests. Plus, starting with fresh, sterile potting soil can significantly reduce the risk of soil-borne diseases and pests.

Container gardening also offers enhanced accessibility, making gardening possible for those who may find traditional gardening physically challenging. Tending to plants in containers eliminates the need for strenuous activities like digging or bending over low beds, making it a more inclusive activity that can be enjoyed by people of all ages and abilities.

Disadvantages Of Fruit Container Gardening

Despite these numerous benefits, fruit container gardening isn't without its drawbacks. One of the main challenges is ensuring adequate hydration for your plants. Containers can dry out much faster than ground soil, especially in warmer climates, requiring frequent watering. Some fruit plants require a lot of moisture, and failure to meet these needs can lead to stressed plants and reduced fruit production.

Limited root space is another disadvantage associated with container gardening. Fruit trees, in particular can quickly become root-bound if the container is too small, stunting their growth and productivity. It's crucial to select dwarf or miniaturized fruit varieties suited for container growth and to repot your plants regularly to give them room to grow.

Finally, the cost can be a deterrent for some. Setting up a container garden can be more expensive than traditional gardening due to the cost of containers, potting soil, and specially bred dwarf or miniature fruit tree varieties. However, with careful planning and budgeting, it's possible to establish an affordable and productive container garden.

While fruit container gardening offers numerous benefits, including adaptability, control over growing conditions, and enhanced accessibility, it also comes with challenges such as regular watering, limited root space, and potentially higher costs. Evaluating these pros and cons can help you determine if container gardening is the right choice for your gardening needs.

BENEFITS & DISADVANTAGES OF FRUIT RAISED BEDS GARDENING

Understanding the benefits and disadvantages of fruit raised bed gardening is essential for several reasons. Similarly to container gardening it allows you to decide whether this form of gardening is suitable for your circumstances, needs, and preferences.

For example, if you live in an area with poor soil quality or drainage issues, knowing that raised beds allow for better soil control and improved drainage could encourage you to adopt this method. On the other hand, being aware of the potential challenges such as the initial time, effort, and cost to set up the beds can help you plan accordingly.

Secondly, this understanding guides your choice of plants. Some fruit plants might thrive better in raised beds than others due to factors like root depth and spread. Knowing the advantages and constraints of raised bed gardening enables you to select fruit varieties that are more likely to succeed in this environment.

Finally, understanding the pros and cons of raised bed gardening influences your care and maintenance practices. Raised beds may require different watering, fertilizing, and pest management strategies compared to ground-level beds and even containers. For instance, they might dry out faster, necessitating more frequent watering. Awareness of these nuances helps you provide the proper care, leading to healthier plants and higher yields.

Recognizing the advantages and drawbacks of cultivating fruit in raised beds is essential for making well-informed choices, choosing appropriate plants, and delivering the best possible care. It gives you the know-how to fully utilize the benefits and lessen the drawbacks, which will ultimately make gardening more fruitful and fulfilling.

Benefits Of Fruit Raised Beds Gardening

Raised bed gardening for fruits provides numerous benefits and is a popular choice among many gardeners. One of the primary advantages is the improved soil conditions that raised beds offer. By creating a raised bed, you have complete control over the soil's composition, allowing you to tailor it to the specific needs of your fruit plants. This can lead to healthier plants and more abundant yields.

Another significant benefit of raised bed gardening is the enhanced drainage it provides. Excess water can quickly drain away, reducing the risk of waterlogging and root rot, which can be detrimental to many fruit plants. Raised beds also warm up faster than the ground in the spring, giving you a head start on the growing season.

Raised beds can also make gardening easier physically, as they require less bending and stooping than traditional in-ground beds. This makes them a great option for older gardeners or those with physical limitations. Additionally, raised beds can help keep out some pests, such as slugs and snails, and prevent soil compaction, as you don't need to walk on the soil to care for your plants.

Disadvantages Of Fruit Raised Beds Gardening

Though these benefits, elevated bed gardening for fruit has a few drawbacks. The initial setup presents one of the biggest obstacles. Building raised beds takes time, effort, and even a big financial investment, particularly if you choose higher-quality materials or larger beds.

Watering can also be challenging, as raised beds can dry out faster than ground-level beds due to improved drainage. This means they may require more frequent watering, particularly during hot weather. It's important to balance this with the risk of overwatering, which can also harm your plants.

Space can be another limitation with raised bed gardening. The finite space within a bed may restrict the size and number of fruit plants you can grow. Some fruit plants have extensive root systems and may not thrive in the limited space of a raised bed.

Fruit raised bed gardening has many advantages, including better drainage, better soil conditions, and easier physical access. However, there are also drawbacks, including initial setup costs and work, the need for watering, and possible space constraints. By weighing these benefits and drawbacks, you can decide if raised bed gardening is the best option for your gardening needs.

TYPES OF CONTAINERS FOR FRUIT GARDENING

Plastic Pots

Plastic pots are vessels made from various types of plastic used in fruit container gardening. They are available in

various sizes, shapes, and colors, offering gardeners a versatile option for cultivating their favorite fruit varieties.

Benefits of using plastic pots in fruit container gardening include:

- Lightweight: Plastic pots are easy to move around, allowing you to adjust their placement based on changing sunlight or weather conditions.
- Moisture Retention: Plastic pots retain moisture well due to their non-porous nature, which is beneficial for many fruit plants that require consistent soil moisture.
- Cost-Effective: Plastic pots are generally less expensive than those made from materials like ceramic or terracotta, making them an economical choice, especially if you need multiple pots.
- Durability: Plastic pots are resistant to breakage, unlike pots made from more fragile materials, increasing their lifespan.

Disadvantages to consider with plastic pots:

- Heat Sensitivity: Plastic pots can become very hot when exposed to direct sunlight, potentially damaging the roots of your plants, particularly those sensitive to heat.
- Risk of Waterlogging: While good at retaining moisture, without adequate drainage, plastic pots can lead to waterlogged soil and potential root damage due to overwatering.
- Environmental Impact: Over time, exposure to the elements, particularly UV light, can cause plastic pots to degrade and become brittle. This not only shortens

their usable life but also raises environmental concerns due to the longevity of plastic waste.

While plastic pots offer benefits such as being lightweight, cost-effective, and durable, they also have drawbacks like potential overheating, risk of waterlogging, and environmental impact. These considerations should be taken into account when deciding whether plastic pots are the right choice for your fruit container gardening needs.

Ceramic or Clay Pots

In container gardening, ceramic or clay pots are made of baked clay used to cultivate fruit plants. They come in various sizes, styles, and patterns and are frequently glazed on the outside for aesthetic appeal. This makes them a desirable choice for gardeners who wish to blend practicality with visual appeal.

Benefits of using ceramic or clay pots in fruit container gardening include:

- Aesthetics: Ceramic or clay pots often have a more traditional and appealing look compared to plastic pots. They come in various colors, designs, and finishes, adding a decorative touch to your garden.
- Temperature Control: Clay pots can help moderate soil temperature. They stay cooler in the heat because they allow air and moisture to pass through their walls.
- Durability: High-quality ceramic or clay pots can last for many years if properly cared for, making them a good long-term investment for your garden.
- Weight: Their heavier weight can benefit top-heavy

plants or in wind-prone areas where lighter pots might tip over.

Disadvantages to consider with ceramic or clay pots:

- Weight: On the contrary, the heavy weight of ceramic or clay pots can be a disadvantage if you need to move your plants frequently.
- Cost: Ceramic or clay pots tend to be more expensive than plastic or metal containers.
- Moisture Loss: Clay pots are porous and can lose moisture quickly, especially in hot weather, requiring more frequent watering.
- Risk of Damage: Ceramic or clay pots can break or crack in cold weather if left outside and susceptible to damage if dropped.

Although ceramic or clay pots have advantages like improved aesthetics, stability, temperature control, and longevity, they also have drawbacks like weight, cost, moisture loss, and damage risk. You should weigh these aspects while determining if clay or ceramic pots are better for your fruit container gardening needs.

Wooden Boxes/Planters

Wooden boxes or planters in fruit container gardening refer to containers made from various types of wood used for cultivating fruit plants. They can range from small, simple boxes to large, intricate planters, and they often add a rustic and natural aesthetic to your garden space.

Benefits of using wooden boxes or planters in fruit container gardening include:

- Aesthetics: Wooden boxes or planters have a natural, rustic look that can enhance the overall ambiance of your garden.
- Insulation: Wood provides good insulation for the soil, helping to protect roots from temperature fluctuations.
- Versatility: Wooden boxes or planters come in a wide range of sizes and styles and can be painted or stained to match any decor.
- Durability: If properly cared for and treated, wooden planters can last for many years.

Disadvantages to consider with wooden boxes or planters:

- Maintenance: Wooden boxes or planters may require more maintenance than other options. They must be properly sealed and regularly treated to prevent rot and insect damage.
- Weight: Larger wooden planters can be heavy and difficult to move around.
- Moisture Retention: Wood can retain moisture, which can lead to rot if not properly managed. It's important to ensure your wooden planter has adequate drainage.
- Cost: High-quality wooden planters can be more expensive than plastic or metal options.

In summary, while wooden boxes or planters offer benefits such as aesthetic appeal, insulation, versatility, and durability, they also present challenges like increased maintenance, potential for heaviness, risk of rot, and higher cost. These factors should be considered when deciding whether wooden boxes or planters are the right choice for your fruit container gardening needs.

Fabric Pots

Fabric pots in fruit container gardening are made from breathable fabric for growing fruit plants. They are a relatively new addition to the gardening world, but their unique properties have quickly made them a popular choice among many gardeners.

Benefits of using fabric pots in fruit container gardening include:

- Root Pruning: When roots reach the edge of a fabric pot, they sense the drier soil exposed to the air, which causes them to form lateral branches. This results in a more fibrous root system, leading to healthier, more productive plants.
- Improved Drainage and Aeration: The porous nature of fabric pots allows for excellent drainage and aeration, reducing the risk of overwatering and promoting healthier root growth.
- Temperature Control: Fabric pots, due to their breathable material, can help keep the root zone cooler in hot weather.
- Portability: Fabric pots are lightweight and often come with handles, making them easy to move around.

Disadvantages to consider with fabric pots:

- Watering Frequency: Due to their breathability and excellent drainage, fabric pots may require more frequent watering compared to other types of pots.
- Durability: While fabric pots are generally tough and long-lasting, they may not last as long as pots made from materials like plastic or ceramic.

- Aesthetics: While functional, fabric pots may not offer the same aesthetic appeal as ceramic, clay, or wooden pots.

While fabric pots provide advantages such as root pruning, enhanced drainage and aeration, temperature control, and portability, they also have drawbacks such as higher watering frequency, the possibility of reduced durability, and a lack of aesthetic appeal. These criteria should be examined while determining whether cloth pots are the best option for your fruit container gardening needs.

Self-Watering Containers

Self-watering containers in fruit container gardening are planters designed with a built-in water reservoir. This reservoir stores water and gradually delivers it to the plant's roots, reducing the need for frequent watering.

Benefits of using self-watering containers in fruit container gardening include:

- Efficiency: Self-watering containers can save time and effort by reducing the frequency of watering needed. They can also conserve water by reducing evaporation and runoff.
- Improved Plant Health: By providing a consistent water supply, self-watering containers can help prevent issues related to overwatering or underwatering, promoting healthier and more productive plants.
- Convenience: These containers are ideal for gardeners who travel frequently or those who simply forget to water regularly.

- Reduced Water Waste: Because water is delivered directly to the plant's roots, less water is wasted through evaporation or runoff.

Disadvantages to consider with self-watering containers:

- Overwatering Risks: If not monitored closely, self-watering containers can potentially overwater plants, especially those that prefer drier soil.
- Limited Sizes and Styles: Self-watering containers may offer less variety in terms of size and style than other types of planters.
- Cost: Self-watering containers can be more expensive than traditional pots or planters.
- Maintenance: These containers may require additional maintenance, such as cleaning the reservoir and wicking system to prevent mold and algae growth.

While self-watering containers offer benefits like efficiency, improved plant health, convenience, and reduced water waste, they also present challenges like risk of overwatering, limited variety, higher cost, and increased maintenance. These factors should be considered when deciding whether self-watering containers are the right choice for your fruit container gardening needs.

Hanging Baskets

Hanging baskets in fruit container gardening are planters designed to hang from a structure, such as a porch, pergola, or balcony railing. These containers are commonly used for growing small fruit plants and vines with a trailing growth habit.

Benefits of using hanging baskets in fruit container gardening include:

- Space-saving: Hanging baskets provide a great solution for gardening in small spaces as they do not take up any ground space.
- Aesthetics: Hanging baskets can add visual interest to your garden, balcony, or patio, especially when filled with colorful fruiting plants.
- Pest Control: Hanging baskets can help keep fruit plants out of reach from some ground-dwelling pests.
- Ease of Harvest: Fruit grown in hanging baskets can often be easier to harvest because the fruit hangs down at eye level.

Disadvantages to consider with hanging baskets:

- Watering Needs: Hanging baskets tend to dry out quickly and therefore may require more frequent watering than other types of containers.
- Limited Space: Hanging baskets offer limited space for root growth, which may restrict the size and number of plants you can grow.
- Weight Restrictions: Weight restrictions may need to be considered depending on the strength of the structure from which they're hanging.
- Exposure: Plants in hanging baskets may be more exposed to wind and elements than those in ground-level containers, which could impact their health.

While hanging baskets have advantages such as reduced space requirements, aesthetic appeal, ease of harvesting, and pest management, they also have drawbacks such as higher watering requirements, restricted space, weight limits, and increased exposure. When choosing if hanging baskets are the best option for your fruit container gardening needs, take these facts into account.

Grow Bags

Grow bags in fruit container gardening are flexible, portable containers made of breathable fabric, often with handles for easy movement. They have become increasingly popular among gardeners for their versatility and affordability.

Benefits of using grow bags in fruit container gardening include:

- Aeration: Grow bags' porous fabric allows roots to breathe, promoting healthier and more robust root growth.
- Drainage: Grow bags offer excellent drainage, reducing the risk of overwatering.
- Temperature Control: Unlike plastic pots, which can overheat in sunny conditions, the fabric of grow bags can help regulate soil temperature.
- Portability: Lightweight and often equipped with handles, grow bags are easy to move around as needed.

Disadvantages to consider with grow bags:

- Watering Frequency: Grow bags may require more frequent watering than other types of containers due to their breathability and excellent drainage.
- Durability: While they are generally quite rugged, grow bags may not last as long as traditional pots when exposed to harsh weather conditions over time.

- Size Limitations: While grow bags come in a variety of sizes, they may not be suitable for larger fruit trees that require a lot of space for root growth.
- Aesthetics: Some gardeners may not find grow bags as visually appealing as ceramic or wooden planters.

In summary, while grow bags offer benefits such as aeration, good drainage, temperature control, and portability, they also present challenges like increased watering frequency, less durability, size limitations, and a lack of aesthetic appeal. These factors should be considered when deciding whether grow bags are the right choice for your fruit container gardening needs.

Barrels or Tubs

Barrels or tubs in fruit container gardening are large containers, often made of wood or plastic, that are used to grow plants. They provide ample space for the roots of fruit trees and bushes, making them an excellent choice for gardeners who wish to cultivate larger fruit varieties without the need for a traditional ground garden.

Benefits of using barrels or tubs in fruit container gardening include:

- Large Volume: Barrels and tubs offer a large volume of soil, which can support larger fruit trees or multiple smaller fruit plants.
- Aesthetics: The rustic look of wooden barrels can add visual appeal to your garden.
- Insulation: The thickness of the barrels or tubs can provide good insulation for the roots against extreme temperature fluctuations.

- Longevity: If properly maintained, wooden barrels can last for many years.

Disadvantages to consider with barrels or tubs:

- Weight: Once filled with soil and plants, barrels and tubs can be quite heavy and difficult to move.
- Drainage: Depending on their design, barrels and tubs may not have adequate drainage, which can lead to waterlogging.
- Cost: Large barrels or tubs, particularly those made from high-quality wood, can be expensive.
- Maintenance: Wooden containers may require regular maintenance, such as sealing, to prevent rot and prolong their life.

Barrels or tubs in fruit gardening come with advantages such as ample space, visual appeal, temperature regulation, and durability. However, they also pose potential difficulties due to their substantial weight, possible drainage problems, elevated cost, and the need for regular maintenance. These elements should be considered when determining if barrels or tubs are the most suitable option for your fruit container gardening endeavors.

Window Boxes

Window boxes in fruit container gardening refer to narrow, rectangular containers that are often affixed under windows or on balcony railings. They are ideal for growing small fruiting plants and herbs, adding both beauty and functionality to your home.

Benefits of using window boxes in fruit container gardening include:

- Aesthetics: Window boxes can add a charming and decorative element to your home's exterior.
- Space-saving: For those with limited space, window boxes offer a solution that doesn't require yard or floor space.
- Accessibility: Plants grown in window boxes are conveniently located for easy care and harvest.
- Microclimate Control: Depending on their location, window boxes may benefit from the microclimate created by your home, such as additional warmth from a sunny wall.

Disadvantages to consider with window boxes:

- Limited Space: Window boxes offer limited space for root growth, which may restrict the size and number of plants you can grow.
- Watering Needs: Due to their small size and exposure to the sun, window boxes may require frequent watering.
- Weight Limitations: Depending on the strength of your window or railing, you may need to consider weight restrictions when filling your window box with soil and plants.
- Exposure: Plants in window boxes can be exposed to harsh weather conditions, including wind and heavy rain, which could impact their health.

To sum up, window boxes provide advantages such as enhancing beauty, saving space, easy accessibility, and the possibility of controlling microclimates. However, they also come with drawbacks such as restricted space, the need for frequent watering, weight constraints, and heightened exposure. These aspects should be weighed carefully when determining if window boxes are a suitable option for your fruit container gardening requirements.

TYPES OF RAISED BEDS FOR FRUIT GARDENING

Wooden Raised Beds

Wooden raised beds in fruit gardening refer to elevated structures, typically made from untreated timber, that are used for growing a variety of fruits. These beds are filled with high-quality soil and compost, providing an optimal environment for root growth.

Benefits of using wooden raised beds in fruit gardening include:

- Improved Soil Conditions: Raised beds allow gardeners to fill them with rich, fertile soil, which can improve growth and yield.

- Better Drainage: Raised beds provide excellent drainage, reducing the risk of waterlogging or root rot.
- Ease of Access: Raised beds' height makes it easier to plant, care for, and harvest fruit without needing to bend or kneel.
- Pest Control: Raised beds can help to deter some ground-dwelling pests, protecting your fruit plants.

Disadvantages to consider with wooden raised beds:

- Cost: Building or buying wooden raised beds can be more expensive than traditional in-ground gardening.
- Maintenance: Wood can deteriorate over time, so wooden raised beds may require regular maintenance or replacement.
- Watering Needs: Raised beds can dry out faster than ground-level soil, so they may require more frequent watering.
- Limited Mobility: Once installed, raised beds are difficult to move.

To sum up, wooden raised beds in fruit gardening provide advantages such as enhanced soil quality, superior drainage, convenient accessibility, and efficient pest management. However, they also come with potential difficulties due to their elevated cost, the necessity for regular upkeep, increased watering requirements, and restricted portability. These aspects should be carefully weighed when determining if wooden raised beds are the most suitable choice for your fruit gardening endeavors.

Composite Raised Beds

Composite raised beds in fruit gardening refer to elevated structures made from a mixture of wood fiber and recycled plastics. This combination creates a durable and eco-friendly material that's ideal for growing fruits.

Benefits of using composite raised beds in fruit gardening include:

- Durability: Composite materials are resistant to rot, insects, and weather-related damage, which can extend the lifespan of your raised beds.
- Eco-Friendly: Composite raised beds are often made from recycled materials, making them a more environmentally friendly choice.
- Low Maintenance: Unlike wooden beds, composite raised beds do not need to be painted or stained and they resist warping and cracking.
- Soil Health: Similar to other raised beds, composite raised beds allow you to control the quality of the soil and drainage, which can lead to healthier fruit plants.

Disadvantages to consider with composite raised beds:

- Cost: Composite raised beds can be more expensive initially than their wooden counterparts.
- Heat Retention: Composite materials can retain heat, which might cause damage to the roots in very hot climates.
- Limited Sizes and Shapes: Composite raised beds are typically available in standard sizes and shapes, which may limit your design options.
- Weight: Composite materials can be heavier than

wood, making these beds more difficult to move once installed.

Composite raised beds bring advantages such as robustness, environmental friendliness, minimal maintenance, and enhanced soil vitality to your fruit gardening. However, they also come with potential hurdles like a steeper initial investment, possible heat conservation, fewer design alternatives, and added weight. These considerations should be thoughtfully evaluated when deciding if composite raised beds align with your requirements for fruit gardening.

Metal Raised Beds

Metal raised beds in fruit gardening refer to elevated structures made primarily from metal materials, such as galvanized steel or aluminum. These types of beds are designed to contain nutrient-rich soil where various kinds of fruit plants can thrive.

Benefits of using metal raised beds in fruit gardening include:

- Durability: Metal raised beds are generally more durable and longer-lasting than their wooden or plastic counterparts. They are resistant to the elements, pests, and decay.
- Thermal Conductivity: Metal raised beds can absorb heat during the day and release it at night, which can help to extend the growing season.
- Low Maintenance: These beds require minimal maintenance as they do not crack, splinter, or rot like wood.
- Aesthetically Pleasing: Metal raised beds often offer a sleek, modern look that can enhance the aesthetic of your garden.

Disadvantages of using metal raised beds:

- Heat Conduction: While beneficial in cooler climates, in very hot areas, metal can overheat the soil, potentially damaging plant roots.
- Potential for Corrosion: Some metals may be rust-prone if not adequately treated or maintained.
- Cost: High-quality metal raised beds can be more expensive upfront compared to other materials.
- Safety Concerns: Metal edges can be sharp, posing a risk if not properly finished or if used around children or pets.

Metal raised beds offer advantages such as longevity, heat conduction, easy upkeep, and visual attractiveness for your fruit gardening. However, they also introduce possible drawbacks like soil overheating, risk of rusting, elevated cost, and safety issues. Carefully balancing these benefits and challenges can assist in deciding if metal raised beds are the appropriate choice for your fruit garden.

Concrete Raised Beds

Concrete raised beds in fruit gardening are elevated structures constructed from concrete blocks or poured concrete. These beds provide a well-defined, robust space filled with nutrient-rich soil that is ideal for cultivating various types of fruit plants.

The benefits of using concrete raised beds in fruit gardening include:

- Durability: Unlike wood or plastic, concrete is incredibly durable and can withstand harsh weather conditions, pests, and rot.

- Thermal Properties: Concrete has the ability to absorb heat during the day and release it at night, which can help extend the growing season.
- Design Flexibility: Concrete raised beds can be custom-made into numerous shapes and sizes, allowing for a more personalized garden layout.
- Low Maintenance: Concrete requires little maintenance; it does not need to be repainted or treated like wood.

Disadvantages of using concrete raised beds:

- Cost: The initial cost of materials and construction for concrete raised beds can be higher than other options.
- Immobility: Concrete beds are difficult to move or change once installed, unlike more flexible materials.
- Alkalinity: Concrete can increase the soil's pH level, which could affect the growth of certain fruits that prefer acidic conditions.
- Heat Retention: In hot climates, concrete may retain too much heat, potentially harming plant roots.

Concrete raised beds offer several advantages for fruit gardening, including their robustness, ability to regulate soil temperature, versatility in design, and low upkeep needs. However, they also present specific challenges, such as a more substantial initial investment, lack of mobility once installed, possible issues with increased soil alkalinity, and potential for retaining too much heat. It's essential to weigh these pros and cons when determining whether concrete raised beds align with your specific fruit gardening requirements.

Stone or Brick Raised Beds

Stone or Brick Raised Beds are sturdy structures used in fruit gardening. They provide a contained area for fruit plants and offer a clear demarcation between the garden and the rest of the yard, creating a specialized space for your garden endeavors.

Benefits of using stone or brick raised beds in fruit gardening include:

- Durability: Stone and brick are highly durable materials and can withstand harsh weather conditions, pests, and rot.
- Aesthetics: These materials offer a traditional cottage garden vibe and can enhance the overall look of your garden.
- Thermal Properties: Stone and brick can absorb heat during the day and release it at night, potentially extending the growing season.
- Flexibility: Stone and brick raised beds can be adjusted in size more easily to fit specific areas.

However, there are also disadvantages to consider:

- Cost: The initial cost of materials and construction can be higher compared to other options.
- Immobility: Once installed, these beds are difficult to move or modify.
- Installation Time: Building stone or brick raised beds can be time-consuming.
- Potential for Soil Drying: These materials can cause the soil to dry out faster, requiring more frequent watering.

While stone or brick raised beds offer benefits like durability, aesthetics, thermal properties, and flexibility, they also come with potential downsides such as higher initial cost, immobility, lengthy installation time, and faster soil drying. These factors should be weighed when deciding if stone or brick raised beds are the right choice for your fruit gardening needs.

Vinyl Raised Beds

Vinyl raised beds in fruit gardening are structures constructed from high-quality, eco-friendly vinyl materials. These elevated platforms create a dedicated space filled with nutrient-rich soil, making them ideal for growing a variety of fruit plants.

The advantages of using vinyl raised beds in fruit gardening include:

- Durability: Made from high-quality vinyl materials, these beds are built to last, providing excellent protection for your fruits and soil.
- Low Maintenance: Vinyl does not require repainting or treatment, making it a low-maintenance option.
- Eco-Friendly: Many vinyl raised beds are crafted from food-grade, BPA/phthalate-free vinyl, ensuring safe food production.
- Ease of Assembly: Most vinyl raised beds are designed for tool-free assembly, making them easy to install.

However, there are also some disadvantages to consider:

- Cost: The initial cost of vinyl raised beds can be higher compared to other options.

- Heat Retention: Vinyl can retain heat, which might be harmful to plant roots in hot climates.
- Sustainability Concerns: While many manufacturers use eco-friendly vinyl, some may still use non-recyclable materials.
- Aesthetic Limitations: Some gardeners prefer the natural look of wood or stone over the synthetic appearance of vinyl.

Vinyl raised beds provide numerous advantages including their robust nature, low upkeep, environmental friendliness, and simple installation process. However, they also carry certain drawbacks such as a greater upfront cost, potential for heat absorption, sustainability concerns, and aesthetic appeal limitations. Each of these factors should be thoughtfully evaluated when determining whether vinyl raised beds are an appropriate choice for your fruit gardening endeavors.

Fabric Raised Beds

Fabric Raised Beds are a unique and innovative approach to fruit gardening. These beds are constructed from specialized fabric materials that provide a contained space for growing fruit plants. These beds offer a dedicated, aerated space filled with nutrient-rich soil that is well-suited for growing a variety of fruit plants.

Benefits of using fabric raised beds in fruit gardening include:

- Promotes Healthy Roots: The aerated fabric container promotes healthy root development through air pruning, leading to better quality fruits and higher yields.
- Flexible Configurations: Fabric raised beds come in

multiple configurations and sizes, offering flexibility according to your gardening needs.

- Improved Drainage: Fabric raised beds provide optimal drainage, beneficial for many garden plants.
- Plant Communication: The shared soil in fabric-raised beds allows plants to communicate and combat attacks via the mycelium network.

Disadvantages associated with fabric raised beds:

- Non-Waterproof: Fabric raised beds are not designed to be waterproof, which may require more frequent watering.
- Potential Root Interference: The roots may interact negatively with the fabric raised bed if placed near existing trees or plants.
- Durability Concerns: While fabric raised beds are generally sturdy, they may not be as long-lasting as other materials like wood or vinyl.

Fabric raised beds offer several advantages such as promoting healthy roots, flexible configurations, improved drainage, and plant communication. However, they also have downsides, like being non-waterproof, possible root interference, and durability concerns. These factors should be weighed carefully when considering fabric raised beds for fruit gardening.

Wattle Raised Beds

Wattle Raised Beds are a traditional form of garden bed that utilizes the technique of weaving flexible branches, typically from willow or other similar woods, to create a sturdy and functional structure for fruit gardening. They offer a charming, rustic aesthetic and serve as a defined space for growing fruit plants.

The benefits of using wattle raised beds in fruit gardening include:

- Sustainability: Wattle raised beds make use of readily available natural materials, making them an eco-friendly option.
- Aesthetics: These beds add a rustic, natural charm to your garden.
- Affordability: Creating a wattle raised bed can be cost-effective if branches and twigs are freely available.
- Composting Option: The 'lasagne composting' method, involving alternating layers of organic materials, can be effectively used in wattle raised beds.

Disadvantages associated with wattle raised beds:

- Durability: Wattle raised beds may not last as long as beds made from more durable materials like wood or vinyl.
- Time-Consuming to Build: The process of weaving the branches and twigs can be labor-intensive and time-consuming.
- Potential for Pest Issues: The organic material can attract pests, which could pose a risk to your fruit plants.

While wattle raised beds provide eco-friendliness, visual charm, cost-effectiveness, and a distinct composting solution, they also present possible challenges like issues with longevity, labor-intensive assembly, and potential pest problems. These aspects warrant careful contemplation when determining if wattle raised beds are suitable for your fruit gardening requirements.

SELECTING WHERE YOUR CONTAINER & RAISED BED FRUIT GARDENS WILL GROW

Setting up your container and raised bed fruit gardens involves many considerations, among which location selection is paramount. The choice of location profoundly influences the well-being and robustness of your fruit plants. Here are some crucial aspects to keep in mind when determining the site for your container and raised-bed gardening.

Sunlight Exposure

Sunlight exposure plays a pivotal role when choosing the location for your container and raised bed fruit garden. Most fruiting plants, including fruit trees, require at least six hours of sunlight daily to flourish and produce optimally. Sunlight is essential for the photosynthesis process, which fuels plant growth and the production of starches and sugars necessary for fruit development.

The importance of sunlight extends beyond just the leaves; it also affects the quality of fruit and nuts. Increased exposure to sunlight has been associated with alterations in the metabolic profile of fruits, shaping their nutritional and sensory properties.

When deciding on the location for your garden, it's essential to observe the patterns of sunlight throughout the day and across different seasons. Identify areas that receive a substantial amount of sunlight for most of the day. Raised beds can offer better exposure to the sun, warming the soil, allowing for a wider variety of plants, and extending the growing seasons. In the case of container gardening, the containers should be placed in locations with significant sunlight exposure. The advantage is the flexibility to move the containers as needed to ensure optimal sun exposure.

Overall, understanding your fruit plants' sunlight needs and strategically placing your raised beds or containers accordingly can significantly enhance your fruit garden's productivity.

Temperature & Microclimate

Temperature and microclimate play a critical role in the success of your container and raised bed fruit garden. Different fruits thrive best in specific temperature ranges and microclimates. For instance, some fruits like apples, cherries, and berries do well in cooler climates, while others such as citrus fruits, peaches, and figs prefer warmer conditions.

Microclimates are small areas within your garden where the climate differs from the overall climate of your yard. These can be influenced by factors such as sun exposure, wind direction, proximity to buildings or bodies of water, and elevation. Understanding these microclimates can help you place your containers and raised beds in locations where they will thrive.

When choosing a location for your fruit garden, consider the temperature requirements of the fruits you plan to grow. Monitor the temperature fluctuations in different parts of your garden throughout the year to identify the most suitable spots.

Raised beds can be beneficial in this regard as they allow for better control of the soil temperature. With containers, you have the flexibility to move them around based on temperature changes and the specific needs of the plants.

Careful consideration of temperature and microclimate when selecting a location for your container and raised bed fruit garden can greatly enhance the health and productivity of your plants.

Pest Control

Pest control is a critical aspect to consider when selecting the location for your container and raised bed fruit garden. Pests such as insects, mites, slugs, and birds can significantly damage plants and reduce yield, making pest management essential for a successful fruit garden.

When choosing a location for your garden, consider factors that can naturally deter pests. For example, placing your garden near plants that attract beneficial insects can help control pest populations. Likewise, interplanting with different vegetables and flowers can discourage pests attracted to large plantings of a single crop.

Raised beds and containers provide unique opportunities for pest control. Their elevated structure can deter some ground-dwelling pests like snails and slugs, and because they're isolated from the main garden, it's easier to manage any pest problems that do arise.

Also, employing physical barriers, such as covers or fences, can be an effective method of preventing pests in your garden. This strategy can be particularly useful in raised beds and containers, where the confined space makes installing and maintaining these barriers easier.

Understanding the types of pests common in your area and their behaviors can also inform your choice of location. For instance, if certain pests are known to frequent shady areas, choose a sunnier spot for your garden.

Considering pest control when choosing the location for your container and raised bed fruit garden will contribute significantly to your garden's health and productivity.

Water Access

Water access is a crucial factor to consider when choosing the location for your container and raised bed fruit garden. Adequate water supply is essential for the growth and productivity of fruit plants, as it facilitates nutrient uptake and helps maintain plant health.

When selecting a location for your garden, ensure it's near a reliable water source. This could be an outdoor tap, a well, or even a rainwater harvesting system. Having a water source nearby makes it easier to provide your plants with the amount of water they need, especially during dry periods.

Raised beds and containers can dry out quickly, especially in hot weather, so they often require more frequent watering than in-ground gardens. Therefore, easy water access becomes even more critical in these types of gardens.

In addition, the location should ideally have good drainage to prevent waterlogging, which can lead to root rot and other diseases. Raised beds and containers naturally offer good drainage due to their elevated structure and the ability to control the soil mix used.

Another aspect to consider is the possibility of using drip irrigation or soaker hoses. These systems deliver water directly to the plant roots and reduce water loss due to evaporation. If you plan to use these systems, choose a location that can easily accommodate them.

Wind Exposure

Wind exposure is an important aspect to consider when choosing the location for your container and raised bed fruit garden. Wind can have both positive and negative effects on plants. On one hand, it can help pollinate flowers and reduce fungal diseases by drying out plant foliage. On the other hand, excessive wind can cause damage to plants, leading to desiccation, breakage, uprooting, and reduced growth.

When selecting a location for your garden, consider its exposure to prevailing winds. If you live in a windy area, choose a spot that's sheltered from the wind by natural features like hills or buildings, or consider installing windbreaks such as fences, hedges, or trellises. Windbreaks can reduce wind speed and protect your plants while also providing a habitat for beneficial insects.

Raised beds and containers are particularly susceptible to wind damage due to their elevated structure and the fact that plants grown in them often have less extensive root systems than those grown in the ground. Therefore, positioning these types of gardens in a sheltered location or securing them with stakes or weights can be beneficial.

Furthermore, consider the wind tolerance of different fruit plants when choosing a location. Some fruit plants are more wind-tolerant than others, so these could be planted in more exposed locations.

Taking into account wind exposure when choosing the location for your container and raised bed fruit garden can significantly impact the health and productivity of your plants.

Accessibility

Accessibility is a crucial factor to consider when choosing the location for your container and raised bed fruit garden. Gardening involves regular maintenance tasks such as watering, pruning, harvesting, and pest control. Having easy access to your garden makes these tasks less physically demanding and more convenient, increasing the likelihood that they are performed regularly and effectively.

When planning your garden, consider how easy it will be to reach all areas. Raised beds and containers should be arranged so that you can reach all plants without straining the soil. This is particularly important for elderly or disabled gardeners, who may benefit from raised beds and containers at a comfortable height.

Also, consider how close the garden is to your house, tools, and water source. A garden closer to the house can be more convenient to maintain and can also deter pests. Ensure there's a clear, safe path to your garden, free of tripping hazards.

Accessibility also involves being able to monitor your garden easily. A well-situated garden allows you to spot problems early and respond quickly.

Considering accessibility when choosing a location for your container and raised bed fruit garden can make your gardening experience more enjoyable and your garden more productive.

Space – Room For Growth

Room for growth is a significant factor to consider when choosing the location for your container and raised bed fruit garden. Fruit plants need adequate space to grow and spread out, both above ground and below ground for their root systems.

When selecting a location for your garden, ensure there is enough space for all your plants to grow without crowding each other. Crowded plants are more susceptible to diseases and pests as poor air circulation can create a moist environment that promotes the growth of harmful fungi and bacteria.

Raised beds and containers provide an excellent solution for managing plant spacing. They allow you to control the arrangement of your plants and ensure they have the space they need. However, it's crucial to choose a size of raised bed or container that matches the growth habit of your fruit plants.

Moreover, consider the vertical space. Some fruit plants, like vining crops, require supports such as trellises or stakes, which must be accommodated in your garden layout. Vertical growing not only saves horizontal space but can also increase productivity and make maintenance and harvesting easier.

Aesthetic Appeal

Aesthetic appeal is an essential factor to consider when choosing the location for your container and raised bed fruit garden. A well-placed and beautifully arranged garden can enhance the overall appearance of your property, create a pleasing view from your home, and provide a space where you can relax and enjoy nature.

When selecting a location for your garden, consider how it will fit into the overall landscape of your property. It should complement other features rather than clash with them. Choose a spot visible from your favorite areas of your home so you can appreciate your garden even when indoors.

Raised beds and containers offer excellent opportunities for creating aesthetically pleasing gardens. They allow you to play with height, color, texture, and arrangement in ways that aren't always possible with traditional in-ground gardens. You could choose containers in different shapes, sizes, and colors to add interest or arrange your raised beds in geometric patterns for a formal look.

Likewise, consider the aesthetic appeal of the plants themselves. To create visual interest, choose a variety of fruit plants with different colors, shapes, and growth habits. Also, remember that fruit plants can be beautiful at all stages of growth, from the blossoming period to the fruit-bearing stage.

Considering the aesthetic appeal when selecting the location for your container and raised bed fruit garden can not only amplify the attractiveness of your property but also heighten your pleasure in gardening.

CHAPTER 2

CONTAINER & RAISED BED FRUIT GARDENS (PREPARATION)

T he importance of preparation for fruit containers and raised bed gardening cannot be overstated. For fruit container gardening, selecting the appropriate container size is a critical step as it determines the root space available for plant growth. Ensuring that the container has adequate drainage is also pivotal to prevent water stagnation, which can lead to root rot. Preparing the soil in the container is another essential step, which involves enriching it with compost or organic matter to provide a nutrient-rich environment conducive for fruiting.

For raised bed gardening, preparation begins with choosing a suitable location with ample sunlight and good air circulation. The raised bed should be of an appropriate height for easy maintenance and to facilitate excellent drainage. Soil preparation is crucial here as well. It should be loose and well-draining, enriched with organic matter such as compost or aged manure to replenish nutrients and improve soil structure, thereby promoting healthy plant growth.

In both scenarios, meticulous preparation significantly influences the success of your gardening endeavor. It directly impacts the health and productivity of the plants, leading to a bountiful harvest of quality fruits. Hence, investing time and effort in preparation is integral to effective fruit container and raised bed gardening.

ESSENTIAL TOOLS FOR CONTAINER & RAISED BED FRUIT GARDENING

Understanding the importance of essential tools for container and raised bed fruit gardening is vital to successful and efficient gardening practices. Each tool has a specific role that aids in creating an optimal environment for your plants to thrive. For instance, using the right containers or raised beds helps to ensure proper drainage and adequate space for root growth, both crucial factors for plant health and productivity.

Tools such as a garden trowel, spade, or fork are needed for soil preparation, planting, and maintenance tasks while pruning shears are vital for managing plant growth and health by removing dead or diseased parts. Watering equipment ensures your plants receive the necessary hydration, a critical factor for their survival and fruit production.

Gloves provide protection during these tasks, and a wheelbarrow can prove indispensable when needing to move large amounts of soil or compost. Speaking of soil, a testing kit is important to keep track of its pH and nutrient levels, allowing you to adjust as needed for your plants' optimal growth.

Lastly, having weeding tools helps maintain the cleanliness and health of your garden by removing invasive plants that could compete with your fruit plants for resources. By understanding why each tool is important, you can improve your gardening practices, leading to a more abundant and healthier fruit harvest.

Garden Trowel

A garden trowel is an indispensable tool for fruit container and raised-bed gardening. This compact, handheld tool is essential for numerous gardening tasks such as digging small holes, transplanting delicate seedlings, and loosening the soil in your containers or raised beds. Its sharp, pointed blade allows you to cut through the soil with precision, making it easier to plant your fruit seeds or seedlings at the correct depth. The trowel is also ideal for adding compost or fertilizer around the base of your fruit plants, ensuring they receive the necessary nutrients for growth and fruit production. In essence, a garden trowel makes planting and maintaining your fruit container or raised-bed garden easier, more efficient, and ultimately more successful.

Hand Fork

A hand fork is a valuable tool for fruit container and raised-bed gardening. Its small size and sturdy prongs make it perfect for working in confined spaces like containers and raised beds. The hand fork is excellent for loosening compacted soil, allowing water and nutrients to penetrate more effectively, which is crucial for the healthy growth of fruit plants. It's also useful for weeding around your plants, as its sharp tines can easily uproot unwanted vegetation without disturbing your fruit plants.

Furthermore, a hand fork is handy when it comes to incorporating compost or fertilizers into the soil, ensuring your fruit plants get the nutrients they need. In essence, a hand fork is a versatile tool that aids in maintaining the overall health and productivity of your fruit container or raised-bed garden.

Spade

A spade is an indispensable tool for fruit container and raised-bed gardening. Its primary function is digging, which is essential for preparing the soil, planting, and transplanting. With its sharp, flat blade, a spade can easily penetrate the soil, making it ideal for creating planting holes or trenches in raised beds. It's also vital for turning over the soil, a crucial step in soil preparation that helps to aerate the soil and mix in organic matter or compost for added fertility. In addition, a spade can be used to edge the garden beds, maintaining a clean and tidy appearance. For all these reasons, a spade is a fundamental tool that aids in promoting the health and productivity of your fruit plants in a container or raised-bed garden.

Pruning Shears

Pruning shears are an essential tool for any fruit container or raised-bed garden. They are specifically designed to cut through plant material, making them perfect for tasks such as removing dead or diseased branches, shaping plants, and controlling growth. For fruit-bearing plants, pruning is a crucial practice that promotes healthier plants and increased fruit production. By removing excess foliage, more energy can be directed towards fruit development.

Additionally, well-pruned plants allow better light penetration and air circulation, reducing the likelihood of disease. Pruning shears provide clean, precise cuts that minimize damage to the plant, promoting quicker healing and reducing the risk of disease entering through the cut site. Therefore, owning a good pair of pruning shears is key to maintaining the health and productivity of your fruit container or raised-bed garden.

Watering Can or Hose

A watering can or hose is an essential tool for maintaining a fruit container or raised-bed garden. Proper hydration is crucial for the health and productivity of any plant, and this is especially true for fruit-bearing plants that require consistent moisture levels to produce juicy, healthy fruits.

A watering can, can provide controlled watering, allowing you to directly water the root zone without wetting the foliage, which can help prevent disease. In larger gardens, a hose is often more practical, enabling you to water large areas quickly and efficiently. Some hoses come with adjustable nozzles that provide a gentle shower for delicate plants or a strong stream for deeper watering. These watering tools ensure that your plants receive the necessary hydration, contributing significantly to their growth and fruit production.

Gardening Gloves

Gardening gloves are a crucial tool for anyone tending to a fruit container or raised-bed garden. These gloves protect your hands from thorns, sharp tools, and potentially harmful organisms in the soil, like bacteria and fungi. When handling various types of fruit plants that may have prickly stems or rough textures, these gloves can prevent scratches and irritation.

They also keep your hands clean, making the cleanup process much easier after a gardening session. Gardening gloves have reinforced fingertips and palms for extra durability, providing a better grip when using tools or lifting heavy objects. In essence, gardening gloves offer an essential layer of protection, enhancing safety and comfort while you work in your fruit garden.

Soil Testing Kit

A soil testing kit is a vital tool for managing a fruit container or raised-bed garden. The health and productivity of your plants are largely determined by the quality and composition of your soil. Fruit-bearing plants, in particular require specific nutrient levels and pH balances to thrive and produce a generous yield. A soil testing kit allows you to determine the exact composition of your soil, including its pH level and the presence of essential nutrients like nitrogen, phosphorus, and potassium.

By understanding your soil's current status, you can make the necessary adjustments, such as adding appropriate fertilizers or other amendments, to create an optimal growing environment. Therefore, a soil testing kit empowers you to tailor your gardening practices to the specific needs of your plants, ultimately leading to healthier plants and a more bountiful harvest.

Weeding Tools

Weeding tools are an essential part of maintaining a healthy and productive fruit container or raised-bed garden. Weeds can compete with your fruit plants for valuable resources such as water, light, and nutrients, potentially hindering the growth and productivity of your plants. Weeding tools, which come in various shapes and sizes to suit different tasks, allow you to effectively remove these unwanted plants from your garden.

Some tools are designed to pull out the entire weed, including roots, to prevent it from regrowing, while others are designed to cut or scrape weeds off at the surface. By regularly using weeding tools, you can keep your garden free of these competing plants, ensuring that your fruit plants have access to all the resources they need to thrive and produce a bountiful harvest.

Wheelbarrow

A wheelbarrow is a critical tool for managing a fruit raised-bed garden, offering practical assistance in numerous gardening tasks. Whether you're moving soil, compost, or garden waste, a wheelbarrow lightens the load making it easier to transport these materials across your garden. This is especially beneficial when setting up or replenishing raised beds or large containers, which often require substantial amounts of soil or compost.

Additionally, during harvest season, a wheelbarrow can be used to collect and transport fruit, reducing the physical strain and time taken to gather your produce. Equally, when pruning or cleaning your garden, a wheelbarrow serves as a convenient receptacle for garden debris. A wheelbarrow enhances efficiency and ease in maintaining your garden, making it an indispensable tool in any fruit container or raised-bed garden.

Garden Rake

A garden rake is an indispensable tool for managing a fruit raised-bed garden. It serves multiple purposes, all of which contribute to the health and productivity of your plants. A garden rake is primarily used to prepare the soil before planting. It helps to break up clumps of soil and level the surface, creating a smooth and even bed for your plants. This ensures that your plant's roots can easily penetrate the soil and access the nutrients they need to grow.

Additionally, a garden rake can be used to gather and remove leaves, and other garden debris from your raised-bed garden, keeping it clean and reducing the risk of disease. It can also be used to spread mulch evenly around your plants, helping to retain moisture and suppress weeds.

Plant Ties or Stakes

Plant Ties or Stakes are essential tools in a fruit container or raised-bed garden, especially for supporting the growth of fruit-bearing plants. As these plants grow and bear fruit, their branches can become heavy and bend or break under the weight. Plant ties or stakes provide the necessary support, keeping the branches upright and preventing damage.

They also help maintain the plant's shape and direct its growth, which can improve air circulation and sunlight exposure, reducing the risk of disease and promoting healthier growth. Furthermore, they make harvesting easier as the fruits are kept off the ground and within easy reach.

Seed Trays or Pots

Seed Trays or Pots are vital tools for a fruit container or raised-bed garden, serving as the perfect starting point for your plants. They provide a controlled environment for seeds to germinate and young plants to grow before they're strong enough to be transplanted into larger containers or beds. This can significantly improve the survival rate of your plants, as they are protected from harsh weather conditions, pests, and diseases during their most vulnerable stage.

Seed trays or pots also allow you to maximize your growing space, as you can start new plants while waiting for space to open up in your garden. Additionally, using seed trays or pots gives you the flexibility to start your gardening season indoors or under cover if outdoor conditions are not yet suitable. Therefore, seed trays or pots are essential tools for successful propagation and efficient use of space in your fruit container or raised-bed garden.

Garden Hoe

A Garden Hoe is fundamental for maintaining fruit container and raised-bed gardens. Its long handle and sturdy blade make it ideal for various tasks, including breaking up compacted soil, creating seed trenches, and most importantly, combating weeds. With its ability to reach deep into the soil, a garden hoe can effectively uproot weeds from your garden beds, preventing them from sapping essential nutrients meant for your fruit plants.

Additionally, using a garden hoe to aerate the soil can promote better water and nutrient penetration, creating an ideal environment for your fruits to thrive. This tool's versatility and efficiency make it indispensable in the upkeep of a healthy and productive garden.

Netting or Fencing

Netting or fencing is an integral tool for fruit container and raised-bed gardens, providing a multitude of benefits. First and foremost, it acts as a protective barrier, keeping pests like birds, rodents, and insects at bay, preventing them from damaging or eating the fruits. It can also serve as a trellis, providing support for climbing or vining fruit plants, helping them grow vertically and efficiently using the limited space in containers or raised beds.

Furthermore, netting or fencing can aid in controlling sun exposure and wind damage, creating a more controlled environment for your fruits to thrive. Hence, this tool is essential for maintaining the health and productivity of your garden.

TYPES OF FRUIT BUSHES & BERRIES

Understanding the different types of fruit bushes is crucial in container and raised-bed gardening as it aids in making informed decisions about what fruits to grow based on factors such as space, climate, and personal preference.

Berry Bushes

Berry bushes are fruit-bearing plants that produce small, pulpy fruits like strawberries, raspberries, blueberries, and blackberries. These plants can range in size from low-growing ground covers to larger shrubs, and they often have brambly or vine-like growth habits. Berry bushes are renowned for their hardiness, adaptability, and the delicious, nutritious fruits they bear.

Understanding berry bushes is crucial in container and raised bed fruit gardening for several reasons. First, many berry bushes are perfectly suited to growing in containers or raised beds due to their compact size and shallow root systems. This allows gardeners with limited space or poor soil quality to still enjoy a bountiful harvest.

Secondly, berry bushes are more disease and pest resistant than other fruit plants, making them an excellent choice for organic gardeners. They also tend to be perennials, meaning they will produce fruit year after year with proper care.

Thirdly, growing berry bushes can provide a continuous supply of fresh, organic berries throughout the growing season. This not only offers health benefits but can also help with grocery costs.

Finally, understanding the specific needs of different types of berry bushes - such as sunlight requirements, preferred soil pH, and pruning needs - can greatly enhance their productivity and longevity. With this knowledge, gardeners can enjoy a bountiful harvest of fresh, home-grown berries right from their backyard.

Stone Fruit Bushes

Stone fruit bushes refer to a group of fruit-bearing plants that produce what are commonly known as stone fruits. This category includes fruits like apricots, cherries, peaches, plums, and nectarines, which are characterized by their large, hard pits or "stones" at the center, surrounded by succulent flesh. These can be grown on trees, but many varieties can also thrive as smaller bushes, making them suitable for container and raised bed gardening.

Understanding stone fruit bushes is crucial in container and raised bed fruit gardening for several reasons. Firstly, many stone fruit varieties have relatively compact growth habits, making them well-suited for container and raised bed gardening where space might be limited. Additionally, their striking spring blossoms add ornamental value, while the fruits they bear are not only delicious but also rich in vitamins and other nutrients.

However, each type of stone fruit bush has specific growing requirements, including sunlight, water, soil pH, and temperature needs. For instance, most stone fruits prefer full sun and well-draining soil, with some needing a certain number of chill hours during winter to ensure good fruit production. Understanding these needs is key to successful stone fruit gardening.

Additionally, growing stone fruits in containers or raised beds allows for better control over soil conditions, easier harvesting, and the ability to move plants around for optimal sun exposure or protection from harsh weather. It also helps prevent soil-borne diseases and pests, which can be a common issue in traditional ground planting.

Understanding stone fruit bushes and their specific needs is vital for successful container and raised bed fruit gardening. With this knowledge, you can enjoy the dual benefits of a visually appealing garden and a bountiful harvest of fresh, home-grown fruits.

Citrus Bushes

Citrus bushes are a type of fruit-bearing plant that produce a variety of citrus fruits, such as lemons, limes, oranges, and grapefruits. These plants are known for their evergreen foliage, aromatic flowers, and their tangy, juicy fruits. Differentiating from larger citrus trees, citrus bushes are usually smaller, making them ideal for container or raised bed gardening.

Understanding citrus bushes is pivotal in container and raised bed fruit gardening for several reasons. Their compact size and adaptability make them well-suited for container or raised bed gardening, allowing even those with limited space to grow their own fruit. Some varieties, like the Lemon-Lime Citrus Bush, offer multiple types of fruit from one plant, adding diversity to your garden without requiring extra space.

Citrus bushes are renowned for their resilience and ability to thrive in various climates, though they do best in warm, sunny locations. They can also be grown indoors during colder months, which makes them a great year-round option for fresh, home-grown fruit.

Additionally, each type of citrus bush has specific needs regarding sunlight, watering, and soil quality. Most prefer well-draining soil and full sun exposure. Understanding these requirements can significantly enhance the health and productivity of your plants.

Growing citrus bushes provides fresh, organic fruit and adds aesthetic appeal to your garden with their vibrant fruit and fragrant blossoms. However, they can be susceptible to certain pests and diseases, so understanding these plants' care and potential challenges is essential for successful container and raised bed fruit gardening.

Tropical Fruit Bushes

Tropical fruit bushes encompass a broad range of fruit-bearing plants that are native to tropical climates. This group includes fruits like bananas, pineapples, mangoes, avocados, and guavas among others. These plants are typically characterized by their need for warm temperatures, high humidity, and ample sunlight.

Understanding tropical fruit bushes is crucial in container and raised bed fruit gardening for many reasons. Firstly, many tropical fruit plants can be successfully grown in containers or raised beds, which offer improved soil drainage and aeration—key factors for their growth. Containers also provide portability, allowing gardeners in cooler climates to move these plants indoors during colder months.

Likewise, growing tropical fruit bushes can add a unique dimension to your garden with their lush foliage and exotic fruits. They can serve as both a source of fresh, home-grown fruit and a decorative element to your outdoor or indoor space.

Additionally, each tropical fruit bush has specific needs concerning light, water, temperature, and soil quality. Understanding these needs can significantly enhance the health and productivity of your plants, leading to a more bountiful harvest.

Container gardening allows you to control the plant's growth and size through pruning and shaping. This aspect is particularly important for tropical fruit bushes, which can grow quite large in their native environments. However, it's important to note that some tropical fruit bushes may be susceptible to certain pests and diseases, so understanding these plants' care and potential challenges is essential for successful container and raised bed fruit gardening.

Vine Fruits

Vine fruits refer to fruits that grow on plants with long, flexible stems that either creep along the ground or climb by clinging to a support with tendrils. The most common example of a vine fruit is the grape - botanically a berry from the deciduous woody vines of the flowering plant genus Vitis. However, the term can also apply to other climbing or trailing fruit plants, such as kiwifruit and passionfruit.

Understanding vine fruits is important in container and raised bed fruit gardening for several reasons. Firstly, many vine fruit plants can be trained to grow upwards on trellises or supports, making them an excellent option for gardeners with limited space. This vertical growth habit allows for efficient use of space, as the plants grow upwards rather than outwards.

Secondly, growing vine fruits in containers or raised beds allows for better control over soil conditions, which can be crucial for these types of plants. Many vine fruits prefer well-draining soil and can suffer from root diseases in waterlogged conditions.

Thirdly, the accessibility of vine fruits grown in containers or raised beds can make maintenance tasks like pruning and harvesting easier. These plants often require regular pruning to stay healthy and productive, and having them at a convenient height can make this task less labor-intensive.

Lastly, vine fruits can add a unique visual appeal to your garden with their climbing growth habit and abundant fruit production. However, they can be susceptible to certain pests and diseases, so understanding these plants' care and potential challenges is essential for successful container and raised bed fruit gardening.

DECIDING WHAT FRUITS TO GROW IN CONTAINERS & RAISED BED GARDENS

When choosing what fruits to grow in containers and raised-bed gardens, there are several key factors to consider. The first is the size of the plant when it's fully grown. Both containers and raised beds have limited space, so it's important to choose fruit plants that won't outgrow their environment. Dwarf or miniature varieties of many fruit trees, such as apples, peaches, and cherries, are well-suited for container gardening as they have been bred to stay small while still producing a good yield of fruit.

The second factor to consider is the plant's sunlight requirements. Most fruit-bearing plants require six to eight hours of direct sunlight each day to produce a good crop. It's essential to choose a location for your container or raised bed where your plants will receive enough light. If you have a shady garden, you might want to consider shade-tolerant fruits like certain types of berries.

Another important consideration is the plant's hardiness zone. Some fruits, like citrus and tropical fruits, can only survive in specific climates. However, growing these fruits in containers can provide the flexibility to move them indoors during colder months, extending their growing range.

The soil type and drainage are also crucial considerations. Most fruit plants prefer well-draining soil, which is easy to provide in a raised bed or container. You'll also need to consider the pH level of your soil, as different fruits have different preferences. For example, blueberries thrive in acidic soil, while figs prefer slightly alkaline conditions.

Lastly, consider your personal taste and how much time you can dedicate to caring for your garden. Some fruit plants, like strawberries, produce fruit quickly and require relatively little maintenance, while others, like apple trees, take longer to bear fruit and require more care. By considering all these factors, you can choose the right fruits for your container or raised-bed garden and enjoy a successful and satisfying harvest.

HOW TO CHOOSE THE RIGHT CONTAINER FOR FRUIT GARDENS

Choosing the right container is a critical aspect of successful fruit gardening. Different fruits have different root systems and growth habits, so selecting a container that suits the specific needs of the plant you intend to grow is important.

Firstly, consider the size of the container. The pot should be large enough to accommodate the mature size of the plant, including its root system. For example, small fruits like strawberries can thrive in smaller pots that are at least 6 to 12 inches in diameter. Larger fruits or dwarf fruit trees, on the other hand, require much larger containers – often 18 inches in diameter or more.

Secondly, pay attention to the material of the container. Plastic pots are lightweight and relatively inexpensive, but they may not provide the best insulation against temperature changes. Clay or ceramic pots are heavier and offer better insulation, but they can break easily and may be more expensive. Wooden containers, such as barrels or raised beds, can be a good choice for larger fruit plants, as they provide ample space and good insulation.

Drainage is another crucial factor. Ensure the container has sufficient drainage holes to prevent waterlogging, which can lead to root rot. If your chosen container doesn't have drainage holes, you can either drill some yourself or layer the bottom of the pot with pebbles or broken pottery to create a space for excess water to pool away from the roots.

Lastly, consider the color of the container. Dark-colored pots absorb more heat, which can lead to overheating in hot climates. Light-colored containers reflect heat and can help keep the root zone cooler.

Remember, the choice of container can significantly influence the health and productivity of your fruit plants. By considering factors like size, material, drainage, and color, you can select the best pot for your particular fruit gardening needs.

HOW TO CHOOSE & BUILD THE RIGHT RAISED BED FOR FRUIT GARDENS

Choosing and building the right raised bed for a fruit garden involves careful consideration of several factors. First, consider the size and depth of the raised bed. The dimensions of your raised bed should correlate with the types of fruit you wish to grow. For example, small fruits like strawberries require less space and can be grown in a bed about 1-2 feet wide and 8 inches deep. Larger fruits, like melons or dwarf fruit trees, require more space and deeper soil, so a bed 3-4 feet wide and at least 12-18 inches deep would be more suitable.

The material you choose for your raised bed also plays a crucial role. Wood, such as cedar or redwood, is a popular choice due to its durability and relatively low cost. However, avoid using treated wood, as it can leach harmful chemicals into the soil. Metal, particularly galvanized steel, is another durable option that provides a modern aesthetic. Plastic or composite materials are lightweight and easy to assemble but may not be as long-lasting or environmentally friendly.

The location of the raised bed is another important factor. Most fruit plants require a minimum of six hours of sunlight each day, so choose an area with plenty of sun. Consider the accessibility of the bed for watering and maintenance purposes. Also, factor in the soil quality underneath the bed; if it's particularly rocky or has poor-quality soil, you may want to opt for a deeper bed or place a layer of landscape fabric at the bottom before filling it with soil.

When building your raised bed, start by clearing and leveling the area where it will be placed. Assemble your chosen materials according to your desired dimensions. Be sure to secure the corners and sides properly to handle the weight of the soil and plants.

It's vital to remember that when building your raised bed, it has a good drainage system. This can be achieved by layering the bottom of the bed with gravel or small stones before adding soil. The soil mix you use should be rich in organic matter to provide the necessary nutrients for fruit growth. A mixture of topsoil, compost, and a slow-release organic fertilizer typically works well.

In conclusion, choosing and building the right raised bed for a fruit garden involves considering the size and depth of the bed, the material it's made from, its location, and the process of building and filling it. With careful planning and execution, a raised bed can provide an excellent environment for growing a variety of fruits.

FUNDAMENTALS OF PREPARING YOUR CONTAINER & RAISED BED SOIL FOR FRUIT GARDENS

Understanding your garden soil is crucial when growing fruits in containers and raised bed gardens. The soil is the primary source of nutrients for your plants, and different fruits have specific soil needs to grow healthily and bear a good fruit yield.

For example, blueberries require acidic soil, while figs prefer slightly alkaline conditions. Knowing your soil's pH level can help you choose which fruits to grow or indicate if you need to amend the soil to suit specific plants.

Moreover, the soil structure, which refers to how particles of sand, silt, and clay are organized, significantly impacts water drainage and retention. Loamy soil, a balanced mix of these particles, is generally ideal as it retains moisture but drains well, preventing waterlogged or dry conditions that can harm your plants.

In container gardening, understanding your soil is even more critical as the plant depends entirely on the pot's medium for its nutritional needs. The soil also hosts beneficial microorganisms that aid in nutrient absorption and help protect plants against diseases.

Additionally, choosing the right soil is a critical step in setting up your container or raised bed fruit garden. For container gardening, garden soil straight from the yard isn't suitable as it can compact easily, hindering root growth and water drainage.

Instead, opt for a high-quality potting mix designed for container plants. These mixes often contain ingredients like peat moss or coconut coir for moisture retention, vermiculite or perlite for drainage, and compost or other organic matter for nutrients. Some even have slow-release fertilizers blended in to feed your plants over time.

For raised bed gardens, you also want a well-draining, nutrient-rich soil but you have a bit more flexibility. You can start with a base of topsoil, which is denser than potting mix and provides more stability for larger plants' roots. Then, enrich it with plenty of organic matter such as compost, well-rotted manure, or leaf mold to boost its fertility and improve its texture.

Ultimately, by understanding and choosing the soil type that is most compatible with your aims and objectives, you're providing a strong foundation that will support your fruit plants' growth and productivity.

CONTAINER & RAISED BED SOIL TYPES

Potting Soil

Potting soil, commonly known as potting mix, is a specialized medium designed to foster the growth of plants in containers. It typically consists of a blend of various ingredients like sphagnum moss, bark, perlite, vermiculite, compost, or coir, which together create an optimal environment for potted plants. Unlike garden soil, which can be heavy and prone to compaction, potting soil is light and well-draining, ensuring that plants receive the necessary water, air, and nutrients.

Benefits of using potting soil in container and raised bed fruit gardens include:

- Excellent Drainage: Overwatering is a common problem in container gardening. Potting soil, with its perlite or vermiculite content, ensures good water flow, preventing waterlogging and root rot.
- Moisture Retention: Despite its excellent drainage, potting soil retains enough moisture to keep plant roots hydrated, thanks to ingredients like sphagnum moss or coir.
- Sterility: Potting soil is generally sterile, reducing the risk of soil-borne diseases and pests. This is particularly crucial in container gardening, where diseases can quickly spread from one plant to another.
- Nutrient-Rich: Potting soil often comes enriched with nutrients or added fertilizers, providing plants with essential nutrients they need for growth.

Despite these benefits, there are a few disadvantages to consider:

- Frequent Watering: Potting soil tends to dry out faster than garden soil, requiring more frequent watering, especially during hot weather.
- Nutrient Depletion: The nutrients in potting soil can get depleted quickly, necessitating regular supplementation with a suitable fertilizer.
- Cost: In raised bed gardening, filling large beds with potting soil can be costly. However, it can be a good choice for filling small raised beds or mixing with garden soil to improve its texture and fertility.

While potting soil has its pros and cons, its many benefits make it a popular choice for both container and raised bed fruit gardening.

Garden Soil

Garden soil, often referred to as topsoil or outdoor soil, is the uppermost layer of the Earth's crust where plants grow. It consists of a mix of organic matter, minerals, gases, liquids, and organisms supporting life together. Garden soil varies greatly depending on its location and is influenced by factors like climate, native flora, and geological processes.

The benefits of using garden soil in raised bed fruit gardens include:

- Nutrient-Dense: Garden soil is usually rich in nutrients, providing a good foundation for plant growth.
- Cost-Effective: Using existing garden soil for raised

beds can be a cost-effective solution, especially for large beds.

- Sustainability: Utilizing garden soil reduces the need for commercially prepared mixes, contributing to sustainability and reducing carbon footprint.

However, there are also some disadvantages of using garden soil:

- Poor Drainage: Garden soil can be heavy and may not drain well, especially if it has a high clay content. This can lead to soggy conditions that are harmful to many plants.
- Disease and Pest Issues: Unlike potting soil, garden soil is not sterile. It may contain soil-borne diseases, pests, and weed seeds.
- Compaction: In container gardening, garden soil tends to compact over time, inhibiting root growth and drainage.

Garden soil has its uses, but for fruit cultivation in containers and raised beds, it might not always be the ideal option. Composted organic matter, perlite, or coir can be added to garden soil to enhance its structure and make it more appropriate for various uses.

Compost

Compost is a product derived from biodegradable materials' controlled aerobic, biological decomposition. It is an organic matter resource that has the unique ability to improve the chemical, physical, and biological characteristics of soils or growing media. Composting is essentially a natural form of recycling, whereby organic materials such as leaves, food scraps, grass clippings, and coffee grounds are broken down into a nutrient-rich soil amendment.

The benefits of using compost in container and raised bed fruit gardens include:

- Soil Enrichment: Compost enriches the soil with nutrients, enhancing the growth and productivity of plants.
- Improved Soil Structure: It helps to improve the structure of the soil, increasing its ability to hold water and promoting root growth.
- Disease Prevention: The beneficial microorganisms in compost can help prevent plant diseases.
- Waste Reduction: Composting is a great way to reduce kitchen and yard waste, contributing to environmental sustainability.

However, there are also some disadvantages to consider:

- Time-Consuming: The composting process can be time-consuming and requires regular turning of the compost pile.
- Potential for Pests: If not managed properly, compost piles can attract pests and rodents.
- Variable Nutrient Content: The nutrient content of compost can vary depending on the materials used, making it difficult to ensure a consistent supply of specific nutrients.

While composting requires effort and careful management, the benefits it offers for both container and raised bed fruit gardening make it a worthwhile practice for many gardeners.

Loamy Soil

Loamy soil is a balanced blend of sand, silt, and clay, often considered the ideal medium for plant growth. It combines the best attributes of each soil type while mitigating their shortcomings. The sand component provides excellent drainage, the silt offers a generous capacity for water retention, and the clay contributes valuable minerals and nutrients. The term "loam" primarily refers to the soil's texture and doesn't denote its acidity or alkalinity.

The benefits of using loamy soil in container and raised bed fruit gardens include:

- Optimal Drainage: Loamy soil has good drainage properties, reducing the risk of waterlogged conditions leading to root diseases.
- Moisture Retention: While it drains well, loamy soil also retains enough moisture to keep plants hydrated.
- Nutrient-Rich: With its clay component, loamy soil is rich in essential nutrients needed by plants.
- Easy to work with: Loamy soil is typically friable, meaning it's crumbly and easy to work with, which is beneficial for root growth.

However, there are also some disadvantages to consider:

- Nutrient Leaching: Due to its good drainage, nutrients can leach out of loamy soil more quickly than they would in heavy clay soils.
- Watering Frequency: While it holds moisture well, loamy soil may still require more frequent watering than heavier soils, especially during hot weather.
- Cost and Availability: High-quality loamy soil can be

expensive and may not be readily available in all regions.

Although loamy soil presents certain difficulties, there are numerous advantages that make it a great option for fruit gardening in both raised beds and containers.

Soilless Mixes

Soilless potting mixes, as the name suggests, are growing mediums that do not contain traditional garden soil. Instead, they consist of a combination of organic and inorganic materials such as peat moss, perlite, vermiculite, coco coir, composted wood chips, and sometimes slow-release fertilizers. These mixes provide an environment for plant roots to grow and receive nutrients while also ensuring good drainage and air circulation.

The benefits of using soilless mixes in container and raised bed fruit gardens include:

- Disease-Free: Soilless mixes are typically sterile, which reduces the risk of soil-borne diseases.
- Improved Drainage and Aeration: These mixes are designed to provide excellent drainage and better aeration, promoting healthy root growth.
- Consistent Texture: Soilless mixes offer a uniform texture, ensuring consistent water and nutrient availability throughout the medium.
- Lightweight: They are lighter than regular garden soil, making them ideal for container gardening.

However, there are also a few disadvantages to consider:

- Cost: Soilless mixes can be more expensive than regular garden soil or compost.
- Nutrient Management: While some mixes come with added fertilizers, others do not. This means gardeners need to supplement their plants regularly with nutrients.
- Watering Frequency: Because of their excellent drainage, soilless mixes may require more frequent watering.

While there are some challenges associated with using soilless mixes, their many advantages make them an attractive option for both container and raised bed fruit gardening.

Enriched Soil Mixes

Enriched soil mixes are a type of garden soil that has been enhanced with additional nutrients and organic matter to improve its fertility. This could include materials like compost, peat moss, manure, bone meal, blood meal, or other natural fertilizers. These enriched soils are designed to provide an optimal growing environment for plants by offering a balanced blend of essential nutrients, good water retention, and excellent drainage.

The benefits of using enriched soil mixes in container and raised bed fruit gardens include:

- Nutrient-Rich: Enriched soil mixes are loaded with essential nutrients that plants need to grow and thrive.
- Improved Soil Structure: These mixes can enhance the

structure of the soil, improving its ability to retain moisture while also ensuring good drainage.

- Time-Saving: Because the soil is already enriched, gardeners may not need to add additional fertilizers as frequently.
- Enhanced Plant Growth: The additional nutrients and organic matter can stimulate plant growth and increase yields.

However, there are also some disadvantages to consider:

- Cost: Enriched soil mixes can be more expensive than regular garden soil.
- Potential for Over-Fertilization: If not used correctly, the high nutrient content can lead to over-fertilization, which can harm plants.
- Quality Variations: The quality and composition of enriched soil mixes can vary greatly depending on the manufacturer.

While using enriched soil mixes requires careful management to avoid over-fertilization, their ability to improve soil structure and deliver a rich blend of nutrients can make them a valuable resource for both container and raised bed fruit gardening.

CREATING ORGANIC SOIL FOR CONTAINER & RAISED BEDS FRUIT GARDENS

Creating organic soil for container and raised bed fruit gardening involves several steps, each aimed at creating a nutrient-rich, well-draining, and biologically active environment for your plants.

The first step in creating organic soil is to source high-quality organic materials. Compost is a key ingredient, providing a rich source of nutrients and beneficial microorganisms. You can make your own compost at home using kitchen scraps, yard waste, and other organic matter or purchase it from a reputable supplier. It's also beneficial to include aged manures, such as cow or chicken manure, which offer additional nutrients and help improve soil structure.

Next, consider adding amendments to improve the physical properties of your soil. Coarse sand improves drainage, while coconut coir or peat moss increases water retention. Both are particularly important for container gardening, where maintaining the right moisture balance is crucial. Organic matter like composted wood chips can also be added to improve soil structure and nutrient content.

Adding bone meal or rock phosphate can provide a slow-release source of phosphorus, an essential nutrient for fruit development. Similarly, greensand or kelp meal can supply trace minerals that are often lacking in garden soils but are necessary for plant health.

Once you have your ingredients, mix them thoroughly to ensure even distribution of nutrients and other soil amendments. The resulting mixture should be dark, crumbly, and smell earthy - signs of a healthy, organic soil. Test the pH of your soil to ensure it falls within the optimal range for fruit plants (typically between 6.0 and 7.0), and adjust if necessary using lime or sulfur.

Finally, fill your containers or raised beds with the prepared soil, leaving some space at the top for watering. Plant your fruit trees or plants according to their specific needs, water thoroughly, and monitor closely for the first few weeks to ensure they are adapting well to their new environment.

Creating organic soil for container and raised bed fruit gardening involves sourcing quality organic materials, adding amendments to improve soil properties, mixing the ingredients thoroughly, testing and adjusting pH, and planting and monitoring your fruit plants. With careful attention to these steps, you can create a thriving organic garden that yields abundant, healthy fruit.

PLANTING & SOWING FRUIT SEEDS IN CONTAINER & RAISED BED GARDENS

Choosing the right planting and sowing methods in container and raised bed fruit gardening is critical for several reasons, each of which contributes to the overall success and sustainability of your gardening efforts. Understanding the nuances of these methods can make a significant difference in plant health, yield and the ecological balance of your garden space.

Firstly, the choice between direct sowing and transplanting seedlings can impact the early development stage of your fruit plants. In container and raised bed setups, space is at a premium, and utilizing it efficiently is key to maximizing production.

Direct sowing is suitable for fruits that do not transplant well or have fast-growing roots, such as strawberries or melons. However, starting seeds indoors and transplanting seedlings can give you a head start on the growing season for slower-growing fruits like tomatoes or peppers. This method allows for better control over the growing conditions during the critical early stages, leading to stronger, more resilient plants.

Secondly, the method of planting also influences soil health and nutrient management. Containers and raised beds have limited soil volumes, making the efficient use of nutrients imperative. The right planting technique can help ensure that plants have access to the nutrients they need without over-crowding or competing excessively with each other.

For instance, companion planting can be an effective strategy in raised beds, where compatible plants are grown together to enhance growth, deter pests, and optimize nutrient use. This symbiotic relationship can lead to healthier plants and higher yields.

Moreover, the physical layout and depth at which seeds or seedlings are planted can significantly affect water usage and drainage – crucial elements in container and raised bed gardening. Properly spaced plants will have adequate room for root development and access to moisture while ensuring good air circulation above the soil, which helps prevent fungal diseases.

The depth at which seeds are sown affects germination rates and the initial root establishment. Too deep, and seeds may not germinate; too shallow, and they may dry out quickly or fail to anchor properly. Each fruit type has its specific needs, emphasizing the importance of understanding and applying the correct sowing depth and spacing guidelines.

Lastly, selecting the appropriate planting method also plays a role in pest and disease management. Raised beds and containers offer the advantage of starting with sterile soil, significantly reducing the risk of soil-borne diseases.

The strategic placement of plants can further minimize the threat of pests and diseases. For example, vertical trellising for vine fruits can improve air circulation, reducing humidity around the plants and subsequently the risk of fungal infections. Similarly, rotating crops in raised beds from year to year can prevent the buildup of pests and diseases that target specific plant families.

In summary, choosing the right planting and sowing methods in container and raised bed gardening is not just about ensuring the immediate survival and growth of plants; it's about optimizing the entire ecosystem of your garden. By considering factors like plant development, soil health, water management, and pest control, you can create productive, sustainable, and enjoyable gardening experiences.

TYPES OF PLANTING & SOWING METHODS IN CONTAINER & RAISED BED FRUIT GARDENS

In container and raised bed fruit gardens, gardeners can employ a variety of planting and sowing methods tailored to the specific needs of their plants and the constraints of their gardening space. These methods help in optimizing plant health, maximizing yield, and ensuring efficient use of space. Here are the different types of planting and sowing methods used in such gardens:

Direct Sowing

Direct sowing is a gardening technique that involves planting seeds directly into the outdoor garden space where they are intended to grow to maturity, rather than starting the seeds indoors and transplanting them outside later. This method can be applied in both traditional in-ground gardens and modern gardening approaches such as container and raised bed gardening.

Direct sowing is particularly appealing for its simplicity and natural alignment with a plant's growth cycle, but like any gardening method, it comes with its own set of advantages and disadvantages.

Benefits of direct sowing in container and raised bed fruit gardens:

- Simplicity and Ease: Direct sowing eliminates the need for indoor seed-starting setups, making it a straightforward and accessible method for gardeners of all skill levels. Seeds are simply planted in their final growing location, reducing the steps involved in the gardening process.
- Reduced Transplant Shock: Some plants are sensitive to root disturbance and can suffer from transplant shock if moved from one location to another. Direct sowing allows plants to establish in place without the stress of being transplanted, potentially leading to healthier, more resilient plants.
- Cost-Effective: Since direct sowing requires fewer supplies (no need for pots, trays, or additional potting soil for starting seeds indoors), it can be a more economical option for gardeners looking to minimize expenses.
- Natural Growth Conditions: Plants grown through direct sowing experience natural fluctuations in environmental conditions from an early stage, which can encourage stronger, more adaptable plants. They adjust to their outdoor environment as they grow, potentially leading to better performance.

Disadvantages of direct sowing in container and raised bed fruit gardens:

- Weather Dependency: Direct sowing is highly dependent on favorable weather conditions. Seeds sown too early can be damaged by frost, while those sown too late may not have enough time to mature before the end of the growing season. This makes timing critical and sometimes challenging.
- Increased Seed Predation: Seeds sown directly into containers and raised beds are more exposed to birds, insects, and other predators that can eat seeds before they have a chance to germinate.
- Variable Germination Rates: Not all seeds will germinate when sown directly, leading to patchy or sparse growth. Gardeners often have to sow more seeds than necessary to account for potential losses and then thin out extra seedlings, which can be wasteful and time-consuming.
- Weed Competition: Especially in raised beds, newly sown seeds may have to compete with weeds for light, nutrients, and water. This competition can hinder the growth of young plants and requires diligent weed management from the gardener.

Direct sowing can be a useful strategy for container and raised bed fruit gardening because it is simple, inexpensive, and provides plants with a natural growth habitat. However, it also faces obstacles such as weather dependency, seed predation, unpredictable germination rates, and weed competition. Gardeners must examine these criteria, as well as their individual gardening context and aims, before deciding whether direct sowing is the best strategy for their garden.

Transplanting Seedlings

Transplanting seedlings is a gardening technique where young plants, started from seeds in a controlled environment such as a greenhouse or indoors, are moved and planted into their final growing location, whether it be in the ground, a container, or a raised bed. This method is particularly popular for fruit gardening, where the early stages of a plant's life might require more controlled conditions to ensure a successful start.

The process involves carefully removing the young plant from its initial pot or tray, making sure to keep the root system intact, and then placing it in a prepared hole in the new growing medium, which has been appropriately enriched with nutrients.

Benefits of transplanting seedlings in container and raised bed fruit gardens:

- Extended Growing Season: Starting seeds indoors allows gardeners to get a head start on the growing season, especially in regions with shorter summers. This is particularly beneficial for fruits that have longer maturation periods, ensuring they can reach harvest before the first frost.
- Improved Germination Rates: By controlling the initial growing conditions, such as temperature, light, and moisture, gardeners can improve germination rates and ensure a more uniform growth among seedlings. This leads to healthier plants that are more likely to thrive when transplanted.
- Reduced Pest and Disease Pressure: Starting seedlings in a controlled environment can reduce the exposure to pests and diseases that are prevalent in

outdoor settings. This can lead to stronger, healthier plants that are better equipped to resist pests and diseases once transplanted.

- Optimized Space Utilization: For gardeners with limited space, starting seeds indoors and then transplanting allows for the maximization of growing space. This is because only the healthiest seedlings are selected for transplanting, avoiding the wastage of space on seeds that do not germinate or seedlings that do not thrive.

Disadvantages of transplanting seedlings in container and raised bed fruit gardens:

- Transplant Shock: One of the main risks associated with transplanting is the shock that plants can experience when moved to a new location. This can temporarily hinder growth as the plant adjusts to its new environment. However, careful handling and appropriate aftercare can mitigate this risk.
- Additional Labor and Resources: Transplanting seedlings requires more effort and resources compared to direct sowing. Starting seeds indoors necessitates additional equipment, such as grow lights and seed starting trays, and the process of transplanting itself is labor-intensive.
- Timing Challenges: Successfully transplanting seedlings requires precise timing. Transplanting too early can expose plants to harmful cold temperatures, while transplanting too late can cause seedlings to become root-bound or outgrow their starter containers, leading to stunted growth.
- Cost: Though not necessarily prohibitive, the initial setup costs for indoor seed starting (e.g., purchasing

grow lights, heating mats, and containers) can add up, making it a potentially more expensive option than direct sowing.

In summary, transplanting seedlings is a valuable technique in container and raised bed fruit gardening, offering advantages such as an extended growing season and healthier plants. However, it does come with its set of challenges, including the potential for transplant shock and the need for additional labor and resources.

Gardeners must weigh these factors against their specific circumstances, goals, and capabilities to determine if transplanting seedlings is the right approach for their garden.

Cuttings

Cuttings, a method of asexual plant reproduction, involve taking a segment of a stem, leaf, or root from a parent plant and enabling it to grow into a new plant. This technique is particularly popular in horticulture for its simplicity and efficiency in propagating a wide range of plants, including many fruit species.

When a cutting is taken, it is placed in a growing medium - such as soil, water, or a specialized propagation mix - where it develops its own root system before being transplanted to a more permanent location, such as a container or raised bed garden.

Benefits of using cuttings in container and raised bed fruit gardens:

- Genetic Uniformity: One of the primary advantages of propagation by cuttings is that the new plants are genetically identical to the parent plant. This ensures that any desirable traits present in the parent, such as fruit size, taste, or disease resistance, are preserved in the offspring.

- Cost-Effectiveness: Propagating plants from cuttings can be more economical than purchasing new plants. For gardeners looking to expand their garden without significant investment, cuttings provide a viable solution.
- Efficiency: Growing plants from cuttings can be faster than starting from seeds, particularly for fruit plants that may have long germination periods. This method allows gardeners to establish new plants quickly and potentially reach production sooner.
- Space-Saving: For those with limited space, such as container and raised bed gardeners, starting plants from cuttings can be a space-efficient way to propagate new plants. Cuttings can be started in small containers or propagation trays and then moved to their final location once rooted.

Disadvantages of using cuttings in container and raised bed fruit gardens:

- Limited Variety: Not all plants can be effectively propagated from cuttings. Some fruit plants may require other methods of propagation to successfully produce viable offspring. This limitation can restrict the variety of plants a gardener can grow using this method.
- Disease Transmission: Since cuttings are genetically identical to the parent plant, they can also inherit any diseases or pests present in the parent. Care must be taken to propagate healthy, disease-free plants to avoid spreading issues to new plants.

- Rooting Challenges: While many plants root easily from cuttings, others may require specific conditions, such as humidity and temperature control, to encourage root development. Without these conditions, cuttings may fail to root, leading to wasted effort and resources.
- Maintenance Requirements: Cuttings often require more attention in their initial stages than plants grown from seeds. They may need regular misting, specific light conditions, and careful handling to ensure successful rooting and growth, which can be time-consuming for the gardener.

Utilizing cuttings for propagation in container and raised bed fruit gardening presents several advantages, such as reduced expenses, consistent genetic characteristics, and streamlined growth processes. Nonetheless, this method is associated with certain drawbacks, including the risk of spreading diseases, a narrower range of plant varieties, challenges in achieving successful root development, and the necessity for more intensive care.

Gardeners are encouraged to weigh these considerations to determine if employing cuttings for propagation aligns with their specific gardening objectives and environmental circumstances.

Layering

Layering is a horticultural technique for plant propagation in which a stem still attached to the parent plant is encouraged to produce roots while it is still above ground. This is achieved by bending a branch to the soil level and partially burying it, leaving the tip exposed. Over time, this buried section of the stem develops its own root system.

Once the new roots are sufficiently developed, the stem can be cut from the parent plant and transplanted as an independent entity. Layering is commonly used with plants that have flexible stems and is particularly popular for propagating certain fruit bushes and vines.

Benefits of using layering in container and raised bed fruit gardens:

- High Success Rate: Layering has a very high success rate compared to other propagation methods, such as cuttings or seeds, because the new plant maintains a connection to the parent plant and continues receiving nutrients and water until it has developed its own root system.
- Simplicity: The process of layering is straightforward and does not require sophisticated equipment or conditions. It can be easily done by gardeners of all skill levels, making it an accessible method for expanding one's garden.
- No Transplant Shock: Since the new plant develops in the location where it will continue to grow, it does not experience the transplant shock that can occur when moving plants from one growing medium to another. This leads to healthier growth and quicker establishment.
- Genetic Uniformity: Similar to cuttings, layering produces plants that are genetically identical to the parent plant. This ensures that any desirable traits present in the parent, such as fruit flavor or disease resistance, are preserved in the offspring.

Disadvantages of using layering in container and raised bed fruit gardens:

- Limited to Certain Plants: Not all plants are suitable for propagation by layering. This method works best with plants that have long, flexible stems that can be easily bent to the ground, such as some berries and vines. This limits the variety of plants that can be propagated using this method.
- Space Requirements: Layering requires sufficient space around the parent plant to accommodate the bending and burying of stems. In container and raised bed gardening, where space may be at a premium, this can be a significant limitation.
- Slower Process: Developing a robust root system through layering can take several months or even a full growing season. This is slower compared to other propagation methods, such as cuttings, which can root and be ready for transplanting more quickly.
- Potential for Damage: The process of bending and securing stems to the ground has the potential to damage both the parent and the new plant if not done carefully. There is also a risk of the buried stem rotting before it can develop roots if conditions are too wet.

To summarize, layering is a propagation technique that provides numerous advantages for container and raised bed fruit planting, including a high success rate, ease, no transfer shock, and genetic homogeneity.

However, it is limited by the types of plants that can be propagated, the amount of space needed, the slower development of new plants, and the possibility of injury during the process. Gardeners should examine these characteristics, as well as their individual gardening situations while considering whether layering is the best propagation method for them.

Grafting

Grafting is a sophisticated horticultural technique where the tissues of two different plants are joined together so they continue to grow as one entity. This process involves taking a scion (the upper part of the graft, selected for its fruiting or flowering qualities) from one plant and attaching it to the rootstock (the lower part, chosen for its robustness and disease resistance) of another. When done correctly, the grafted parts fuse over time, combining the desirable traits of both the scion and rootstock into a single plant.

Grafting is a method widely used in the propagation of fruit trees, allowing for the reproduction of specific fruit varieties and the enhancement of plant characteristics such as disease resistance, yield, and adaptability to different soil types and climates.

Benefits of grafting in container and raised bed fruit gardens:

- Disease Resistance: Grafting allows gardeners to select rootstocks that are resistant to certain soil-borne diseases and pests, thereby reducing the need for chemical interventions and promoting healthier plants.
- Improved Yield: By combining the qualities of two different plants, grafting can lead to higher fruit yields. The rootstock can provide vigor and a well-established root system capable of supporting more abundant fruit production.

- Faster Fruit Production: Grafted plants often reach fruit-bearing maturity quicker than those grown from seed. This is particularly advantageous in container and raised bed gardening, where space and time may be limited.
- Size Control: Certain rootstocks are selected for their dwarfing properties, which are ideal for container and raised bed gardens. Dwarf rootstocks limit the size of the grafted plant, making it easier to manage and more suitable for small spaces.
- Adaptability: Grafting enables the cultivation of fruit varieties that might not be well-suited to the local climate or soil conditions. The rootstock can offer increased resilience and adaptability, allowing for a broader range of fruits to be grown.

Disadvantages of grafting in container and raised bed fruit gardens:

- Technical Skill Required: Grafting is a more complex propagation technique that requires knowledge, skill, and practice to perform successfully. Incorrectly executed grafts may fail to take, resulting in wasted effort and resources.
- Initial Cost: While grafting can save money in the long term by producing more robust plants, the initial investment in purchasing grafted plants or the materials needed for DIY grafting can be higher than other methods of propagation.
- Maintenance Needs: Grafted plants can require more careful maintenance, especially in the early stages after grafting. The graft union needs to be protected from physical damage and monitored for signs of disease or failure to ensure successful establishment.

- Limited Availability: The desired scion and rootstock varieties may be unavailable for those looking to perform their own grafting. This can restrict the range of plants that a gardener can graft and grow in their garden.

In summary, grafting presents a valuable technique for container and raised bed fruit gardening, offering benefits such as disease resistance, improved yield, faster fruit production, size control, and adaptability. However, it also poses challenges, including the need for technical skills, higher initial costs, increased maintenance needs, and potentially limited availability of plant materials. Gardeners considering grafting should weigh these factors against their gardening goals, resources, and expertise to determine if it is the right approach for their garden.

Square Foot Gardening

Square Foot Gardening (SFG) is an innovative, space-saving method of planning and organizing the growing area in your garden. This approach divides the garden space into small square segments, typically 1x1 foot each, within a grid layout.

This method is designed to create an efficient, highly productive garden in a limited space, making it particularly appealing for those with small gardens or for incorporating into container and raised bed gardening systems. The Square Foot Gardening Foundation highlights that this method can be learned quickly, emphasizing its accessibility to gardeners of all skill levels.

Benefits of square foot gardening in container and raised bed fruit gardens:

- Efficient Use of Space: By dividing the garden into small, manageable squares, gardeners can optimize the use of available space, enabling them to grow a variety of plants in a compact area. This is especially beneficial for container and raised bed gardens where space may be limited.
- Reduced Water Usage: Square Foot Gardening is designed to be water-efficient. With plants closely spaced in a confined area, water is directed precisely where it's needed, reducing waste and ensuring that plants receive adequate moisture without excess.
- Lower Maintenance: The dense planting in SFG reduces the space available for weeds to grow, thereby decreasing the time and effort required for weeding. Additionally, the raised beds commonly used in SFG are easier on the back, as they require less bending over.
- Cost-Effective: The initial setup of a square-foot garden can be more economical compared to traditional row gardening.
- Improved Soil Conditions: SFG encourages the use of a specific soil mix (often a combination of peat moss, vermiculite, and compost) that promotes healthy plant growth. This mix can be easily controlled and amended as needed, which is particularly advantageous in container gardening.

Disadvantages of square foot gardening in container and raised bed fruit gardens:

- Initial Setup Time and Expense: While overall more cost-effective, the initial setup of a Square Foot Garden can require a significant investment of time and resources. Building or purchasing raised beds, soil mix, and grid materials can add up.
- Limited Root Space for Some Plants: Certain fruit plants with extensive root systems may find the confined space of a square foot segment restrictive. This can limit the types of fruits that can be successfully grown using this method.
- Planning and Organization: To maximize the benefits of SFG, careful planning is necessary to ensure that each square is used efficiently throughout the growing season. This might be daunting for beginners or those looking for a more laid-back gardening approach.
- Watering Challenges: While SFG is designed to be water-efficient, the dense planting can sometimes lead to uneven water distribution, with some plants receiving too much and others too little. This requires careful monitoring and adjustment.

Square Foot Gardening presents a highly effective, streamlined, and user-friendly approach for those engaged in gardening within containers and raised beds. Key benefits of this method are optimized space use, reduced water usage, decreased upkeep, affordability, and improved soil quality.

However, gardeners must weigh potential drawbacks, including the initial investment of time and money, limitations on root growth for certain plants, the necessity for meticulous planning and management, and challenges related to irrigation. By carefully evaluating these factors, you can assess if Square Foot Gardening aligns with your gardening objectives and available resources.

Vertical Gardening

Vertical gardening is an innovative gardening technique that focuses on growing plants upwards rather than spreading them out horizontally. This approach uses various structures such as trellises, stakes, wall-mounted planters, and tower gardens to support the vertical growth of plants. It's a method that's gaining popularity among urban gardeners, those with limited outdoor space, and anyone looking to add an aesthetic appeal to their gardening endeavors.

Benefits of vertical gardening in container and raised bed fruit gardens:

- Space Efficiency: Vertical gardening maximizes the use of vertical space, allowing gardeners with limited ground area to grow more plants. This is particularly advantageous for container and raised bed gardens where horizontal space is at a premium.
- Improved Plant Health: Elevating plants off the ground can lead to better air circulation around the foliage, reducing the risk of diseases such as powdery mildew or leaf spot. Additionally, vertical structures can provide plants with more access to sunlight, which is beneficial for growth and fruit production.
- Ease of Harvest: Vertical gardening can make harvesting easier and more accessible. By growing plants at a higher level, bending and stooping are minimized, making it a more comfortable experience, especially for those with mobility issues.

- Aesthetic Appeal: Vertical gardens can add visual interest and beauty to any gardening space, whether it's a balcony, patio, or backyard. They can be used to create living walls, privacy screens, or simply to bring a touch of nature to urban environments.
- Pest Management: Growing plants vertically can help reduce exposure to certain pests found in the soil, potentially leading to healthier plants and higher yields.

Disadvantages of vertical gardening in container and raised bed fruit gardens:

- Structural Support Requirements: Implementing a vertical garden requires additional structures such as trellises, cages, or towers. These not only represent an initial investment but also need to be sturdy enough to support the weight of mature plants and fruits.
- Watering Challenges: Vertical gardens may require more frequent watering as they can dry out faster than traditional gardens, especially in containers and raised beds. Ensuring even water distribution can also be more challenging, as water tends to flow downwards, potentially leaving upper plants drier.
- Limited Plant Options: While many plants thrive in a vertical setting, not all fruits are suited to this method of gardening. Large or heavy fruiting plants may struggle without sufficient support, and some root systems may not develop as fully in confined spaces.
- Maintenance and Upkeep: Vertical gardens can require regular maintenance to ensure structures remain secure and plants are properly supported. Pruning, tying, and training plants to grow upwards can also add to the gardener's workload.

In summary, vertical gardening offers an effective solution for maximizing limited space, improving plant health, easing harvest, enhancing aesthetic appeal, and managing pests in container and raised bed fruit gardening. However, gardeners must consider the requirements for structural support, the challenges of watering and plant selection, and the increased maintenance that comes with adopting this approach.

Companion Planting

Companion planting is a time-honored gardening technique that involves growing different plant species in close proximity to each other for the mutual benefit of the plants involved. This practice is rooted in the understanding that certain plants can complement each other in various ways, such as enhancing growth, improving flavor, repelling pests, providing shade, and even fixing nitrogen in the soil.

Benefits of companion planting in container and raised bed fruit gardens:

- Pest Management: One of the most significant advantages of companion planting is its ability to naturally reduce pest populations. Certain plants can repel specific pests or attract beneficial insects that prey on common garden pests. For instance, marigolds are known to deter nematodes and other pests, making them an excellent companion for fruit plants susceptible to these invaders.
- Improved Pollination: Companion planting can also enhance pollination rates by attracting pollinators to the garden. Flowers and herbs interplanted with fruit crops can draw bees, butterflies, and other pollinating insects, thereby increasing the yield of fruit-bearing plants.

- Optimized Use of Space: In container and raised bed gardens, space is often limited. Companion planting allows gardeners to maximize their use of available space by pairing plants with complementary growth habits — for example, planting tall plants to provide shade for heat-sensitive shorter plants.
- Soil Health: Some companion plants can improve soil health by fixing nitrogen—a critical nutrient for plant growth. Legumes, such as peas and beans, have a symbiotic relationship with nitrogen-fixing bacteria, which can benefit neighboring plants by enriching the soil with nitrogen.
- Disease Suppression: The diversity encouraged by companion planting can help reduce the spread of plant diseases. By avoiding large monocultures, which can be breeding grounds for specific pathogens, gardeners can create a healthier, more resilient garden environment.

Disadvantages of companion planting in container and raised bed fruit gardens:

- Complex Planning: Implementing a successful companion planting strategy requires careful planning and knowledge of plant relationships. Gardeners need to research which plants are compatible and which combinations should be avoided, which can be time-consuming and complex for beginners.
- Space Limitations: While companion planting can optimize space usage, it can also lead to overcrowding if not planned correctly. In containers and raised beds, competition for resources like light,

water, and nutrients can become an issue if plants are too closely spaced.

- Watering Challenges: Different plants have varying water needs, and when diverse species are planted together, it can be challenging to meet these needs without overwatering some plants and underwatering others. This is particularly relevant in container gardening, where soil moisture levels can vary significantly.
- Risk of Unintended Consequences: Although many plant relationships are beneficial, some combinations can be detrimental. For example, certain plants may stunt the growth of their neighbors or attract pests that harm companion species. Without thorough research, gardeners may inadvertently create problems in their garden.

The practice of companion planting presents numerous advantages for those engaged in container and raised bed fruit gardening, such as effective pest control, enhanced pollination, efficient utilization of space, improved soil quality, and reduced disease occurrence. Nonetheless, these benefits are accompanied by certain challenges including intricate planning requirements, possible constraints on space, complexities in watering, and the possibility of adverse outcomes.

Through meticulous selection of plant pairings and attentiveness to the unique requirements and synergies of their plants, you can leverage the positive aspects of companion planting to cultivate a fruitful and ecologically sustainable garden environment.

CHAPTER 3
BERRY BUSHES: CONTAINER & RAISED BED GARDENS – STRAWBERRIES

S trawberries, with their vibrant red hue and sweet, juicy flavor, are a quintessential favorite that can add both beauty and bounty to any garden. Ideal for fruit containers and raised bed gardening, these versatile berries are not only delicious but also remarkably easy to grow, making them a perfect choice for gardeners of all experience levels. Whether nestled in compact containers on a sunny patio or sprawling elegantly in a well-structured raised bed, strawberries thrive in well-drained, fertile soil and require minimal space to produce an abundant harvest. This makes them an excellent option for those looking to maximize their yield in limited areas, bringing the delight of fresh, home-grown strawberries right to your doorstep.

Planting strawberries in containers and raised beds brings numerous benefits to your garden, making it an increasingly popular choice among gardening enthusiasts. One of the primary advantages is the enhanced control over the soil quality and composition.

Strawberries thrive in well-drained, fertile soil with a slightly acidic pH, conditions that are easier to maintain and adjust in containers and raised beds compared to traditional ground planting. This method also significantly reduces the risk of soil-borne diseases and pest infestations, such as slugs and snails, which can decimate strawberry plants.

Additionally, the elevated nature of raised beds and the mobility of containers make it simpler to manage weeds and harvest fruits without straining your back. These methods allow for extended growing seasons since the soil in containers and raised beds warms up faster than ground soil in the spring and can be covered easily during unexpected frosts.

For those with limited space, gardening with strawberries in containers and raised beds maximizes green space efficiently - turning patios, balconies, and small yards into productive areas whilst cultivating and ensuring a bountiful harvest of healthy strawberries.

THE RIGHT SOIL TO GROW STRAWBERRIES IN CONTAINER & RAISED BEDS

Creating the right soil conditions is crucial for successfully growing strawberries in fruit containers and raised beds, as these conditions directly influence the health, yield, and flavor of the strawberries. Strawberries prefer well-drained, loamy soil rich in organic matter, which ensures that the roots have access to both moisture and air.

For container and raised bed gardening, a mix of high-quality potting soil, compost, and a slow-release fertilizer will provide the nutrients these plants crave. Incorporating perlite or vermiculite can enhance drainage, preventing waterlogged conditions that lead to root rot, a common issue in poorly drained soils.

The pH level of the soil is another vital aspect to consider when cultivating strawberries. These fruits thrive in slightly acidic soil with a pH range of 5.5 to 6.8. Before planting, it's advisable to test the soil pH using a home testing kit or by seeking the services of a local extension office.

If the soil is too alkaline, incorporating elemental sulfur can help lower the pH, while if it's too acidic, adding garden lime can raise the pH to the desired level. Adjusting the soil pH to the optimal range ensures that strawberry plants can absorb the necessary nutrients effectively.

Likewise, maintaining the fertility of the soil in containers and raised beds is essential for the continued health of strawberry plants. Since these environments can deplete nutrients quicker than in-ground gardens, regular applications of a balanced, organic fertilizer throughout the growing season are beneficial. Additionally, mulching with straw or pine needles not only helps retain soil moisture and regulate temperature but also keeps the fruits clean and minimizes the risk of fungal diseases by preventing soil splash.

Lastly, because containers and raised beds warm up faster in the spring compared to ground soil, they allow for an earlier start to the growing season. However, this also means that the soil can dry out more quickly, especially during hot weather. Therefore, ensuring consistent moisture without overwatering is key. A drip irrigation system or a regular watering schedule that allows the soil to dry slightly between waterings will promote strong root development and prevent water stress, leading to healthier plants and a more bountiful harvest.

The right soil conditions for growing strawberries in fruit containers and raised beds involve a well-drained, nutrient-rich, slightly acidic soil mix, careful pH management, regular fertilization, and adequate moisture control. By meeting these requirements, gardeners can look forward to enjoying sweet, succulent strawberries straight from their garden.

HOW TO SOW STRAWBERRIES IN CONTAINERS & RAISED BEDS GARDENS

Correct Season To Sow Strawberries In Containers & Raised Beds Gardens

Selecting the correct season to sow strawberries in fruit containers and raised bed gardens is fundamental for ensuring a healthy growth cycle and maximizing yield. In most temperate regions, early spring, just after the last frost date, is the ideal time to plant strawberries. This period typically falls between late March and early April, when the soil has warmed up enough to support root development. Yet, the cooler temperatures enable the plants to establish without the stress of midsummer heat.

For gardeners looking to get a head start or extend their growing season, especially in cooler climates, strawberries can be sown in late summer or early fall. Planting during these times allows for an autumn establishment, giving the plants a robust start before going dormant in winter and then resuming vigorous growth in spring. This method can particularly benefit June-bearing varieties, producing an entire crop the following year.

Everbearing and day-neutral strawberries, on the other hand, planted in early spring, can yield fruit from summer through to the first frosts of fall, offering a continuous harvest. When growing strawberries in containers and raised beds, there's an added advantage of manipulating the microclimate to some extent.

For instance, moving containers indoors or under cover can protect early or late plantings from unexpected frosts. Thus, while early spring remains the prime planting season for strawberries in containers and raised bed gardens, strategic planning and the use of these gardening methods can provide flexibility and extend the growing and harvesting window for these cherished fruits.

Plant Needs & Requirements

Germinating strawberries from seeds to seedlings correctly is a critical step in the cultivation process, especially when growing in containers and raised beds. This initial phase sets the foundation for the health and productivity of the strawberry plants. Proper germination ensures that the strawberry plants develop a robust root system, which is essential for absorbing nutrients and water efficiently. A strong start is even more crucial in the contained environments of containers and raised beds, where resources are finite compared to open ground. Correctly germinated seedlings are more resilient to environmental stressors such as fluctuations in moisture levels, temperature changes, and limited space for root expansion. Furthermore, healthy germination leads to vigorous seedlings that are better equipped to compete with weeds and resist pests and diseases, reducing the need for chemical interventions.

Achieving optimal germination involves controlling soil temperature, maintaining consistent moisture without waterlogging, and providing adequate light—all factors that are more manageable in the controlled settings of containers and raised beds.

This attention to detail during the germination stage pays off with a more uniform and timely harvest, maximizing the yield from each plant. Therefore, investing time and care into correctly germinating strawberry seeds to seedlings not only improves the overall success rate but also enhances the quality and quantity of the strawberries produced, making it an invaluable step in the cultivation process.

Germinating strawberry plants from seeds to seedlings is a meticulous process that requires attention to detail and patience. The first step in this process involves preparing the right kind of soil mix. A light, well-draining soil blend rich in organic matter is ideal for strawberry seeds. Mixing potting soil with peat and sand can create an optimal environment for germination.

Once the soil is ready, sow the strawberry seeds on the surface, lightly pressing them into the soil without covering them, as they need light to germinate. Next, water the seeds gently using a fine mist to ensure the soil is moist but not soggy.

Strawberry seeds germinate best at temperatures between 60°F to 75°F (15°C to 24°C). Maintaining this temperature range is crucial, and using a heat mat can help to provide consistent warmth, especially if germinating seeds indoors during cooler months.

Additionally, the seeds require ample light during this period. Placing the seed tray in a brightly lit area or under grow lights for about 8-10 hours a day will encourage germination. Under these conditions, strawberry seeds typically begin to germinate within 2 to 3 weeks, though some can take a bit longer depending on the variety and germination conditions.

After the seeds have sprouted and the seedlings have developed their first true leaves—leaves that appear after the initial sprout leaves—it's an indication that they are gradually getting ready to be transplanted. However, it's important to allow the seedlings to grow strong enough in their initial trays or containers, which usually takes about another 3-4 weeks.

During this time, continue to provide them with sufficient light and maintain the soil moisture at a consistent level, gradually reducing the temperature to more closely mimic outdoor conditions if they are being moved to an outdoor raised bed or container garden.

The strawberry seedlings are ready to be transplanted into containers or raised bed gardens when they are about 2-3 inches tall and have developed a robust set of leaves. Before transplanting, it's essential to acclimate the seedlings to outdoor conditions by gradually exposing them to outside temperatures and sunlight over a week, a process known as hardening off. This helps prevent transplant shock and eases their transition to a new growing environment. When transplanting, ensure that the soil in the containers or raised beds is rich in organic matter and well-draining to support the young plants' growth.

In summary, successful germination of strawberry seeds involves preparing the right soil mix, ensuring the correct temperature and light conditions, and carefully nurturing the seedlings until they are strong enough for transplantation. By following these steps meticulously, you can look forward to establishing healthy strawberry plants in your containers and raised beds, leading to a fruitful harvest.

Spacing & Measurement

Proper spacing and measurements when transplanting strawberry seedlings into fruit containers and raised bed gardens are crucial for several important reasons. Firstly, adequate spacing ensures that each plant receives enough sunlight, air, and nutrients from the soil, which are essential for healthy growth and development. Crowded plants compete for these resources, which can lead to stunted growth and reduced fruit production.

Secondly, appropriate spacing helps maintain good air circulation around the plants, reducing the risk of fungal diseases such as powdery mildew and leaf blight that thrive in moist, congested conditions.

Additionally, well-spaced plants allow for easier access when it comes to maintenance activities such as watering, fertilizing, and harvesting, making the gardening process more efficient and enjoyable. In containers, ensuring that each plant has enough room to grow is also vital for root development;

cramped conditions can constrain root growth, affecting the plant's overall health and productivity.

Finally, proper measurements and spacing are key to aesthetic appeal, creating visually pleasing arrangements in containers and raised beds that enhance the gardening space.

For raised bed gardens, strawberry plants typically require about 12-18 inches of space between plants. This spacing allows each strawberry plant to spread out as it grows, ensuring that each plant has enough room to develop a healthy root system and foliage without competing with its neighbors for resources. Between rows, a distance of 24-36 inches is recommended to allow for easy access for maintenance activities such as weeding, watering, and harvesting.

The precise spacing may vary depending on the variety of strawberries being planted; for example, June-bearing strawberries might need more space between plants compared to everbearing or day-neutral varieties, which can be planted slightly closer together due to their continuous, less vigorous growth habit.

In the case of fruit containers, the size of the container dictates how many strawberry seedlings can be planted within it. A standard rule of thumb is to plant one strawberry plant for every 6-8 inches of surface area. For example, a 12-inch diameter pot can comfortably support 2-3 plants, ensuring they have enough space to grow without overcrowding.

When using larger containers or planter boxes, maintain the same per-plant spacing as you would in a raised bed, observing the 12–18-inch spacing guideline. This ensures that even in a container, strawberry plants have ample room to develop robust root systems and healthy foliage.

Additionally, choosing containers with sufficient depth is important, as strawberries have relatively shallow roots; a depth of 8-12 inches is typically adequate.

It's also worth noting that the layout of plants in raised beds can follow either a traditional row format or a staggered (or hexagonal) pattern, which can maximize space efficiency while still maintaining proper spacing. In containers, arranging plants near the edge with equal spacing allows for even growth and fruit production, with the center of the container acting as a communal space for roots to expand.

Overall, adhering to these spacing and measurement guidelines when planting strawberry seedlings in both fruit containers and raised bed gardens not only optimizes the health and productivity of the plants but also makes maintenance easier, ensuring that your gardening efforts yield the sweetest rewards.

Ideal Temperatures & Sun Requirements

The ideal temperatures and sun requirements play a pivotal role in the successful cultivation of strawberries in fruit containers and raised bed gardens, significantly affecting their growth, fruit production, and overall health. Strawberries thrive in full sunlight, needing at least 6 to 8 hours of direct sun daily to produce the best yields.

Sunlight is essential for photosynthesis, the process by which plants convert light energy into chemical energy, fueling their growth and enabling them to develop fruits. Furthermore, the optimal temperature range for growing strawberries falls between 60°F and 80°F (15°C to 27°C). Within this range, strawberry plants can efficiently perform metabolic activities necessary for vigorous growth and fruiting.

Temperatures that are too low can slow down growth and delay fruiting, while excessively high temperatures can lead to plant stress, reduced fruit quality, and even plant death. Maintaining these ideal temperature and sunlight conditions ensures that strawberry plants can photosynthesize effectively, leading to strong, healthy plants and an abundant harvest of sweet, juicy strawberries.

Therefore, when planning a strawberry garden in containers or raised beds, choosing a location that meets these sun exposure requirements and monitoring the microclimate to protect plants from extreme temperatures are key strategies for maximizing your strawberry crop's potential.

MAINTAINING YOUR CONTAINER & RAISED BED STRAWBERRIES

Maintaining strawberries in fruit containers and raised bed gardens is paramount for several compelling reasons. Regular maintenance, including appropriate watering, fertilizing, and pruning, ensures that strawberry plants remain healthy, vigorous, and productive throughout their growing season. Proper watering keeps the soil moist but not waterlogged, preventing root rot and stress from drought, while fertilization supplies essential nutrients that support growth and fruit production.

Additionally, pruning old leaves and runners helps direct the plant's energy into producing large, sweet fruits rather than excessive foliage or offspring plants. This maintenance routine also involves monitoring for pests and diseases, which, if left unchecked, can quickly devastate a crop.

Beyond these practical aspects, maintaining your strawberry plants can extend their productive lifespan, allowing for multiple fruitful seasons from perennials in raised beds and maximizing the yield and quality of the berries in both containers and raised gardens.

Essentially, diligent care and maintenance of strawberry plants are the cornerstones of a successful and rewarding strawberry gardening experience, ensuring a bountiful harvest of fresh, flavorful strawberries right from your garden.

Pruning & Thinning Your Strawberries

Pruning and thinning strawberries grown in containers and raised bed gardens are crucial practices for ensuring the health and productivity of the plants. This process involves removing dead or diseased leaves, trimming back excessive runners, and thinning out overcrowded plants. These actions are vital for several reasons.

Firstly, they help to improve air circulation around and within the plant, significantly reducing the risk of fungal infections and other diseases that can thrive in damp, stagnant conditions. Secondly, by removing unproductive or excessive growth, pruning allows the plant to direct more energy towards fruit production rather than maintaining unnecessary foliage or runners. This results in larger, more flavorful strawberries. Thinning overcrowded plants ensures that each strawberry plant has enough space to access the sunlight, nutrients, and water it needs to thrive, preventing competition between plants that can lead to stunted growth and poor yield.

Additionally, pruning and thinning make it easier to inspect the plants regularly for pests and diseases, allowing for early detection and management. Overall, regular pruning and thinning are integral to maintaining a healthy, productive strawberry garden, leading to bountiful harvests from your container or raised bed gardens.

Pruning and thinning strawberries grown in containers and raised bed gardens are essential tasks that should be carried out with precision and at the right time to ensure the health and productivity of the plants. The best time for these activities is after the plants have finished fruiting, usually in late summer or early fall. This timing allows the plants to recover and prepare for the next growing season. Additionally, any dead or diseased foliage should be removed as soon as it is noticed throughout the growing season to prevent the spread of disease.

Pruning involves cutting back the foliage and removing any runners, which are long shoots that extend from the main plant and have the potential to root and form new plants. While runners can be beneficial for propagating new plants in a contained environment like a container or raised bed, they can lead to overcrowding and competition for resources.

Use clean, sharp scissors or pruning shears to cut the runners close to the base of the main plant. It's also important to remove any leaves that are damaged, diseased, or dying to improve air circulation and reduce the risk of fungal infections.

Thinning is slightly different and involves selectively removing entire plants that are too close together. In containers and raised beds where space is limited, ensuring each strawberry plant has enough room is crucial. If they are too close, gently dig up and remove the excess plants, being careful not to disturb the roots of the remaining plants. This can be done in the early spring before the plants begin their vigorous growth or after the harvest when you're already pruning the plants.

Both pruning and thinning are important not just for the health of the plants but also for their productivity. By focusing the plants' energy on fruit production rather than sustaining excess foliage or producing runners, you can enjoy a more fruitful harvest.

Watering Your Container & Raised Bed Strawberries

Watering strawberries in containers and raised bed gardens is paramount for several reasons, underpinning the health and productivity of these beloved plants. Strawberries have shallow root systems, making them particularly vulnerable to water stress, which can drastically affect their growth and fruiting potential.

In containers and raised beds, soil dries out more quickly than in-ground, necessitating regular and careful watering to maintain consistent soil moisture levels. Adequate water is essential for sustaining the plants' basic metabolic functions and ensuring the development of juicy, full-flavored fruits.

Uneven or insufficient watering can lead to problems such as poor fruit development, increased susceptibility to diseases, and physiological issues like blossom end rot; however, it's crucial to balance this by avoiding overwatering, which can lead to root rot and fungal diseases due to lack of air in the soil.

Watering strawberries in containers and raised beds correctly involves understanding both the frequency and quantity of water required to keep these plants healthy and productive. For strawberries, maintaining a consistent moisture level is key; their shallow roots do not fare well under either drought or waterlogged conditions.

Generally, strawberries need about 1 to 2 inches of water per week, but this can vary based on temperature, plant size, and the growth stage. During hot, dry spells, more frequent watering may be necessary to prevent stress, whereas cooler, cloudy periods may require less.

For container-grown strawberries, it's vital to check the soil moisture daily, especially in warm weather. Containers can dry out quickly, sometimes needing water twice a day during peak summer heat. A good rule of thumb is to water when the top inch of soil feels dry to the touch. Ensure that containers have adequate drainage holes to prevent water from pooling at the bottom, which can lead to root rot and other issues. When watering, do so thoroughly, allowing water to run out of the drainage holes at the bottom of the container, ensuring the roots receive adequate moisture.

Raised bed strawberries also require careful attention to watering. Because raised beds have improved drainage, they can dry out faster than ground-level gardens, necessitating regular monitoring of soil moisture.

Early morning is the best time to water, as it allows leaves to dry out during the day, reducing the risk of fungal diseases. Using a soaker hose or drip irrigation system for raised beds can be particularly effective, delivering water directly to the base of the plants and keeping foliage dry. This method also conserves water by reducing evaporation and runoff.

It's essential to adjust your watering strategy in both containers and raised beds as the plants enter different growth stages. During the establishment phase and flowering, consistent moisture is crucial for the development of strong plants and the formation of fruit. However, once fruits begin to ripen, slightly reducing watering can help concentrate sugars in the berries, enhancing flavor.

Always ensure that the watering approach you adopt accounts for environmental conditions and plant needs, aiming for deep, infrequent watering sessions that encourage robust root growth over superficial, frequent sprinkling. This approach ensures that strawberries develop a healthy root system capable of accessing water and nutrients efficiently, supporting overall plant health and fruit production.

Organic Fertilization For Container & Raised Bed Strawberries

Organic fertilization plays a crucial role in the cultivation of strawberries in containers and raised bed gardens, primarily due to its comprehensive approach to plant nutrition and soil health. Unlike synthetic fertilizers, organic fertilizers release nutrients slowly, providing strawberries with a steady supply of essential nutrients as they grow. This gradual feeding mimics the natural nutrient uptake process of plants, reducing the risk of over-fertilization and nutrient burn, which can be detrimental in the confined spaces of containers and raised beds.

Organic fertilizers also improve soil structure and increase its water-holding capacity, which is vital for the shallow root system of strawberries. They enrich the soil with organic matter, encouraging the proliferation of beneficial microorganisms that aid in nutrient breakdown and absorption as well as helping to suppress soil-borne diseases. By using organic fertilization methods, gardeners not only ensure that their strawberry plants are nourished in a more balanced and sustainable way but also contribute to a healthier, more vibrant ecosystem within their garden.

This approach supports the production of high-quality, flavorful strawberries while maintaining the environmental integrity of the gardening practice, making organic fertilization an essential component of successful container and raised bed strawberry cultivation.

One effective type of organic fertilizer for strawberries is compost. Compost, made from decomposed organic matter like leaves, kitchen scraps, and manure, is rich in nutrients and beneficial microorganisms. It improves soil structure, which helps retain moisture and provides a slow release of nutrients as plants need them. You can mix compost into the soil before planting strawberries and top-dress the soil with additional compost during the growing season to continue supplying nutrients.

Another suitable organic fertilizer for strawberries is well-aged manure, particularly from cows, horses, or chickens. Manure adds essential nutrients such as nitrogen, phosphorus, and potassium to the soil, vital for plant growth and fruit development.

It's important to use aged or composted manure to avoid introducing pathogens to your garden and to prevent burning plants with too much nitrogen. Apply aged manure to the soil a few weeks before planting and again as a top dressing mid-season to nourish the plants.

Worm castings are also an excellent organic fertilizer option for strawberry plants in containers and raised beds. Worm castings are the end product of the decomposition process carried out by earthworms. This organic matter is rich in water-soluble nutrients, making it an easily accessible food source for plants. Worm castings can improve soil structure, increase water retention, and help suppress diseases. They can be mixed into the soil at planting time and added around the base of plants throughout the growing season.

Fish emulsion and seaweed extracts are liquid organic fertilizers that provide a quick nutrient boost to strawberry plants. These fertilizers are high in nitrogen and trace minerals, promoting strong vegetative growth and helping plants recover from transplant shock. They can be diluted with water and applied to the soil or used as a foliar spray during the growing season. It's best to apply these liquid fertilizers every 2-4 weeks, following the manufacturer's instructions for dilution rates.

When fertilizing strawberries in containers and raised beds, timing and application methods are important. Apply solid fertilizers like compost, manure, and worm castings at planting time and again as a mid-season boost.

For liquid fertilizers like fish emulsion and seaweed extracts, begin applications in early spring when plants start actively growing and continue through the summer as needed. Constantly water the soil well after applying solid fertilizers to help distribute nutrients and avoid applying fertilizers directly to leaves or fruit to prevent burning.

By selecting the appropriate organic fertilizers and applying them at the right times, you can ensure that your container and raised bed-grown strawberries receive the nutrients they need to thrive and produce delicious fruits.

PROTECTING YOUR CONTAINER & RAISED BED STRAWBERRIES

Extreme Temperatures

Protecting strawberries grown in containers and raised beds from extreme temperatures is essential for maintaining their health, ensuring vigorous growth, and achieving optimal fruit production. Strawberries are particularly sensitive to temperature fluctuations, which can impact their flowering patterns, fruit set, and overall yield.

In regions with hot summers, high temperatures can stress plants, leading to poor fruit development, while in colder climates, frost can damage or kill the plants. Implementing strategies to moderate temperature extremes is key to cultivating thriving strawberry plants.

Utilizing shade cloth or row covers can be highly effective in shielding strawberries from the scorching summer heat. These materials can be strategically placed to provide partial shade during the hottest parts of the day, ideally allowing morning sunlight while protecting plants during peak afternoon heat. This practice helps prevent heat stress, which can cause blossoms to drop and negatively affect fruit size and taste. Additionally, mulching with organic materials like straw or wood chips around the plants can help maintain cooler soil temperatures and retain moisture, further reducing heat stress on the plants.

Equally, in cooler climates or during unexpected cold snaps in spring or fall, protecting strawberries from frost is crucial. Floating row covers or frost blankets can be draped over the plants at night to trap ground heat and shield the plants from freezing temperatures.

For container-grown strawberries, simply moving the containers indoors or to a sheltered area can provide necessary protection from cold weather. It's also beneficial to use mulch to insulate the roots, offering an extra layer of defense against sudden drops in temperature.

Watering practices can also play a role in temperature management. Watering in the early morning during hot weather ensures that plants are hydrated before the heat of the day, reducing the risk of heat stress. In anticipation of a frost, watering the soil around the plants can help it retain heat, mitigating the impact of sudden cold.

Protecting strawberries from extreme temperatures not only safeguards the plants themselves but also ensures the production of high-quality fruits. Stress from heat or cold can significantly impact the flavor, size, and texture of strawberries, making temperature management a critical aspect of care.

By implementing protective measures, you can extend the growing season, improve yield, and enjoy delicious, home-grown strawberries despite challenging weather conditions. Adapting these strategies to the specific needs of your garden, considering local climate conditions and seasonal variations will contribute to the success and sustainability of your strawberry cultivation efforts.

Protecting Container & Raised Bed Strawberries From Pests

Opting for organic methods to protect container and raised bed grown strawberries from pests is important not only for the health of the plants but also for the safety of consumers and the environment. Organic pest management embraces the use of natural predators, barriers, and botanical sprays that work harmoniously with nature, reducing the reliance on synthetic chemicals that can harm beneficial insects, soil health, and water quality.

This approach ensures that strawberries remain free from potentially harmful residues, aligning with the growing consumer demand for organically produced foods known for their healthfulness and superior flavor. Furthermore, organic practices enhance biodiversity, encourage a balanced ecosystem where pests are naturally regulated, and promote the sustainability of gardening spaces.

By protecting strawberries organically, you ensure a safe, nutritious crop while stewarding the environment responsibly, preserving it for future generations. This methodological shift towards organic pest management reflects a broader commitment to health, sustainability, and ecological balance, crucial elements for thriving container and raised bed gardens.

Strawberries grown in containers and raised beds, while advantageous for managing soil conditions and improving drainage, are not immune to the threat of pests. These pests can range from tiny insects to larger critters, all capable of causing significant damage to strawberry plants. Common pests include aphids, spider mites, slugs, snails, and birds.

Aphids and spider mites suck sap from the plants, weakening them and potentially spreading diseases. Slugs and snails, on the other hand, are notorious for eating large holes in the fruit and leaves, often under the cover of darkness. Birds, attracted by the ripe berries, can decimate a crop in a very short period if left unchecked.

Protecting strawberries organically involves implementing strategies that prevent these pests from becoming a problem without resorting to synthetic chemicals. For aphids and spider mites, one effective organic method is the introduction of natural predators such as ladybugs and lacewings into the garden. These beneficial insects feed on the pests, naturally reducing their numbers.

Another method is spraying the plants with a mixture of water and neem oil or insecticidal soap, which can deter or kill these pests without harming the plant. It's important to apply these treatments in the evening to avoid harming beneficial pollinators and to minimize the impact on the plants themselves.

Slugs and snails can be managed by creating barriers around the strawberry plants. Copper tape or sharp grit can discourage these pests from climbing into the beds or containers. Additionally, setting up beer traps – shallow containers filled with beer near the plants – can attract and drown slugs and snails. Regularly clearing the garden area of debris and weeds can also reduce hiding places for these pests, making your strawberry garden less attractive to them.

For bird protection, netting is the most effective organic solution. Covering the plants with a fine mesh net can prevent birds from accessing the fruits while still allowing sunlight, rain, and pollinators through. Ensure the net is secured well and lifted above the plants to prevent birds from reaching the strawberries through the mesh.

Lastly, practicing crop rotation and companion planting can significantly reduce pest issues in container and raised bed gardens. Planting garlic or onions near strawberries can repel some pests while rotating crops each year minimizes disease buildup and disrupts the life cycle of pests that have become established in the soil.

By integrating these organic pest management strategies, gardeners can protect their strawberries effectively, ensuring a healthy, productive, and sustainable garden. It's important to monitor plants regularly for signs of pest activity and intervene early with the least invasive methods possible, gradually escalating to more comprehensive measures if necessary. This approach not only protects the strawberry plants but also contributes to a healthier garden ecosystem overall.

Protecting Container & Raised Bed Strawberries From Diseases

Protecting strawberries grown in containers and raised beds from diseases organically is paramount for several reasons. Firstly, organic methods ensure the health and safety of the produce, eliminating the risk of chemical residue that can harm humans and beneficial garden inhabitants. Diseases such as powdery mildew, botrytis gray mold, and verticillium wilt can devastate a strawberry crop, reducing both yield and quality.

By employing organic preventive measures, such as proper spacing for air circulation, using clean potting soil, and practicing crop rotation, you can significantly reduce the occurrence of these diseases. Additionally, organic approaches, like applying compost teas or using resistant strawberry varieties, strengthen the plants' natural defenses, promoting a more vibrant, resilient garden ecosystem. This supports the biodiversity necessary for a healthy garden and contributes to a more sustainable agricultural practice overall.

Protecting strawberries from diseases organically thus ensures that the fruits are safe and nutritious to eat, while also safeguarding the environment and supporting the well-being of the garden ecosystem.

Strawberries grown in containers and raised beds are susceptible to several diseases that can significantly impact their health and productivity. Common diseases include powdery mildew, which appears as a white powdery substance on leaves and stems, causing the foliage to wither and die.

Botrytis gray mold is another prevalent issue, especially in cool, wet conditions, leading to fruit rot and yield loss. Verticillium wilt, a soil-borne fungal disease, results in the wilting and death of plants by obstructing the water conducting systems within the plant. Lastly, leaf spot and leaf blight can cause dark spots on leaves, weakening the plant over time.

To organically protect strawberries from these diseases, you can adopt a multifaceted approach focused on prevention, cultural practices, and natural treatments. Starting with disease-resistant varieties is a fundamental step, as these plants are bred to be less susceptible to common pathogens.

Proper spacing between plants ensures good air circulation, reducing the humidity that fosters fungal growth. Using clean, sterile potting mix for container-grown strawberries and ensuring raised beds have well-draining soil can prevent the onset of root rot and other moisture-related diseases.

Maintaining cleanliness around the garden is also crucial. Removing debris and fallen leaves minimizes the habitats for fungi and bacteria to thrive. Regularly inspecting plants for early signs of disease allows for prompt removal of affected parts, preventing the spread to healthy foliage or fruits. Crop rotation, even in small-scale container gardening, can help break the life cycle of soil-borne pathogens.

For managing diseases without synthetic chemicals, organic fungicides based on copper or sulfur can be effective when used as a preventive measure before symptoms appear. Applying compost tea or baking soda sprays can offer a mild fungicidal effect for surface-level issues like powdery mildew. Introducing beneficial microorganisms through quality compost or mycorrhizal fungi inoculants can enhance the plant's resilience by boosting the soil's biological health.

Another organic strategy involves using mulches, such as straw or wood chips, to reduce soil splash, which can spread spores to the lower leaves of plants. This helps keep the area clean, retains soil moisture, and regulates temperature, creating unfavorable conditions for disease proliferation.

By combining these organic practices, you can effectively manage and mitigate diseases in your strawberry crops, ensuring a healthy, productive garden. These methods align with sustainable gardening principles, promoting a balanced ecosystem while producing safe, nutritious fruits free from chemical residues.

HARVESTING CONTAINER & RAISED BED STRAWBERRIES

The timeline for strawberries to reach harvest readiness in containers and raised beds largely depends on the variety planted and the conditions under which they are grown. Generally, strawberries fall into three main types: June-bearing, everbearing, and day-neutral. June-bearing strawberries typically produce a single, large crop per year over a period of 2-3 weeks, usually in late spring to early summer, depending on the local climate.

Everbearing varieties produce two smaller crops, one in late spring/early summer and another in late summer/early fall. Day-neutral strawberries can produce fruit throughout the growing season, provided temperatures remain between 35°F and 85°F.

From planting, June-bearing strawberries usually take about a year before they bear fruit, as most gardeners remove flowers during the first year to encourage stronger plant development. Everbearing and day-neutral plants, on the other hand, can start producing fruit a few months after planting.

For instance, if planted in early spring, these plants may begin yielding strawberries by early to mid-summer of the same year. It's important to note that proper care in terms of watering, feeding, and disease prevention plays a crucial role in the speed and abundance of the harvest.

Harvesting strawberries at the right time is essential for enjoying their full flavor. Strawberries are ready for harvest when entirely red, with no white or green spots, and the fruit is plump. Unlike some fruits, strawberries do not ripen after being picked, so it's best to wait until they're fully ripe before harvesting.

The best time to pick strawberries is in the morning when they are still cool. To harvest, gently grasp the stem just above the berry between the forefinger and the thumbnail and pull with a slight twisting motion. Leaving a short portion of the stem attached can help improve the berry's shelf life. Regular picking encourages plants to produce more fruit, so it's beneficial to harvest every two to three days during peak production.

After harvesting, strawberries should be gently washed in cool water and allowed to dry before being stored in the refrigerator, where they can be kept for a few days. However, for the best flavor, strawberries are most delightful when consumed fresh, soon after picking. Container and raised bed gardens offer the advantage of easier access and control over the growing environment, which can lead to a rewarding and fruitful strawberry harvest with the right care and attention.

CONTAINER & RAISED BEDS STRAWBERRIES NOTES

Start: Seeds or Seedlings.

Germination: 2-3weeks, at temperatures between 60°F to 75°F (15°C to 24°C).

Seed Life: 3 Years.

Soil Type: Well-drained, loamy soil rich in organic matter - pH between 5.5 to 6.8.

Seed Spacing: ¼" depth.

Seedling Spacing:

Containers - One strawberry plant per every 6-8 inches of surface area. For example, a 12-inch diameter pot can support 2-3 plants.

Raised Beds - 12-18 inches of space between plants.

Sunlight: 6 – 8hrs full sunlight daily.

Growing Temperatures: Temperatures between 60°F and 80°F (15°C to 27°C).

Duration Till Harvest:

June-bearing Strawberries - June-bearing strawberries usually take about a year before they bear fruit. Everbearing / Day-neutral Strawberries - Everbearing and day-neutral plants can start producing fruit a few months after planting. If planted in early spring, these plants may begin yielding strawberries by early to mid-summer of the same year.

CHAPTER 4

BERRY BUSHES: CONTAINER & RAISED BED GARDENS – RASPBERRIES

R aspberries are a delightful and versatile fruit that adapts remarkably well to container and raised bed gardening, offering an appealing option for gardeners with limited space or those seeking to optimize their yield in a controlled environment. These lush, perennial plants are known for their delectable fruit, rich in vitamins, antioxidants and fiber, making them as nutritious as they are delicious. Whether you choose red, black, golden, or purple varieties, raspberries can thrive and produce bountiful harvests with the right care, even outside of traditional in-ground garden settings.

Container and raised bed gardening allows for enhanced soil management, improved drainage, and easier access for maintenance and harvesting, creating an ideal microclimate for these berry plants. By adopting such cultivation methods, you can enjoy the sweet rewards of fresh raspberries grown right at home, turning balconies, patios, and small gardens into productive berry patches that entice both the palate and the eye.

Planting raspberries in containers and raised beds offers a multitude of benefits that can significantly enhance your gardening experience and improve the health and productivity of your plants. One of the primary advantages is the ability to control the growing medium, ensuring that the soil has the perfect balance of nutrients, drainage, and pH levels, which raspberries require for optimum growth. This level of control helps prevent common soil-borne diseases and pests, which can be particularly problematic in traditional in-ground gardens.

Containers and raised beds also allow for better air circulation around the plants, reducing the risk of fungal diseases. For gardeners with limited space, container and raised bed gardening makes it possible to grow raspberries in small areas, including patios, balconies, or urban gardens, maximizing the use of available space while still enjoying a bountiful harvest.

Furthermore, the elevated nature of raised beds can make tending to the plants easier on the back and knees, making gardening more accessible and enjoyable.

THE RIGHT SOIL TO GROW RASPBERRIES IN CONTAINER & RAISED BEDS

Creating the right soil conditions is paramount when growing raspberries in containers and raised bed gardens, as these conditions directly influence plant health, berry quality, and yield. Raspberries prefer a well-drained, loamy soil rich in organic matter, which ensures a balance of moisture retention and aeration essential for their root systems.

To achieve this ideal soil structure in containers and raised beds, a mix of garden soil, compost, and a coarse material like perlite or sand can be used. This combination promotes good drainage while still holding enough moisture to keep the roots hydrated.

The pH level of the soil is another critical factor for raspberry plants. They thrive in slightly acidic conditions, with an optimal pH range of 5.5 to 6.5. Before planting, testing the soil's pH is advisable to ensure it falls within this range. If the soil is too alkaline, incorporating sulfur can help lower the pH, while if it's too acidic, adding garden lime will raise the pH to a more suitable level. Adjusting the pH not only affects nutrient availability but also maximizes plant uptake, enhancing growth and fruit production.

In addition to the physical properties and pH of the soil, nutrient content is vital for supporting healthy raspberry plants. A balanced, slow-release fertilizer rich in nitrogen, phosphorus, and potassium at the beginning of the growing season can promote vigorous growth and ample fruiting.

However, because raspberries are sensitive to high nitrogen levels, especially in container environments where nutrients are more concentrated, it's important to apply fertilizers according to recommended rates and to incorporate organic matter regularly. Organic materials, such as compost or well-rotted manure, not only provide a slow release of nutrients but also improve soil structure and encourage beneficial microbial activity.

For gardeners opting for containers and raised beds, ensuring adequate depth is crucial since raspberries have a relatively deep root system. Additionally, mulching with organic materials like straw or wood chips can help conserve soil moisture, suppress weeds, and maintain even soil temperatures, further creating an ideal growing condition for raspberries.

Overall, paying close attention to creating and maintaining the right soil conditions in containers and raised beds can significantly impact the success of growing raspberries. By providing well-drained, slightly acidic soil rich in organic matter, ensuring proper nutrient levels, and considering the specific needs of the raspberry variety, you can enjoy bountiful harvests of these delicious fruits.

HOW TO SOW RASPBERRIES IN CONTAINERS & RAISED BEDS GARDENS

Correct Season To Sow Raspberries In Containers & Raised Beds Gardens

The correct season to sow raspberries, particularly when dealing with container and raised bed gardens, is a critical factor that can significantly influence the establishment and productivity of your plants. Typically, the best time for planting raspberries in most temperate regions is early spring, just as the ground thaws and after the risk of severe frost has passed. This timing allows the plants to establish a robust root system and acclimate to their new environment before the onset of the vigorous growth phase in late spring and summer.

For those in warmer climates where frost is minimal or nonexistent, late fall planting can also be advantageous. This takes advantage of cooler temperatures and winter rainfall to help establish young plants, giving them a head start before the spring growing season.

When planting bare-root raspberry canes, which is common for both container and raised bed gardening, ensure they are planted while dormant, typically between late fall and early spring depending on your local climate conditions. Keep in mind that container-grown raspberries may have slightly more flexibility in planting times, as the soil in containers tends to warm up more quickly than ground soil and can be moved to protect the plants from late or unexpected frosts.

Regardless of timing, preparing your containers or raised beds with the right soil conditions—well-drained, slightly acidic, and rich in organic matter, before planting is essential for successfully establishing and growing raspberry plants.

Plant Needs & Requirements

Germinating raspberries from seeds to seedlings correctly when growing in containers and raised beds is a crucial step that lays the foundation for the health and productivity of the plants. This process demands patience and precision, as raspberry seeds have a naturally slow and somewhat erratic germination rate, requiring stratification to break dormancy.

Correct germination ensures that the seedlings develop a robust root system, which is vital for absorbing nutrients and water, particularly in the confined spaces of containers and raised beds where resources are limited.

Properly germinated seedlings are also more likely to grow into robust plants that can withstand environmental stresses such as temperature fluctuations, pests, and diseases. Furthermore, starting raspberries from seeds allows gardeners to cultivate a wider variety of species that might not be readily available as pre-grown nursery plants, offering an opportunity to experiment with different flavors, colors, and harvest times.

Ensuring that these initial stages of life are carefully managed helps establish vigorous plants that will yield abundant fruit harvests for years to come, making the meticulous process of germinating raspberries from seeds well worth the effort for container and raised bed gardeners.

Germinating raspberries from seeds to develop into healthy, fruit-bearing bushes involves a meticulous process, requiring attention to detail from seed selection to the transplantation of seedlings into containers or raised bed gardens.

The initial step in this process is the stratification of raspberry seeds, a crucial pre-sowing treatment that mimics the natural winter conditions the seeds would experience in the wild. Stratification involves mixing the raspberry seeds with a moist medium, such as sand or peat moss, and then refrigerating them for about 4 to 6 weeks. This cold treatment breaks the seeds' dormancy, enhancing their germination rate.

Following stratification, the seeds are sown in trays or pots filled with a well-draining seed starting mix. It's essential to keep the soil moist but not soaked and provide the seeds with ample indirect light. Raspberry seeds germinate best at temperatures between 60°F to 75°F (15°C to 24°C), a range that promotes optimal growth without encouraging the development of mold or fungi. Keeping the soil consistently moist and maintaining the correct temperature can be achieved by covering the seed trays with a clear plastic lid or wrap, which also helps to retain humidity.

Germination can take anywhere from 2 to 6 weeks, depending on the variety and the conditions provided. Once the seeds have sprouted and the seedlings begin to show their first true leaves—a stage beyond the initial sprout or 'cotyle-don' stage—they are ready for the next crucial phase, which is thinning. Thinning involves removing weaker seedlings to ensure the stronger ones have enough space and resources to grow. This step is typically performed when seedlings are about an inch tall.

The raspberry seedlings are ready to be transplanted into larger containers or raised beds when they have developed a sturdy stem and several sets of true leaves, usually measuring around 2 to 3 inches in height. This stage often occurs approximately 8 to 12 weeks after sowing. Transplanting at this phase allows the young plants to acclimate to more extensive growing conditions gradually.

When moving the seedlings, it's important to handle them gently by the leaves rather than the stem to avoid damage. In their new environment, whether it be a container or a raised bed, ensuring good drainage, access to full sunlight, and protection from strong winds will help the young raspberry plants establish themselves and continue their maturity.

Throughout these stages, patience and careful attention to the needs of the raspberry plants—such as maintaining the appropriate moisture levels, providing sufficient light, and ensuring the temperature remains within the ideal range—are crucial for successful germination and the establishment of healthy, productive raspberry bushes in containers and raised bed gardens.

Spacing & Measurement

Proper spacing and measurements are critical when transplanting raspberry seedlings into containers and raised bed gardens, primarily because these factors significantly influence the health and productivity of the plants. Raspberries are known for their vigorous growth and can become overcrowded if not given sufficient space, leading to poor air circulation around the plants.

This lack of airflow can create a humid environment that promotes the development of fungal diseases, such as botrytis or powdery mildew, which can severely impact plant health and berry yield. Additionally, adequate spacing ensures that each plant receives enough sunlight, which is essential for photosynthesis and the development of solid and productive canes.

When planting raspberry seedlings in fruit containers and raised bed gardens, paying close attention to spacing and measurements is essential for ensuring the plants' optimal growth and fruit production. For container planting, each raspberry plant requires a container that is at least 18-24 inches deep and equally wide to accommodate its root system without crowding. This size allows enough room for the roots to spread and access the nutrients and water they need to thrive.

If multiple raspberry plants are planted in a single container, ensure that each plant has ample space, ideally using a 24-36 inches diameter container for two plants, to prevent overcrowding and competition for resources.

In raised bed gardens, the desired spacing between raspberry plants is about 18-24 inches apart within rows, with rows spaced about 4-6 feet apart. This arrangement allows each plant enough space to grow and develop a strong root system while ensuring adequate air circulation to minimize the risk of fungal diseases.

Row spacing is particularly important for allowing easy access to maintenance activities such as pruning, weeding, and harvesting and providing enough room for the raspberry canes to spread over time.

For both containers and raised beds, it's also crucial to consider the mature size of the raspberry variety being planted, as some may require more space than others. Erect varieties of raspberries, which tend to grow more vertically, may be planted slightly closer together than trailing or semi-erect varieties, which have a wider spread.

Additionally, providing support structures such as trellises or stakes at the time of planting can help manage the growth and spread of the plants, making them easier to maintain and harvest.

Overall, giving raspberry seedlings the right amount of space and carefully considering the dimensions of their growing environment are vital steps in establishing a healthy and productive raspberry garden. Proper spacing not only impacts the plants' health and fruit yield but also makes the garden more manageable and enjoyable for the gardener. By adhering to these guidelines, you can look forward to bountiful raspberry harvests season after season.

Ideal Temperatures & Sun Requirements

Ideal temperatures and sun requirements play a pivotal role in the successful cultivation of raspberries, especially when they are grown in fruit containers and raised bed gardens. These factors significantly influence the plant's ability to photosynthesize, flower, and ultimately fruit. Raspberries thrive in moderate climates and require full sun exposure for at least 6 to 8 hours a day to produce the highest yields. Full sun not only promotes strong, healthy growth but also enhances fruit quality and taste. The desired temperature range for growing raspberries falls between 55°F and 75°F (13°C to 24°C). Within this range, raspberry plants can efficiently carry out photosynthesis and respiration, essential processes for growth and fruit development.

Temperatures that are too high or too low can stress the plants, leading to poor fruit sets, reduced yields, or even plant death. Nighttime temperatures are also crucial; cool nights coupled with warm days are ideal for raspberry production, as they help improve fruit quality and flavor. For gardeners in regions with hotter climates, providing some afternoon shade can help protect the plants from excessive heat, ensuring they remain within their optimal temperature range.

By paying close attention to these temperature and sun exposure requirements, you can create the ideal conditions for your raspberry plants to flourish in containers and raised bed gardens, leading to abundant and tasty harvests.

MAINTAINING YOUR CONTAINER & RAISED BED RASPBERRIES

Maintaining raspberries in fruit containers and raised bed gardens is crucial for ensuring the longevity, health, and productivity of the plants. Regular maintenance tasks such as pruning, watering, fertilizing, and monitoring for pests and diseases play pivotal roles in the life cycle of raspberry plants. Raspberry bushes can become overgrown without proper care, leading to poor air circulation and sunlight penetration. These are vital for fruit development and can significantly increase the likelihood of fungal infections and pest infestations.

Additionally, raspberries have specific water and nutrient requirements that, if not met, can result in weak growth and reduced fruit yield. Pruning is especially important for removing dead or diseased canes and supporting new growth, where fruit is produced. These maintenance activities become even more critical in containers and raised beds, where space and resources are more limited than in traditional garden settings.

Pruning & Thinning Your Raspberries

Pruning and thinning are essential practices for managing raspberries grown in containers and raised bed gardens, crucial for both the health of the plants and the quality and quantity of fruit they produce.

Pruning involves removing dead, diseased, or weak canes and those that have already fruited, depending on the variety of raspberry. This process helps to improve air circulation and sunlight penetration throughout the plant, reducing the risk of fungal diseases and encouraging the growth of strong, healthy canes that will produce fruit in the following season.

Thinning, on the other hand, involves selectively removing some of the new canes to prevent overcrowding within the container or bed. Overcrowded plants compete for light, nutrients, and water, which can lead to poor fruit development and increased susceptibility to disease and pest issues. By reducing the number of canes, thinning ensures that the remaining ones have adequate space to grow and access to sufficient resources, leading to a healthier plant and higher quality fruit.

Additionally, in the confined spaces of containers and raised beds, where conditions are better controlled but also more restricted, these practices are particularly important for maintaining the balance between vegetative growth and fruit production, ensuring that the plants remain productive and manageable over time.

The timing and method when pruning and thinning raspberries can vary based on the type of raspberry—summer-bearing or fall-bearing, nevertheless the overarching goal is to encourage vigorous growth and bountiful fruit production.

For summer-bearing raspberries, which produce fruit on the previous year's canes (floricanes), pruning should be done in late winter or early spring before new growth begins. This involves removing all the canes that bore fruit the previous summer, as they will not produce again and could contribute to overcrowding and disease if left in place. Cut these canes down to ground level.

Additionally, any weak, damaged, or diseased canes should be removed to allow more space and resources for the more vigorous canes. Thinning is also crucial; leave only the strongest 4-6 canes per square foot to ensure adequate air circulation and sunlight exposure.

Fall-bearing raspberries, on the other hand, produce fruit on the current year's growth (primocanes). For these varieties, gardeners have two options. The first is to cut all canes to ground level in late winter or early spring; this will result in a single, late summer or fall harvest.

The second option is to prune by removing only the portions of the canes that fruited in the fall, leaving the rest of the cane to produce an early summer crop the following year, followed by pruning back to the ground after the summer harvest for a fall harvest as well. This dual-cropping method requires more precise pruning but can yield two harvests.

When pruning and thinning raspberries in containers, the same general rules apply, but special attention must be paid to the limited space. Canes should be selected and pruned with care to avoid overcrowding, which is more acute in the confined space of a container. Ensure that the remaining canes have adequate room to grow and that air circulation is not impeded by the container's walls.

For both container and raised bed gardens, use sharp, clean pruning tools to make clean cuts close to the ground or the base of the plant, and remove pruned material from the area to minimize the risk of disease transmission. After thinning, a balanced fertilizer can be applied to support new growth, following label instructions for rates and application methods.

These practices, while time-consuming, are critical for sustaining healthy raspberry plants that can produce abundant, flavorful fruit. Regular pruning and thinning not only manage plant size and shape but also play a vital role in disease and pest management strategies, thereby contributing significantly to the success of the garden.

Watering Your Container & Raised Bed Raspberries

Watering raspberries grown in containers and raised beds is a pivotal aspect of their care, underpinning the health and productivity of these plants. In containers and raised beds, raspberries have limited access to natural soil moisture, making them more reliant on regular watering to meet their hydration needs. These growing environments can dry out more quickly than in-ground gardens, especially during warm, sunny days or windy conditions, which increases the evaporation rate.

Consistent, adequate watering ensures that raspberry plants can absorb the necessary nutrients from the soil, maintain healthy growth, and develop a robust root system. This is especially crucial during the fruiting season when the plants are producing berries, as insufficient water can lead to poor fruit quality, reduced yield, and increased susceptibility to stress and disease.

Proper hydration helps to keep the soil evenly moist but not waterlogged, promoting optimal conditions for raspberry plants to thrive and produce an abundant harvest of juicy, flavorful berries. Therefore, regular monitoring and adjusting watering schedules according to weather conditions and soil moisture levels are essential practices for gardeners aiming to cultivate successful crops of container and raised bed-grown raspberries.

Watering raspberries in containers and raised beds requires a balanced approach to ensure the plants receive enough moisture without becoming waterlogged. The amount and frequency of watering depend on several factors including the weather, the plant growth stage, and the growing medium used.

For container-grown raspberries, it's crucial to provide a consistent water supply because the limited soil volume can dry out quickly, especially in the summer heat. During the growing season, these plants typically need watering once or twice a day to maintain evenly moist soil.

It's essential to use containers with adequate drainage holes to prevent water from pooling at the bottom, which can lead to root rot and other diseases. A general rule is to water until excess moisture begins to drain from the bottom of the container, ensuring the roots have received sufficient hydration.

Raised bed gardens tend to retain moisture better than containers but still require careful monitoring, as their elevated position can also lead to quicker drying compared to traditional garden beds. In the peak of summer or during dry spells, raspberry plants in raised beds might need watering every other day. The goal is to keep the soil consistently moist to a depth of about 1-2 inches. This can usually be achieved by applying about 1 to 2 inches of water per week, but this may increase during particularly hot or windy weather.

The timing of watering is another critical consideration. It's best to water raspberries early in the morning. This allows the water to penetrate deeply into the soil, reaching the roots while minimizing evaporation losses. Morning watering also helps leaves to dry out quickly, reducing the risk of fungal diseases that thrive in moist conditions.

During the fruiting period, raspberries have increased water demands. Adequate watering during this time is vital to ensure the development of plump, juicy berries. However, after the harvest season, you can reduce the watering frequency as the plants enter dormancy, especially in areas where fall and winter provide natural precipitation.

Monitoring the top few inches of soil for dryness can be a practical guide for when to water. If the top inch of soil feels dry to the touch, it's time to water. Adapting your watering schedule according to the plants' needs, rather than sticking rigidly to a calendar schedule, will promote healthier growth and better fruit production.

Organic Fertilization For Container & Raised Bed Raspberries

Organic fertilization plays a crucial role in supporting the health and productivity of raspberries grown in containers and raised beds. Utilizing organic fertilizers provides a slow-release source of nutrients that mimics the natural soil fertility, offering a balanced supply of essential nutrients that raspberries need for growth, flowering, and fruiting.

Unlike synthetic fertilizers, which can sometimes lead to nutrient runoff or soil imbalances, organic options improve soil structure and increase its water-holding capacity, both of which are particularly beneficial in the confined environments of containers and raised beds. These organic matter-based amendments also encourage beneficial microbial activity in the soil, which aids in nutrient absorption by raspberry roots and helps in the natural breakdown of organic matter into plant-available nutrients.

This process is vital in containers and raised beds where soil life is limited compared to in-ground gardens. Additionally, organic fertilization aligns with sustainable gardening practices, minimizing the impact on the environment by reducing chemical inputs and potentially harmful runoff into waterways.

By nourishing raspberry plants with organic fertilizers, you can foster healthier, more resilient plants that are capable of producing abundant, flavorful berries while contributing to the long-term health of the soil ecosystem within your containers and raised beds.

Organic fertilizers come from natural sources and include compost, manure, bone meal, blood meal, fish emulsion, and seaweed extracts, each offering different nutrients essential for raspberry plants.

Compost is a versatile organic fertilizer that provides a broad range of nutrients alongside improving soil structure and moisture retention. Well-composted organic matter can be mixed into the soil before planting raspberries and used as a top dressing around existing plants in the spring to slowly release nutrients throughout the growing season. It's especially beneficial in containers and raised beds, where it helps maintain soil health and fertility within the confined space.

Manure, particularly from cows, horses, and chickens, is another excellent source of nutrients, including nitrogen, phosphorus, and potassium. It should be well-rotted or composted before use to avoid burning the plants or introducing pathogens into the soil. A thin layer applied in early spring provides nutrients for raspberry plants as they enter a period of active growth.

Bone meal is a slow-release fertilizer high in phosphorus, supporting strong root development and berry production in raspberry plants. It can be incorporated into the soil at planting time and added annually in early spring to containers and raised beds to encourage healthy growth.

Blood meal is a high-nitrogen organic fertilizer, excellent for promoting vegetative growth in the early stages of raspberry plant development. It should be applied sparingly, especially in containers, to avoid nitrogen burn, ideally mixed into the soil before planting or as a top dressing in early spring.

Fish emulsion and seaweed extracts are liquid organic fertilizers that provide a quick nutrient boost to raspberry plants, ideal for mid-season applications when berries are forming. They can be diluted and applied directly to the soil or used as foliar sprays for fast absorption, typically every 2-4 weeks during the growing season.

When fertilizing raspberries in containers and raised beds, it's essential to apply organic fertilizers according to the product instructions and the plants' specific needs. Over-fertilization can lead to excessive vegetative growth at the expense of fruit production, while under-fertilization can result in poor yields and weak plants. A balanced approach, starting with a soil test to determine specific nutrient needs, allows you to tailor your fertilization strategy, ensuring raspberries receive the proper nutrients at the right time for optimal growth and fruiting.

PROTECTING YOUR CONTAINER & RAISED BED RASPBERRIES

Extreme Temperatures

Protecting raspberries grown in containers and raised beds from extreme temperatures is essential for maintaining the health of the plants and ensuring a successful harvest. Both high and low temperature extremes can stress raspberry plants, leading to reduced fruit production, poor fruit quality, and even plant death. Therefore, implementing strategies to moderate temperature fluctuations is crucial to raspberry care in container and raised bed gardens.

During the hot summer months, raspberries, especially those in containers, are vulnerable to overheating. The soil in containers can heat up quickly, damaging the root system and inhibiting the plant's ability to absorb water and nutrients. To protect them from excessive heat, positioning containers in locations where they can receive partial afternoon shade can help reduce temperature stress.

Using light-colored containers or wrapping darker containers with reflective materials can also help by reflecting rather than absorbing heat. Additionally, applying a layer of mulch over the soil surface helps retain moisture, reduces temperature fluctuations, and keeps roots cooler.

For raspberries in raised beds, mulching plays a similar protective role against high temperatures. Incorporating organic mulches like straw, wood chips, or leaf litter not only cools the soil but also adds organic matter as it decomposes, improving soil health over time. During particularly intense heatwaves, temporary shade structures like shade cloth can be used to provide relief to both container and raised-bed raspberries, reducing the intensity of direct sunlight.

Cold temperatures present a different challenge, particularly for raspberries in containers, as their roots are more exposed to cold than those in the ground. Moving containers to a sheltered location, such as against the house or inside an unheated garage, can provide some temperature moderation to safeguard these plants in winter.

Wrapping containers in insulating materials like burlap or bubble wrap further protects roots from freezing. For raspberries in raised beds, applying a thicker layer of mulch after the ground has frozen can help insulate the soil, minimizing freeze-thaw cycles that can damage roots.

Watering practices also need adjustment according to temperature conditions. In hot weather, ensuring that raspberries have adequate water is crucial to prevent heat stress. However, watering should be reduced as temperatures cool down in autumn to prepare the plants for dormancy.

Protecting raspberries from extreme temperatures is vital for their survival and productivity. By taking measures to shield them from the heat and cold, you can ensure your raspberry plants remain healthy, vigorous, and capable of producing delicious berries year after year. These efforts not only extend the life of the plants but also enhance the quality and quantity of the fruit they produce, making temperature protection a worthwhile endeavor in container and raised bed raspberry cultivation.

Protecting Container & Raised Bed Raspberries From Pests

Protecting container and raised bed grown raspberries from pests organically is crucial for several reasons. Utilizing organic pest control methods aligns with sustainable gardening practices, ensuring that the food produced is safe for consumption without the residue of synthetic chemicals. It also preserves the ecological balance within the garden, encouraging a beneficial relationship between plants and insects.

Many synthetic pesticides not only harm targeted pests but can also detrimentally affect pollinators, such as bees, and other beneficial organisms that contribute to the health of the garden by controlling pest populations naturally. Additionally, organic pest management strategies often focus on preventative measures, such as selecting disease-resistant raspberry varieties, proper spacing for improved air circulation, and maintaining healthy soil, which inherently reduces the plants' vulnerability to pest infestations.

By fostering a healthy, balanced ecosystem within containers and raised beds, you can mitigate pest problems in a way that supports plant health, yields high-quality fruits, and protects the environment and your health.

Container and raised bed grown raspberries can fall prey to various pests, each with the potential to impact the health and productivity of the plants. Some common pests include aphids, spider mites, raspberry beetles, and Japanese beetles.

These pests can cause damage ranging from defoliation and fruit damage to transmitting diseases.

Aphids are small, green, or black insects that suck sap from the leaves, causing them to curl and weaken the plant. An organic approach to controlling aphids involves introducing natural predators such as ladybugs or lacewings into the garden. These beneficial insects can significantly reduce aphid populations.

Another effective strategy is to spray infested plants with a strong stream of water to knock aphids off the plants or use an organic insecticidal soap or neem oil solution, which is less harmful to beneficial insects.

Spider mites, another common pest, are tiny spider-like pests that can cause leaves to appear speckled and eventually lead to leaf loss. Increasing humidity around the plants can deter spider mite outbreaks since they thrive in dry conditions. Regularly inspecting the underside of leaves and applying a neem oil spray can help control their populations organically.

Raspberry beetles affect the fruit, laying eggs on the flowers, which then hatch into larvae that burrow into the berries. To combat these pests organically, gardeners can use pheromone traps to catch adult beetles and prevent them from laying eggs. Regularly removing any affected fruit can also help break the pest's life cycle.

Japanese beetles are voracious eaters that can quickly defo-liate raspberry bushes and damage fruit. Handpicking beetles off plants early in the morning when they are less active and dropping them into soapy water is an effective organic control method. Applying neem oil to the foliage can also deter these pests without harming beneficial insects.

Aside from these specific control methods, general practices can strengthen raspberry plants against pest attacks organically. Encouraging biodiversity by planting a variety of flowers and herbs can attract beneficial insects that prey on raspberry pests.

Using mulch not only retains moisture and suppresses weeds but also can provide a habitat for predatory insects. Keeping the area around raspberry plants clean and free of debris reduces hiding places for pests and can prevent infestation. Crop rotation, even within the limited space of containers and raised beds, can prevent the build-up of soil-borne pests and diseases.

Organic pest management focuses on prevention, employing physical, biological, and cultural methods to keep pest populations under control while preserving the health of the garden ecosystem. By implementing these organic practices, gardeners can protect their raspberries from pests and enjoy bountiful harvests without resorting to synthetic chemicals.

Protecting Container & Raised Bed Raspberries From Diseases

Protecting container and raised bed grown raspberries from diseases organically is crucial for sustaining both plant health and environmental integrity. Organic disease management practices focus on preventing problems before they start, emphasizing the importance of maintaining a balanced ecosystem within the garden.

This approach helps produce healthy, chemical-free raspberries and preserves the beneficial microorganisms in the soil that support plant growth and resilience. By avoiding synthetic fungicides and pesticides, gardeners ensure that their gardening practices do not contribute to soil degradation, water contamination, or harm to non-target species such as bees and other pollinators essential for plant reproduction.

Furthermore, organic methods, such as crop rotation, proper pruning for air circulation, and using resistant varieties, enhance the natural defense mechanisms of raspberries against diseases. This proactive and holistic strategy towards disease management in raspberries aligns with sustainable gardening principles, ultimately yielding safer, more nutritious fruits while protecting the garden's surrounding environment.

Container and raised bed grown raspberries, like those planted in traditional gardens, are susceptible to a range of diseases that can compromise plant health and fruit production. Some of the most common diseases include Botrytis fruit rot (gray mold), powdery mildew, and root rot. These diseases affect the yield and quality of the raspberries and can weaken the plants, making them more susceptible to pest infestations and other diseases.

Botrytis fruit rot, or gray mold, is a fungal disease that thrives in cool, humid conditions. It affects the fruit, covering it in a gray, fuzzy mold, and can spread rapidly if not controlled. To manage this disease organically, it's crucial to maintain good air circulation around the plants by spacing them adequately and pruning them regularly to remove any dead or diseased material.

Applying a thin layer of straw mulch can help reduce humidity around the fruit. Furthermore, watering the plants at their base rather than overhead reduces moisture on the fruit and leaves, discouraging mold growth.

Powdery mildew presents as a white, powdery coating on the leaves and can lead to leaf distortion and poor fruit development. This fungal disease prefers warm, dry conditions with high humidity. To prevent it organically, choose resistant raspberry varieties and ensure they're planted in well-draining soil to reduce standing water. Increasing air flow through pruning and proper plant spacing is also effective. For treatment, organic options include spraying affected plants with a mixture of baking soda and water or applying sulfur-based fungicides, which are considered organic.

Root rot is another serious concern, particularly for raspberries grown in containers or poorly draining raised beds. It can be caused by various fungi and results in wilting plants that do not recover with watering. Preventing root rot organically involves ensuring good drainage in containers and raised beds, using well-composted organic matter to improve soil structure, and avoiding over-watering.

If root rot is detected, removing the affected plants to prevent the spread of the disease is often necessary. Crop rotation and allowing soil to dry out between waterings can also help prevent its recurrence.

In addition to these strategies, practicing crop rotation—even in container gardening—can be beneficial. Rotating where raspberries are planted each year helps prevent the build-up of soil-borne pathogens. Employing companion planting can also boost the garden's overall health; for example, planting garlic or chives near raspberries can deter certain pests and potentially reduce disease risk due to their natural antifungal properties.

Organic disease management in raspberry cultivation focuses on prevention, cultural practices, and the use of organic remedies to create a balanced ecosystem that supports plant health. By adopting these practices, you can successfully grow raspberries in containers and raised beds, enjoying fresh, healthy fruits without resorting to chemical treatments.

HARVESTING CONTAINER & RAISED BED RASPBERRIES

The timeline for harvesting container and raised bed grown raspberries largely depends on the variety planted—summer-bearing or everbearing—and the specific conditions under which they are grown. Summer-bearing raspberries typically produce fruit once a year in early to mid-summer, usually around June or July, depending on the climate.

After planting, it might take a year for these plants to start producing fruit, with peak productivity reached in their second and third years. Everbearing raspberries, on the other hand, can produce two crops annually—one in late spring/early summer and another in late summer/fall. They might offer a modest harvest in their first year post-planting, with significant yields from the second year onwards.

When it comes to harvesting raspberries, timing and technique are crucial for ensuring the highest quality fruit. Raspberries are ready to harvest when fully colored (red, black, golden, or purple, depending on the variety) and detach easily from the plant with a gentle tug.

Ripe berries are soft to the touch, and attempting to pull unripe berries will meet with resistance. It's important to harvest raspberries carefully to avoid crushing them. The best approach is to hold the fruit gently between your fingers and thumb, twisting slightly to allow the berry to come off the plant. Using shallow containers for collecting the berries will prevent them from getting squashed under their own weight.

Harvesting should be done regularly, ideally every couple of days, to ensure that berries are picked at the peak of ripeness. This not only maximizes the flavor and nutritional content of the raspberries but also helps reduce issues with pests and diseases, as overripe fruit can attract unwanted visitors and contribute to fungal diseases.

Morning is the best time for harvesting, as the berries are firmer and cooler, making them less likely to be damaged during the process. However, avoid picking wet berries, as moisture can promote mold growth and decrease their shelf life.

After harvesting, raspberries should be processed promptly. They are highly perishable and best enjoyed fresh within a day or two of picking. Raspberries can be refrigerated for longer storage but should be kept dry and in a single layer to prevent molding and bruising. For even longer preservation, raspberries can be frozen, dried, or made into jams and preserves.

In container and raised bed gardens, ensuring that raspberry plants have adequate support, proper nutrition, and sufficient water is vital for encouraging healthy growth and abundant fruit production. These practices, along with regular monitoring for pests and diseases, will contribute significantly to the success of your raspberry harvest.

CONTAINER & RAISED BEDS RASPBERRIES NOTES

Start: Seeds or Seedlings.

Germination: 2 to 6 weeks, at temperatures between 60°F to 75°F (15°C to 24°C).

Seed Life: 3 Years.

Soil Type: Well-drained, loamy soil rich in organic matter - pH range of 5.5 to 6.5.

Seed Spacing: ¼" depth.

Seedling Spacing:

Containers - Raspberry plant requires a container at least 18-24 inches deep and equally wide to accommodate its root system without crowding.

Raised Beds - The desired spacing between raspberry plants is about 18-24 inches apart within rows, with rows spaced about 4-6 feet apart.

Sunlight: 6 – 8hrs full sunlight daily.

Growing Temperatures: The desired temperature range for growing raspberries falls between 55°F and 75°F (13°C to 24°C).

Duration Till Harvest:

Summer-bearing raspberries - These raspberries typically produce fruit once a year in early to mid-summer, usually around June or July, depending on the climate. After planting, it might take a year for these plants to start producing fruit, with peak productivity reached in their second and third years.

Everbearing raspberries - These raspberries can produce two crops annually—one in late spring/early summer and another in late summer/fall. They might offer a modest harvest in their first-year post-planting, with significant yields from the second year onwards.

CHAPTER 5
BERRY BUSHES: CONTAINER & RAISED BED GARDENS – BLACKBERRIES

Blackberries offer a rewarding and flavorful addition to any container or raised bed gardening endeavor, bringing both the beauty of their blossoming flowers and the delicious bounty of their fruits to small and urban spaces alike. These versatile berries are well-suited to container and raised bed cultivation, providing gardeners with limited space the opportunity to harvest home-grown, succulent fruits right from their patio, balcony, or backyard. With a range of varieties available, from thornless to trailing types, blackberries can be tailored to fit different garden sizes and preferences.

Cultivating blackberries in containers and raised beds not only simplifies weed and pest management but also allows for better control over the soil quality and moisture levels, ensuring healthier plants and more bountiful yields. By choosing the right variety and providing some basic care, you can enjoy the dual benefits of an attractive landscape feature and the pleasure of freshly picked blackberries throughout the summer.

Planting blackberries in containers and raised bed gardens offers numerous benefits that can enhance the overall health and productivity of your garden. Firstly, this approach allows for better control over the soil environment, enabling gardeners to tailor the soil composition to meet the specific needs of blackberry plants, ensuring optimal growth and fruit production.

Containers and raised beds also improve drainage, reducing the risk of root rot and other water-related diseases that commonly affect blackberries. These gardening methods can also help circumvent the challenges posed by poor native soil and limited space, making it possible to grow lush, fruitful blackberry bushes in various settings.

Another significant advantage is the ease of management and maintenance. Raised beds and containers elevate the plants, making them more accessible for pruning, harvesting, and monitoring for pests and diseases. This method also facilitates the containment of blackberry plants, known for their vigorous growth and potential to become invasive. By confining the plants to containers or raised beds, you can enjoy the bountiful harvests of blackberries without worrying about them overtaking the garden. Overall, container and raised bed gardening can lead to healthier plants, higher yields, and a more manageable and enjoyable gardening experience.

THE RIGHT SOIL TO GROW BLACKBERRIES IN CONTAINER & RAISED BEDS

The success of growing blackberries in fruit container and raised bed gardens largely hinges on creating the right soil conditions. Blackberries thrive in well-drained, fertile soils that are rich in organic matter. The ideal soil for blackberries should have a slightly acidic pH between 5.5 and 6.5. This pH range maximizes nutrient availability and promotes healthy root development. Before planting, it's beneficial to test the soil's pH and adjust accordingly using elemental sulfur to lower the pH or garden lime to raise it if needed.

For container-grown blackberries, choosing a high-quality potting mix designed for fruits can provide a good starting point. These mixes usually offer the right balance of drainage and water retention while being light enough to encourage root growth. It's essential to ensure that the container has adequate drainage holes to prevent water from pooling at the bottom, leading to root rot.

Additionally, incorporating a slow-release, balanced fertilizer into the potting mix can help support the plants' growth and fruit production throughout the season.

In raised beds, enhancing the native soil with compost or well-rotted manure can significantly improve soil structure and fertility. Organic matter not only adds vital nutrients back into the soil but also improves its ability to retain moisture without becoming waterlogged. For raised beds built over poor or compacted soil, filling them with a blend of topsoil, compost, and a portion of sand or perlite can create an optimal growing environment for blackberries. This mixture ensures good drainage and aeration, key factors in preventing root diseases and promoting healthy plant growth.

Mulching around blackberry plants in containers and raised beds offers several benefits, including moisture retention, temperature regulation, and weed suppression. Organic mulches like straw, pine bark, or shredded leaves can also contribute to the soil's overall fertility as they decompose. However, it's crucial to keep the mulch a few inches away from the plant stems to prevent moisture from accumulating against them and potentially causing stem rot.

Regular monitoring and amendments based on the plants' performance are necessary for maintaining the right soil conditions throughout the growing season. Over time, continuous cropping can deplete the soil's nutrients, making annual soil tests and subsequent fertilization adjustments beneficial for sustained berry production.

By diligently managing the soil conditions in your container and raised bed gardens, you can enjoy bountiful harvests of sweet, juicy blackberries for many years.

HOW TO SOW BLACKBERRIES IN CONTAINERS & RAISED BEDS GARDENS

Correct Season To Sow Blackberries In Containers & Raised Beds Gardens

The correct season to sow blackberries in fruit container and raised bed gardens primarily depends on your geographical location and the climate conditions prevalent there. Generally, the ideal time for planting blackberries is in the early spring, just as the ground thaws and the threat of frost has passed. This timing ensures that the plants have ample time to establish their root systems before the onset of hot summer weather or, in cooler climates, before the ground freezes in winter.

In regions with milder winters, planting can also be successful in the fall, allowing the plants to establish during the cooler months and burst into growth come spring. This autumn planting strategy can lead to an earlier start in the growing season, potentially yielding an earlier harvest. It's essential to choose a time when the soil can be worked easily and when young plants won't be subjected to extreme heat or cold shortly after planting.

For container-grown blackberries, the flexibility is greater, as containers can be moved to protect the plants from harsh conditions if necessary. Regardless of the timing, ensuring that blackberry plants are well-watered and protected from extreme elements as they settle into their new environment is crucial for their long-term success and productivity in both container and raised bed gardens.

Plant Needs & Requirements

Germinating blackberries from seeds to seedlings correctly is a foundational step when growing them in containers and raised bed gardens for several reasons. Firstly, proper germination ensures the development of strong, healthy seedlings that are more capable of withstanding the transition to outdoor conditions and resisting pests and diseases. A well-started plant will establish itself more quickly, leading to a robust root system crucial for nutrient uptake and overall plant health.

Additionally, by controlling the germination environment—such as maintaining consistent moisture levels, adequate warmth, and sufficient light—you can optimize the growth conditions, leading to a higher germination rate and more uniform plant growth. This early stage of care also allows you to select the strongest seedlings for planting, ensuring that only the most vigorous plants make it into your containers or raised beds.

Likewise, understanding and applying the correct germination techniques for blackberries can save time and resources by reducing the need for replanting due to initial failure. In essence, successful germination sets the stage for the entire growing cycle, influencing not just survival but also the future yield and quality of the blackberries produced in container and raised bed gardens.

Germinating blackberries from seeds requires patience and attention to detail, as the process is more intricate than planting nursery starts. The first step in the germination process is to stratify the seeds, a method that simulates winter conditions to break the seeds' dormancy.

To do this, mix the blackberry seeds with slightly moistened peat moss or sand and place them in a sealable plastic bag. Then, store the pack in the refrigerator for approximately 8-12 weeks. This cold treatment is crucial for stimulating germination once the seeds are planted.

After stratification, the seeds are ready to be sown in a germination mix. Use shallow trays or pots filled with a sterile, fine-textured, and well-draining seed starting mix. Sow the seeds on the surface and lightly press them into the mix without covering them, as blackberry seeds need light to germinate. The trays or pots should then be placed in a warm, brightly lit area, but not in direct sunlight, which can be too intense.

Blackberry seeds germinate best at temperatures between 68°F to 75°F (20°C to 24°C). Maintaining this temperature range is essential for encouraging germination, which can take anywhere from 2-4 weeks, depending on conditions. During this period, keep the soil consistently moist but not waterlogged by using a spray bottle to gently mist the surface. Covering the trays or pots with a clear plastic dome or wrap can help retain moisture and warmth but be sure to ventilate occasionally to prevent mold growth.

Once the blackberry seedlings emerge and develop their first true leaves (the second set of leaves after the initial seed leaves or cotyledons), they can be carefully transplanted into individual pots filled with a high-quality potting mix. This allows the young plants to grow in a controlled environment where nutrients, water, and light can be closely managed. It's important to handle the delicate seedlings gently, especially when teasing apart their roots during transplanting.

The seedlings are ready to be moved to their final containers or raised bed gardens when they have established a robust root system and are sturdy enough to withstand outdoor conditions. This typically occurs when the seedlings are about 4-6 inches tall and have several sets of true leaves.

However, before transplanting outdoors, it's crucial to harden off the seedlings by gradually exposing them to outdoor conditions over a week. This process helps them adjust to the sunlight, temperatures, and winds they will encounter in the garden.

Spacing & Measurement

Proper spacing and measurements when transplanting black-berry seedlings into fruit containers and raised bed gardens are crucial for several reasons. First, it ensures that each plant has enough room to grow and spread without competing for essential resources such as sunlight, water, and nutrients.

Blackberries are known for their vigorous growth habit and, if planted too closely, can become overcrowded, leading to reduced air circulation around the plants. This lack of space and airflow can create a humid environment conducive to the development of fungal diseases, such as powdery mildew and leaf spot, which can severely affect the health and productivity of the plants.

Appropriate spacing allows for easier access for maintenance activities, including pruning, weeding, and harvesting, making the gardening process more efficient and enjoyable. In containers, ensuring that the pot size is adequate for the mature size of the blackberry variety being grown is essential to prevent root crowding and to accommodate the plant's extensive root system, which in turn supports healthy top growth and fruit production.

Equally, in raised bed gardens, adhering to recommended spacing guidelines not only optimizes plant health and yield but also helps in managing the spread of the plants, keeping the garden orderly and productive. Proper planning and execution of spacing and measurements when transplanting blackberry seedlings ultimately lead to healthier plants, higher quality fruit, and a more bountiful harvest.

When planting blackberry seedlings in fruit containers and raised bed gardens, understanding and implementing the desired spacing and measurements is critical to ensure the health and productivity of the plants. For container planting, choosing the right size is essential. Each blackberry plant should be housed in a container that is at least 18-24 inches in diameter and equally deep to accommodate the spreading root system. This size allows sufficient room for growth while ensuring that the soil retains moisture yet drains well, preventing root rot.

If you wish to plant multiple blackberries in a single container, opt for larger sizes, such as half wine barrels or similarly sized commercial planters, and maintain a spacing of at least 18 inches between each plant to prevent over-crowding.

The spacing and measurements taken differ in the context of raised bed gardens, focusing more on row and plant spacing. Blackberry plants should be spaced about 4-6 feet apart within a row to give them ample room to grow and spread. If you're planting multiple rows of blackberries, space the rows 8-10 feet apart to ensure easy access for maintenance, harvesting, and adequate airflow between the plants. This spacing helps in minimizing disease pressure and allows for better light penetration, which is critical for fruit production.

When designing your raised bed for blackberries, consider the mature size of the variety being planted. Erect varieties may need less space between plants (about 3-4 feet) compared to more sprawling, semi-erect, or trailing varieties that require the full 4-6 feet.

Implementing trellises or support systems within the beds can also influence your spacing decisions. Supports should be installed when planting to avoid damaging the roots later on and provide immediate assistance to the growing plants.

Lastly, the depth of the raised bed is another important measurement to consider. A minimum depth of 12-18 inches is recommended for blackberry plants, allowing enough soil for roots to grow deep and robust. This depth supports optimal plant health by facilitating good drainage and providing plenty of room for organic matter, which blackberries thrive on.

Adhering to these specified spacing and measurements when planting blackberry seedlings in fruit containers and raised bed gardens can create an environment that maximizes growth potential, encourages healthy development, and ultimately leads to a bountiful harvest of blackberries.

Ideal Temperatures & Sun Requirements

The ideal temperatures and sun requirements play a pivotal role in the successful cultivation of blackberries in fruit containers and raised bed gardens, directly influencing plant health, growth, and fruit production. Blackberries thrive in full sun, needing at least 6 to 8 hours of direct sunlight daily to produce the highest yields and sweetest fruit.

Adequate sunlight is crucial for photosynthesis, the process by which plants convert light energy into chemical energy, fueling growth and fruit development. The desired temperature range for growing blackberries is between 75°F to 85°F (24°C to 29°C) during the day. Night temperatures ideally should be lower, around 60°F to 70°F (15°C to 21°C), to help plants rest and recover. These conditions mimic the blackberry's natural environment, promoting vigorous growth and optimal fruiting.

Blackberries are relatively hardy, but extreme temperatures can be detrimental. High temperatures, especially when combined with insufficient watering, can lead to stress, blossom drop, and reduced berry size, while very low temperatures can damage the plants, particularly new growth and flower buds. In container gardening, the soil temperature can fluctuate more than in the ground, making it essential to monitor and mitigate extreme conditions, such as moving containers to shaded areas during heat waves or providing insulation during unexpected cold snaps.

Ensuring that blackberries receive the right amount of sunlight and are grown in an environment with ideal temperatures is key to achieving a bountiful harvest. Proper container and raised bed siting, attentive water management, and seasonal adjustments to plant positioning or protection measures can all help maintain these optimal growing conditions. By meeting these fundamental needs, you can enjoy the rewards of healthy plants and delicious, home-grown blackberries.

MAINTAINING YOUR CONTAINER & RAISED BED BLACKBERRIES

Maintaining blackberries in fruit containers and raised bed gardens is crucial for several reasons, each contributing to the longevity, health, and productivity of the plants. Regular maintenance, including pruning, watering, fertilizing, and pest management, ensures that blackberry bushes remain vigorous and can produce bountiful harvests year after year.

Pruning is particularly important as it helps stimulate new growth, increase air circulation, and reduce disease occurrence by removing old or diseased canes. Proper watering keeps the soil moist but not waterlogged, preventing root rot and stress from drought, both of which can significantly impact fruit quality and yield.

Fertilizing according to the plant's growth stage supports healthy development and fruit production, addressing the nutritional demands of blackberries grown in limited soil volumes of containers and raised beds.

Additionally, consistent monitoring and treatment for pests and diseases keep the plants healthy and productive. Without regular maintenance, blackberries can quickly become overgrown or succumb to environmental stresses, pests, or diseases, which can decrease the lifespan of the plants and reduce the quantity and quality of the fruit.

By investing time in maintaining your blackberry plants, you can enjoy the rewards of fresh, home-grown berries and robust plants that contribute to the beauty and bounty of your gardens.

Pruning & Thinning Your Blackberries

Pruning and thinning blackberries grown in containers and raised bed gardens are essential practices for several reasons, paramount among them being the promotion of plant health and fruit quality. These maintenance tasks directly influence the air circulation and light penetration each plant receives, two critical factors that can significantly impact the incidence of diseases and the efficiency of photosynthesis.

By selectively removing old, diseased, or excessively crowded canes, gardeners can reduce the risk of fungal infections and pest infestations, which thrive in dense, damp foliage. Furthermore, pruning stimulates the growth of new canes, which are often more vigorous and productive than their predecessors. This renewal process ensures that the plants remain productive year after year, channelling their energy into the growth of healthy canes and the production of large, sweet berries.

Thinning, on the other hand, involves removing weaker canes to reduce competition for nutrients, water, and sunlight, thereby allowing the stronger canes to thrive and produce more fruit. In container environments, where space and resources are inherently limited, these practices are even more critical to prevent overcrowding and ensure that each plant has ample room to grow.

Properly executed, pruning and thinning enable blackberries in containers and raised beds to reach their full potential, providing bountiful harvests and enhancing the overall aesthetics of the garden space.

Pruning and thinning blackberries grown in containers and raised bed gardens are essential tasks that should be carried out with care and at the right time to ensure the health and productivity of the plants. The timing of these activities largely depends on the variety of blackberries—whether they are erect, semi-erect, or trailing types and whether they bear fruit on first-year canes (primocanes) or second-year canes (floricanes).

For varieties that fruit on second-year canes, pruning is best done immediately after harvest in late summer or early fall. This involves removing the canes that have just fruited, as they will not produce again and could become a source of disease if left in place. In contrast, primocane varieties, which bear fruit on canes grown in the current season, can be pruned in late winter or early spring before new growth begins. This pruning focuses on thinning out weaker canes and cutting back tops to encourage branching and more fruit production.

The process of pruning involves several steps. First, identify and remove any dead, diseased, or damaged canes at their base to prevent the spread of pathogens. Next, thin the plants by removing smaller, weaker canes, leaving only the most vigorous ones to grow; this typically means leaving about four to six of the strongest canes per plant.

For semi-erect and trailing varieties, it may also be necessary to tie the canes to a support structure to encourage upward growth and make harvesting easier. Aim to space the remaining canes evenly when thinning to improve airflow and light penetration throughout the plant, reducing the risk of diseases.

Thinning should not be overlooked in container-grown black-berries, where space is even more limited. For these plants, it's crucial to monitor their growth closely and be more aggressive in removing excess canes to prevent overcrowding. Ensuring there is enough room between the plants allows for better air circulation and easier access for maintenance and harvesting.

Lastly, always use clean, sharp tools when pruning and thinning to make clean cuts that heal quickly. Disinfect your tools between cuts if you're dealing with diseased plants to prevent the spreading of infection. Following these guidelines for when and how to prune and thin blackberries in containers and raised bed gardens will help keep your plants healthy, manageable, and productive, leading to bountiful harvests of delicious berries.

Watering Your Container & Raised Bed Blackberries

Watering blackberries grown in containers and raised bed gardens is fundamental to their survival and productivity, as water is essential for almost every physiological process within the plant, including photosynthesis, nutrient transport, and temperature regulation.

Unlike blackberries grown directly in the ground, those in containers and raised beds depend entirely on the gardener for their water needs, as their roots cannot reach beyond their confined space to access additional moisture. Consistent and adequate watering ensures that the plants can develop a strong root system, which is vital for supporting healthy foliage, flower development, and, ultimately, fruit production.

Blackberries require a steady supply of moisture, especially during fruit setting and growth phases, to produce plump, juicy berries. Insufficient water can lead to stress, reduced vigor, blossom drop, and fruit that is small and dry. However, it's equally important to avoid overwatering, which can lead to root rot and other diseases due to poor drainage.

Thus, maintaining a balanced watering regime that keeps the soil consistently moist but not waterlogged is crucial for the thriving growth of container and raised bed-grown blackberries, highlighting the importance of watering practices in achieving a successful harvest.

Determining how much and when to water blackberries grown in containers and raised bed gardens requires a careful balance. Water needs can vary based on several factors, including the plant's growth stage, weather conditions, and the specific growing medium used. For blackberries, the key is to maintain consistently moist soil without allowing it to become waterlogged, as both underwatering and overwatering can stress the plants and impact their health and fruit production.

During the growing season, especially in the warmer months, container-grown blackberries may need to be watered daily, as containers can dry out quickly due to limited soil volume and increased exposure to heat. Raised bed gardens, with their larger soil volume, might retain moisture longer, but they still require monitoring and possibly watering every couple of days.

The exact watering frequency should be determined by checking the top inch or two of soil for moisture; if the soil feels dry to the touch, it's time to water. Early morning is the best time to water, as this allows any moisture on the leaves and fruit to dry during the day, reducing the risk of fungal diseases. Additionally, watering at this time ensures that the plants have adequate moisture to withstand the heat of the day.

The amount of water provided at each watering session is also crucial. For containers, watering until water begins to drain out of the bottom ensures that the entire root ball has been saturated. However, it's essential to ensure that containers have proper drainage to prevent excess water from sitting at the bottom and causing root rot.

In raised beds, a slower, deep watering technique is preferred to encourage deeper root growth. This can be achieved by using soaker hoses or drip irrigation systems, which deliver water directly to the base of the plants, minimizing water loss due to evaporation and reducing moisture on the leaves.

As blackberries approach ripening, managing water becomes even more critical. Consistent watering during this period prevents the fruit from becoming dry or too sour. However, overwatering at this stage can dilute the sugars in the berries, affecting their flavor. After the harvest season, reducing watering slightly helps signal to the plants that the growing season is over, allowing them to harden off and prepare for dormancy.

Attentive watering practices, tailored to the changing needs of blackberries throughout their growth cycle and adjusted for environmental conditions, are vital for nurturing healthy plants and ensuring a bountiful, tasty harvest. By providing just the right amount of water at the right times, you can help your blackberries in containers and raised beds thrive throughout the season.

Organic Fertilization For Container & Raised Bed Blackberries

Organic fertilization plays a crucial role in the sustainable and healthy growth of blackberries in containers and raised beds, offering a myriad of benefits that synthetic fertilizers cannot match.

Organic fertilizers, derived from natural sources such as compost, manure, bone meal, or seaweed, release nutrients slowly into the soil, mimicking the nutrient availability found in a blackberry plant's natural habitat. This slow-release mechanism prevents the risk of nutrient burn, common with synthetic fertilizers, which can damage the root systems of plants in the confined spaces of containers and raised beds.

Additionally, organic fertilizers improve soil structure and increase its water-holding capacity, which is particularly beneficial in container gardening, where soil can dry out quickly and nutrients are leached away with frequent watering. They also enhance the biological activity within the soil, promoting the presence of beneficial microorganisms that aid in nutrient breakdown and absorption, improving overall plant health and resilience to diseases and pests.

By using organic fertilizers, you not only support the vigorous growth and productivity of your blackberries but also contribute to a more sustainable and eco-friendly gardening practice, ensuring the long-term health of the soil and environment.

For gardeners cultivating blackberries in containers and raised beds, selecting the right type of organic fertilizer is key to nurturing healthy, productive plants. Organic fertilizers not only supply essential nutrients in a natural and eco-friendly manner but also improve soil health over time, making them an ideal choice for blackberry cultivation in confined spaces.

One effective organic fertilizer option for blackberries is compost. Rich in a variety of nutrients, compost improves soil structure, which is crucial for container and raised bed gardening where soil can become compacted. It enhances moisture retention while providing a slow release of nutrients, mimicking the natural decomposition process found in nature.

Applying a 2-3 inch layer of compost around the blackberry plants in early spring can kickstart the growing season by enriching the soil with essential nutrients as temperatures rise and plants begin active growth.

Another excellent organic fertilizer for blackberries is well-aged manure, particularly from poultry or cattle. Manure is high in nitrogen, which supports leafy growth, an important factor for blackberries that need strong foliage to support fruit production. It should be applied sparingly and well ahead of the growing season, ideally in late fall or early winter, to allow the manure to break down and integrate into the soil, minimizing the risk of burning plant roots.

Fish emulsion and seaweed extracts are also favored organic fertilizers among blackberry growers, especially for container-grown plants. These liquid fertilizers provide a quick, nutrient-rich boost during the critical phases of flowering and fruiting. They're typically diluted in water according to package instructions and applied directly to the soil around the plants.

For best results, use these liquid fertilizers every 4-6 weeks during the growing season, from early spring until late summer, to support sustained growth and berry production.

Bone meal is another valuable organic fertilizer, particularly rich in phosphorus, which supports root development and fruit formation. Sprinkling bone meal around the base of blackberry plants in early spring can encourage vigorous root growth, enhancing the plant's ability to uptake water and nutrients throughout the growing season.

When applying organic fertilizer, it's crucial to ensure even distribution around the plant, avoiding direct contact with stems and leaves to prevent burn injury. Watering the fertilizer after application helps to carry the nutrients down into the soil, where they can be accessed by the plant roots. For container-grown blackberries, be mindful of the limited soil volume and adjust the quantity of fertilizer accordingly to avoid over-fertilization, which can be just as harmful as under-fertilization.

Incorporating organic fertilizers into your gardening practice supports the health and productivity of your blackberries and contributes to the sustainability of your gardening ecosystem. By choosing natural and organic options, you're investing in your soil's long-term fertility and your plants' vitality.

PROTECTING YOUR CONTAINER & RAISED BED BLACKBERRIES

Extreme Temperatures

Protecting container and raised bed-grown blackberries from extreme temperatures is crucial to ensure a bountiful harvest. Blackberries are remarkably resilient plants that can bear fruit in various conditions but are not invulnerable to the whims of weather.

Extreme cold can damage or kill blackberry canes, while excessive heat may stress the plants, leading to poor fruit development or reduced yields. Therefore, understanding how to shield these plants from temperature extremes is essential for any gardener looking to enjoy the rich, succulent fruits of their labor.

Mulching plays a vital role in protecting against cold temperatures. Applying a thick layer of organic mulch around the base of the blackberry plants in containers and raised beds can significantly reduce ground freezing, thus insulating the roots.

Materials such as straw, pine needles, or wood chips are excellent choices, offering a natural buffer against the cold. Additionally, when extreme cold snaps are forecasted, covering the plants with frost blankets or burlap can provide an extra layer of warmth, ensuring that the canes survive through winter to produce fruit in the following season.

In the face of sweltering heat, it's crucial to maintain consistent moisture levels in the soil. Containers and raised beds can dry out much faster than in-ground plantings, particularly during hot spells. Regular watering, ideally in the early morning or late evening to reduce evaporation, helps keep the plants hydrated.

Using soaker hoses or drip irrigation systems in raised beds can also facilitate deep water penetration to the roots, where it's most needed. For containers, consider double potting or placing them in locations that receive partial shade during the hottest parts of the day to prevent overheating.

Another strategy involves the use of reflective mulches or white plastic covers around the plants. These materials reflect sunlight away from the soil, keeping it cooler and reducing the heat stress on the plants. In addition, installing temporary shade cloth over the blackberries during peak sun hours can protect them from heat damage, especially for young plants that are still establishing themselves.

The importance of protecting blackberries from extreme temperatures cannot be overstated. Stress from cold or heat not only impacts the current season's yield but can also affect the plant's overall health, longevity, and fruiting potential in subsequent years.

Vigilant gardeners who take steps to mitigate temperature extremes can enjoy the rewards of their efforts in the form of larger, more flavorful blackberry harvests. Through these practices, you can ensure that your blackberry plants remain productive and vibrant, contributing to a diverse and resilient garden ecosystem.

Protecting Container & Raised Bed Blackberries From Pests

Protecting container and raised bed-grown blackberries organically from pests is crucial for several reasons. Firstly, organic pest control methods safeguard the health of the plants and the well-being of the garden ecosystem, including beneficial insects, soil microbiota, and, ultimately, the gardeners themselves. The use of chemical pesticides can lead to a host of undesired consequences, such as the buildup of harmful residues in the soil and on fruit, the potential harm to non-target species like bees and butterflies, and the risk of contaminating water sources.

Furthermore, pests can cause significant damage to blackberry plants by stunting their growth, reducing fruit yield, and in severe cases, killing the plants. By employing organic pest control strategies, such as introducing natural predators, using botanical insecticides, or applying physical barriers, you can effectively manage pest populations, ensuring your blackberry plants remain healthy and productive.

Container and raised bed-grown blackberries, while reducing some challenges of traditional gardening, are still susceptible to various pests that can compromise the health and productivity of the plants. Understanding which pests pose a threat and implementing organic strategies to manage them is crucial for maintaining a healthy blackberry garden.

One common pest that targets blackberries is the spider mite. These tiny arachnids feed on the undersides of leaves, causing them to turn yellow and drop prematurely. In severe infestations, they can significantly weaken the plants, reducing fruit yield and quality.

To combat spider mites organically, one effective method is introducing natural predators into the garden, such as ladybugs or lacewing larvae, which feed on the mites. Regularly spraying the plants with water can also help dislodge mites and reduce their numbers.

Aphids are another pest that can be problematic for blackberries grown in containers and raised beds. These small, sapsucking insects cluster on new growth and the undersides of leaves, excreting a sticky substance known as honeydew that can attract other pests and promote sooty mold growth.

Organic control measures include spraying the plants with a mixture of water and neem oil, a natural pesticide that disrupts the aphids' life cycle without harming beneficial insects. Additionally, encouraging the presence of aphid predators, like ladybugs and parasitic wasps, can provide long-term control by keeping aphid populations in check.

Japanese beetles can also pose a threat to blackberry plants, feeding on the leaves and sometimes the berries themselves, leaving behind skeletonized foliage and damaged fruits. Handpicking beetles off the plants early in the morning when they are less active and dropping them into a bucket of soapy water is a straightforward organic solution.

Applying neem oil or kaolin clay to the plants can act as a deterrent, making the leaves less appealing to these pests.

To protect container and raised bed grown blackberries from these pests organically, an integrated approach works best. Encouraging biodiversity in the garden by planting a variety of flowers and herbs can attract beneficial insects that prey on common pests.

Installing bird feeders and providing water sources can also draw natural predators that help keep pest populations under control. Employing physical barriers, such as fine mesh netting or row covers, can prevent pests from reaching the plants while allowing light, water, and air to circulate freely.

Regular monitoring is key to organic pest management. By closely monitoring your blackberry plants, you can detect early signs of pest activity and address issues promptly before they escalate.

Employing a combination of preventative measures and timely interventions enables you to protect your blackberries from pests organically, ensuring a healthy and productive garden without the need for chemical pesticides. This approach not only safeguards the plants but also contributes to a healthier ecosystem and a more bountiful harvest.

Protecting Container & Raised Bed Blackberries From Diseases

Protecting container and raised bed-grown blackberries from diseases organically is crucial for many reasons, paramount among them being the safety and health of both the plants and the consumers.

Organic disease management practices preserve the natural ecosystem within the garden, preventing the contamination of soil and water resources with chemical fungicides and pesticides, which can be harmful to beneficial insects, wildlife, and even humans in the long term.

By employing organic methods, such as crop rotation, proper spacing for adequate air circulation, and resistant varieties, you can effectively reduce disease pressure and promote a more resilient garden ecosystem. These sustainable practices support the broader goals of environmental stewardship and contribute to producing high-quality, nutritious fruits free from harmful residues.

In essence, organic disease protection in blackberry cultivation aligns with a holistic approach to gardening that prioritizes plant, environmental, and human health equally, ensuring that the garden is a source of safe, wholesome produce.

While container and raised bed-grown blackberries enjoy some advantages over in-ground cultivation, they are not immune to diseases. If not addressed organically and proactively, these issues can compromise plant health, fruit quality, and yields. Recognizing the diseases that commonly affect blackberries and implementing organic preventative measures are key to ensuring a healthy and productive crop.

One prevalent disease affecting blackberries is powdery mildew. This fungal disease manifests as white, powdery spots on leaves, stems, and sometimes fruits. It thrives in humid conditions and can significantly reduce plant vigor.

To manage powdery mildew organically, it's important to prioritize air circulation around the plants. This can be achieved by spacing plants appropriately and practicing regular pruning to remove diseased or dead material, which also removes the fungal spores.

Applying a foliar spray made from baking soda mixed with horticultural oil or liquid soap can create an environment less conducive to fungal growth. Additionally, incorporating sulfur-based fungicides, which are acceptable in organic gardening, can help control outbreaks when used as a preventive measure before the disease appears.

Another disease that can impact blackberries is anthracnose, caused by a fungus that results in small, purplish spots on canes that eventually turn grayish with tiny black dots. The disease progresses to girdle canes, killing them above the infection point. Cultivating disease-resistant blackberry varieties is a fundamental organic control strategy for anthracnose.

Regular removal and destruction of infected canes and debris, along with careful watering practices to avoid wetting foliage, can significantly reduce the spread of this disease. For organic treatment options, copper-based fungicides can be effective when applied early and as part of a regular disease management schedule.

Botrytis cinerea, or gray mold, is another challenge, particularly in wet, cool conditions. It affects blossoms, young shoots, and developing fruits, covering them in a fuzzy gray mold. Ensuring good air circulation is crucial for prevention, alongside avoiding overhead watering to keep the plant parts dry.

Organic mulches can help reduce spore splashing from the soil onto the plant. Lime sulfur sprays and biological controls, such as Bacillus subtilis or Trichoderma harzianum, can offer organic solutions for managing gray mold when applied according to product instructions and as part of a comprehensive disease management plan.

Focusing on plant health through proper nutrition is foundational to protect blackberries from diseases organically. Balanced feeding with organic fertilizers encourages vigorous growth, making plants less susceptible to diseases. Utilizing compost and well-aged manures not only feeds the plants but also introduces beneficial microorganisms to the soil that can outcompete or inhibit pathogens. Crop rotation and allowing adequate space between plants for airflow are simple yet effective cultural practices that reduce disease risk. Implementing these organic strategies creates a robust defense against diseases, ensuring the blackberry garden remains productive and sustainable.

HARVESTING CONTAINER & RAISED BED BLACKBERRIES

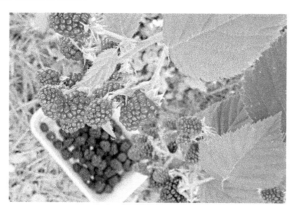

The timeline for harvesting container and raised bed grown blackberries can vary based on several factors, including the variety of blackberries, local climate, and the specific conditions of the container or raised bed. Generally, blackberries planted in containers or raised beds will follow a similar growth cycle to those planted directly in the ground but can benefit from the controlled environment to potentially bear fruit slightly earlier.

Blackberries typically follow a biennial growth pattern; the canes (or 'primocanes') grow vegetatively in their first year, then bear fruit in their second year as 'floricanes' before dying back after fruiting. From planting, blackberries can take between 1 to 2 years to begin producing fruit.

Once the flowering occurs, which usually starts in late spring to early summer, the berries will take approximately 35-45 days to reach maturity and be ready for harvest. This period can be influenced by the weather, with warmer temperatures speeding up the ripening process. Most blackberry varieties are ready to harvest from midsummer to early autumn, depending on the local climate and the time of bloom.

When it comes to harvesting blackberries, the key is to wait until the fruit is fully ripe. Unlike some fruits, blackberries do not continue to ripen once picked, so harvesting at the right time is crucial for flavor. Ripe berries will be plump, firm, and fully black. They should come off the stem with a gentle tug; if they resist, they're likely not ripe enough. Harvesting in the morning when the temperatures are cooler can help preserve the quality of the fruit.

It's advisable to wear gloves while picking blackberries to protect your hands from the thorns found on most traditional blackberry canes and to use shallow containers for collecting the berries to avoid crushing them under their own weight. Since blackberries are delicate and perishable, they should be handled gently and cooled as soon as possible after harvesting to extend their shelf life.

After harvesting, blackberries should be cooled quickly to maintain their quality. They should be stored in a refrigerator if not used immediately and can last up to a week when stored properly. However, for the best flavor and texture, using them within a few days is recommended. Washing the berries should be done before use to prevent them from becoming soggy and reduce the risk of spoilage.

For those interested in preserving their harvest, blackberries can be frozen, dried, or used in jams, jellies, and other preserves. Freezing is a straightforward option that preserves the taste and nutritional value of the berries.

Simply wash the blackberries gently, pat them dry, spread them out on a baking sheet to freeze individually, and then transfer them to airtight containers or freezer bags.

Growing blackberries in containers and raised beds offers you the opportunity to enjoy these delicious fruits even with limited space. By understanding the growth cycle and proper harvesting techniques, you can maximize your yield and enjoy fresh blackberries throughout the season.

CONTAINER & RAISED BEDS BLACKBERRIES NOTES

Start: Seeds or Seedlings.

Germination: 2 to 4 weeks, at temperatures between 68°F to 75°F (20°C to 24°C).

Seed Life: 3 Years.

Soil Type: Well-drained, fertile soils rich in organic matter - pH range of 5.5 to 6.5.

Seed Spacing: ¼″ depth.

Seedling Spacing:

Containers – Blackberries plant requires a container at least 18-24 inches deep and equally wide to accommodate its root system without crowding.

Raised Beds - Desired spacing between Blackberry plants is about 18-24 inches apart within rows, with rows spaced about 4-6 feet apart.

Sunlight: 6 – 8hrs full sunlight daily.

Growing Temperatures:

The desired temperature range for growing blackberries is between 75°F to 85°F (24°C to 29°C) during the day. Night temperatures ideally should be lower, around 60°F to 70°F (15°C to 21°C).

Duration Till Harvest:

First Year - Blackberries focus on establishing a robust root system and vegetative growth in their first year.

Second Year - You can expect a more substantial harvest in the second year. Blackberries produce fruit on canes that grew the previous year (known as floricanes). The yield and timing will depend on the variety and local climate, but generally, the fruit ripens in mid to late summer. For those in warmer regions, this may occur slightly earlier in the year, while cooler climates might see a later start to the blackberry season.

Third Year - Blackberry plants enter their peak production phase, which can last several years, with annual harvests that typically span 3 to 5 weeks during summer. The precise duration of the harvesting window and the abundance of fruit are influenced by the plant's health, weather conditions, and the specific blackberry variety.

CHAPTER 6
STONE FRUIT BUSHES: CONTAINER & RAISED BED GARDENS – CHERRY BUSHES

C herry bushes are an excellent addition to fruit containers and raised bed gardens, offering the delightful combination of ornamental beauty and delicious, home-grown fruit. Unlike their larger tree counterparts, cherry bushes are compact, making them ideal for small gardening spaces such as patios, balconies, and urban gardens. These versatile plants thrive in well-drained soil and benefit from the controlled environment that containers and raised beds provide - allowing for easier soil quality, moisture, and nutrient management.

With varieties that boast both sweet and sour flavors, cherry bushes are perfect for fresh eating, baking, and preserving. Their springtime blossoms add a burst of color to any garden setting, while their dense foliage and manageable size make them easy to prune and maintain.

These setups can help mitigate common gardening issues such as soil-borne diseases and pest invasions, offering a healthier environment for cherry bushes. By isolating the plants from ground-level threats and providing well-aerated soil, gardeners can effectively manage plant health and productivity. The mobility of containers allows for strategic placement to maximize sunlight exposure and protection from harsh weather, further enhancing the growth potential of cherry bushes.

Ultimately, utilizing containers and raised beds to grow cherry bushes not only optimizes growing conditions but also enhances the aesthetic appeal and functional value of your garden.

THE RIGHT SOIL TO GROW CHERRY BUSHES IN CONTAINER & RAISED BEDS

Creating the right soil conditions is paramount for the successful growth of cherry bushes in fruit containers and raised bed gardens. Cherry bushes thrive in well-draining, loamy soil rich in organic matter, ensuring their roots receive adequate oxygen while retaining enough moisture to support healthy growth. The ideal soil pH for cherry bushes ranges between 6.0 and 7.0, which is slightly acidic to neutral. This pH range allows the plants to efficiently absorb essential nutrients such as nitrogen, phosphorus, and potassium, critical for their development, flowering, and fruit production. Before planting, it is beneficial to test the soil pH and adjust it if necessary, by incorporating amendments like lime to raise the pH or sulfur to lower it.

In containers, using a high-quality potting mix specifically formulated for fruiting plants can provide an excellent starting point. This mix should be light, airy, and well-draining, often containing components such as peat moss, perlite, and compost. Adding a slow-release organic fertilizer to the mix can ensure that the cherry bushes receive a steady supply of nutrients throughout the growing season.

Additionally, incorporating compost or other organic matter into the soil enhances its fertility and structure, promoting healthier root growth and increasing the soil's ability to retain moisture without becoming waterlogged. Regularly refreshing the top layer of soil with compost or aged manure can help maintain nutrient levels and soil health over time.

For raised bed gardens, preparing the soil thoroughly before planting is essential. A blend of garden soil, compost, and well-rotted manure can create a nutrient-rich environment that supports vigorous growth. Raised beds should also have good drainage to prevent water from pooling around the roots, which can lead to root rot and other issues.

Elevating the soil in raised beds can improve drainage naturally, but it's still crucial to monitor soil moisture levels, especially during periods of heavy rain or drought. Mulching the soil surface with organic materials such as straw or wood chips can help retain moisture, regulate soil temperature, and suppress weed growth, all of which contribute to a healthier growing environment for cherry bushes.

Achieving the right soil conditions also involves ongoing care and monitoring. Regularly checking the soil moisture is vital, particularly in containers where the soil can dry out more quickly than in the ground. Watering deeply and consistently ensures that the entire root zone is hydrated, but it's important to avoid overwatering, which can suffocate the roots and lead to disease. During the growing season, supplementing with organic fertilizers tailored for fruiting plants can provide additional nutrients, supporting the plant's energy needs for fruit production.

By carefully managing soil conditions, you can create an optimal growing environment for cherry bushes in containers and raised beds, leading to healthier plants and more bountiful harvests. Tailoring the soil to meet the specific needs of cherry bushes ensures that these plants can thrive in their confined spaces, bringing the joy of home-grown cherries within easy reach.

HOW TO SOW CHERRY BUSHES IN CONTAINERS & RAISED BEDS GARDENS

Correct Season To Sow Cherry Bushes In Containers & Raised Beds Gardens

The correct season to sow cherry bushes in fruit containers and raised bed gardens is primarily during the early spring or fall when weather conditions are most favorable for establishing young plants. Early spring planting allows cherry bushes to settle in and start developing a robust root system before the intense heat of summer arrives. This timing ensures that the plants can take full advantage of the growing season, producing strong vegetative growth and setting the foundation for future fruiting.

Alternatively, planting in the fall offers the advantage of cooler temperatures and typically increased rainfall, which can reduce transplant shock and provide a less stressful environment for the plants. The soil is still warm from the summer months, encouraging root development while the above-ground growth slows down, focusing energy on establishing a healthy root system.

Regardless of the season chosen, it's crucial to ensure that the plants avoid extreme weather conditions—planting too early in spring risks exposure to late frosts, while planting too late in fall may not allow enough time for roots to establish before winter. By choosing the optimal season, you can give your cherry bushes the best start, leading to healthier, more fruitful plants in their containers and raised bed gardens.

Plant Needs & Requirements

Germinating cherry bushes from seeds to seedlings correctly is crucial because it sets the foundation for healthy plant development and successful fruit production. Proper germination ensures that the seedlings emerge strong and vigorous, with a robust root system capable of thriving in the confined spaces of containers and raised beds.

This initial phase of growth is particularly sensitive to environmental conditions such as temperature, light, and moisture, all of which need to be carefully managed to avoid issues like damping-off, poor root establishment, or stunted growth. Starting with healthy, well-germinated seedlings also reduces the risk of transplant shock when moving them into their final growing location, allowing for a smoother transition and quicker adaptation to their new environment.

Additionally, correct germination practices help ensure uniformity in plant size and growth rate, which is important for maintaining an aesthetically pleasing garden and maximizing space efficiency in raised beds and containers. By giving cherry bushes the best possible start through meticulous germination, you can improve the chances of a bountiful and high-quality harvest, making the most of your gardening efforts and resources.

Germinating cherry bushes from seeds to seedlings involves several precise steps to ensure the seeds develop into healthy plants ready for transplantation. The process begins with seed stratification, a crucial step for breaking the dormancy of cherry seeds and mimicking the natural winter conditions they would experience in the wild.

To stratify the seeds, place them in a moist medium such as sand or peat moss and store them in the refrigerator at temperatures between 33°F and 41°F (1°C to 5°C) for approximately 60 to 90 days. This cold treatment helps to soften the seed coat and signal the embryo inside the seed that it is time to begin germination.

After the stratification period, the seeds can be sown in a suitable germination medium. Use a well-draining seed starting mix, a blend of peat moss, vermiculite, and perlite. Plant the seeds about 1/2 inch deep and keep the soil consistently moist but not waterlogged. It's essential to provide the right temperature for germination; cherry seeds typically germinate best at temperatures between 70°F and 75°F (21°C to 24°C).

Using a heat mat can help maintain these optimal temperatures if you're sprouting seeds indoors. Ensure the seeds receive adequate light by placing them in a bright location or under grow lights set for about 12-16 hours per day.

Once the seeds have germinated, which can take several weeks, the seedlings will start to develop their first true leaves. This stage indicates that the young plants are beginning to establish themselves and can be cared for more intensively. Continue to provide consistent moisture, ensuring that the seedlings do not dry out while avoiding overwatering.

As the seedlings grow, they will benefit from being fertilized with a diluted organic fertilizer to support their development. Gradually acclimate the seedlings to outdoor conditions by placing them outside for a few hours each day, increasing the duration gradually over a week or two. This hardening-off process reduces transplant shock when the seedlings are moved to their final growing location.

Cherry seedlings are typically ready for transplantation into containers or raised bed gardens when they have developed a strong root system and several sets of true leaves. This generally occurs 8 to 12 weeks after germination. Select containers at least 18 inches in diameter and depth to accommodate the root growth and provide good drainage.

For raised beds, ensure the soil is well-prepared with a mix of quality garden soil, compost, and organic matter to provide a nutrient-rich environment. Transplant the seedlings carefully, disturbing the roots as little as possible. Plant them at the same depth they were growing in their seedling trays and water thoroughly after planting to help settle the soil around the roots.

By following these detailed steps for germinating cherry bushes seeds, you can ensure your young plants are healthy and well-prepared for growth in containers and raised beds. The attention to detail during the early stages of germination and seedling care will pay off in the form of robust, productive cherry bushes that can thrive and produce bountiful harvests in their confined growing spaces.

Spacing & Measurement

Spacing and measurements when transplanting cherry bush seedlings into fruit containers and raised bed gardens are crucial for several reasons. Proper spacing ensures that each plant has adequate room to grow, essential for healthy root development and optimal access to nutrients, water, and sunlight. Crowding can lead to competition among plants, resulting in stunted growth and reduced fruit production.

Likewise, well-spaced plants allow for better air circulation around the foliage, which helps prevent fungal diseases and pest infestations by reducing humidity levels and promoting faster drying of leaves after watering or rainfall. In containers, considering the size and depth is equally important to accommodate the mature spread of the root system without causing root-bound conditions, which can impede growth and fruiting.

Adequate spacing also facilitates easier maintenance tasks such as weeding, pruning, and harvesting, making gardening more efficient and enjoyable. By adhering to recommended spacing guidelines, gardeners can create a healthier and more productive environment for their cherry bushes, leading to abundant harvests of high-quality fruits.

When planting cherry bush seedlings in fruit containers, the desired spacing and measurements are essential for ensuring healthy growth and optimal fruit production. For container gardening, each cherry bush should be planted in an individual container at least 18-24 inches deep and 20-24 inches wide. This size allows sufficient room for the root system to expand and prevents the plant from becoming root-bound, impeding growth and fruiting. Using a high-quality potting mix enriched with organic matter ensures good drainage and nutrient availability. Additionally, placing containers in a location that receives at least 6-8 hours of direct sunlight per day is crucial for the plants' photosynthetic needs and overall health.

In raised bed gardens, proper spacing is equally important to provide each cherry bush with ample room to thrive. Typically, cherry bushes should be spaced about 3-4 feet apart within the raised bed. This distance allows for adequate air circulation around each plant, reducing the risk of fungal diseases and pest issues.

It also ensures that each plant has enough space to develop a robust canopy, vital for maximizing fruit production. The raised bed should be at least 18 inches deep to accommodate the roots and filled with well-draining soil rich in compost or other organic matter to support healthy growth.

When planning the layout of your raised bed garden, consider accessibility for maintenance tasks such as weeding, pruning, and harvesting. Ensuring there is enough space between rows—typically around 4-5 feet—allows for easy movement without damaging the plants.

Raised beds should be positioned to receive full sun exposure, similar to containers, as cherry bushes require substantial sunlight for fruit development. Installing a drip irrigation system can help maintain consistent soil moisture levels, which is essential for cherry bushes, particularly during fruiting periods.

Proper spacing and measurements are vital for the health of individual plants and the overall productivity and ease of managing your cherry bush garden. Crowded plants can lead to increased competition for resources, resulting in weaker growth and lower yields. Whether in containers or raised beds, thoughtful planning and attention to detail in planting will significantly enhance the success and enjoyment of your cherry bush gardening endeavors.

Ideal Temperatures & Sun Requirements

The importance of ideal temperatures and sun requirements when growing cherry bushes in fruit containers and raised bed gardens cannot be overstated, as these factors are critical to the successful cultivation and fruiting of the plants.

Cherry bushes thrive best in temperatures ranging from 60°F to 75°F (15°C to 24°C), which favor robust growth and optimal fruit development. Consistent exposure to these temperatures helps prevent stress on the plants, reducing the risk of issues such as poor flowering or fruit set.

Furthermore, cherry bushes require full sun, needing at least 6 to 8 hours of direct sunlight each day to maximize photosynthesis, which fuels their growth and fruit production. Insufficient sunlight can lead to weak, spindly growth and diminished yields. Ensuring that cherry bushes receive ample sunlight also aids in disease prevention, as sunlight helps keep foliage dry and reduces the likelihood of fungal infections.

For container-grown cherry bushes, positioning the containers in a location that receives unobstructed sunlight is essential. Similarly, in raised bed gardens, selecting a sunny spot and arranging the beds to capture maximum sunlight throughout the day will ensure that each plant thrives and produces an abundant harvest. Maintaining the right temperature range and providing adequate sun exposure can create an environment where cherry bushes flourish, leading to healthier plants and more bountiful fruit production.

MAINTAINING YOUR CONTAINER & RAISED BED CHERRY BUSHES

Maintaining your cherry bushes is crucial for ensuring their health, longevity, and productivity. Regular maintenance tasks such as watering, pruning, fertilizing, and monitoring for pests and diseases are vital in keeping the plants vigorous and capable of producing high-quality fruit.

Consistent watering helps keep the soil evenly moist, which is essential for preventing stress that can lead to poor growth and reduced fruit yields. Pruning removes dead or diseased branches, encourages better air circulation, and promotes the growth of new, productive shoots. Fertilizing provides the necessary nutrients that may be depleted from the soil over time, supporting ongoing growth and fruit production.

Vigilant monitoring for pests and diseases allows for early intervention, preventing infestations from spreading and causing significant damage. Additionally, maintaining an appropriate mulch layer can help regulate soil temperature, retain moisture, and suppress weeds. By diligently caring for your cherry bushes, you ensure they remain robust and productive, leading to a rewarding gardening experience and a plentiful harvest.

Pruning & Thinning Your Cherry Bushes

Pruning and thinning cherry bushes grown in containers and raised bed gardens are essential horticultural practices that significantly impact plant health, fruit quality, and yield. Pruning involves selectively removing dead, diseased, or overcrowded branches to enhance air circulation and light penetration throughout the canopy.

This reduces the risk of fungal infections and pest infestations, creating a more robust and resilient plant. Thinning, on the other hand, involves removing some of the developing fruit to ensure the remaining cherries have enough space and resources to grow to their full size and quality. Both practices help to balance the plant's energy distribution, directing it towards the production of healthier, larger fruits rather than supporting excessive foliage or an overabundance of small, underdeveloped cherries.

Additionally, pruning and thinning can help maintain the desired shape and size of the cherry bushes, making them easier to manage within the confined spaces of containers and raised beds. By fostering stronger structures and preventing overcrowding, these practices ultimately lead to more productive and visually appealing plants, ensuring a bountiful harvest of high-quality cherries year after year.

Pruning and thinning cherry bushes are vital tasks that should be performed with careful timing and technique to maximize their benefits. The best time to prune cherry bushes is during the late winter or early spring, while the plants are still dormant before new growth begins. This timing allows the wounds to heal quickly as the plant enters its active growing phase.

Pruning during dormancy also makes it easier to see the structure of the bush and make precise cuts. Begin by removing any dead, damaged, or diseased branches to prevent the spread of infections and to open the canopy for better air circulation. Next, thin out any crossing or over-crowded branches to ensure light can penetrate the entire plant, which is crucial for fruit development and overall health.

When pruning, use clean, sharp pruning shears to make clean cuts close to the main stem or just above a healthy bud. This helps promote healing and reduces the risk of disease entry. For container-grown cherry bushes, maintaining a balanced shape is important, as it ensures even growth and prevents the plant from becoming too top-heavy.

In raised beds, more robust pruning might be necessary to keep the bushes within their designated space and to encourage a more controlled, upright growth habit. Always aim to preserve the natural form of the cherry bush while removing excess growth that may hinder its productivity.

Thinning is another crucial practice that should be conducted after the initial fruit set in late spring or early summer. Thinning involves selectively removing some of the developing fruits to prevent overcrowding, which allows the remaining cherries to grow larger and ripen more evenly.

For optimal results, thin the fruits so there is about 4 to 6 inches of space between each cherry. This spacing ensures that each fruit has enough room to develop without competing for nutrients and sunlight. Thinning also reduces the weight load on the branches, preventing breakage and promoting the health and longevity of the cherry bush.

During the thinning process, carefully inspect each cluster of cherries and gently twist off the smaller or misshapen fruits, leaving the healthiest ones to mature. It's important to perform thinning early enough in the season before the fruits have fully developed, as this will give the remaining cherries ample time to benefit from the reduced competition.

Regularly monitor the cherry bushes throughout the growing season for additional thinning needs, especially if the bush appears overloaded with fruit. By consistently pruning and thinning your cherry bushes, you not only improve the quality and size of your harvest but also enhance the overall vigor and aesthetic appeal of the plants, ensuring they remain productive and healthy for years to come.

Watering Your Container & Raised Bed Cherry Bushes

Watering cherry bushes grown in containers and raised bed gardens is a critical aspect of their care that directly influences their health, growth, and fruit production. Consistent and adequate watering is essential because it ensures that the plants receive the moisture they need to support their metabolic functions, including photosynthesis and nutrient uptake.

In containers, the soil tends to dry out more quickly than in traditional garden beds due to limited volume and increased exposure to air, making regular watering crucial to prevent drought stress, which can lead to wilting, leaf drop, and poor fruit development.

Similarly, raised bed gardens, although better at retaining moisture than containers, still require vigilant watering practices to maintain soil moisture levels, especially during hot, dry periods. Proper watering helps maintain an even soil moisture level, preventing fluctuations that can cause root damage or stress the plants, ultimately leading to reduced fruit quality and yield.

Additionally, well-hydrated cherry bushes are more resilient against pests and diseases, as water helps strengthen their natural defenses. By ensuring consistent watering, you can foster robust, productive cherry bushes that yield abundant, high-quality fruit.

Watering cherry bushes involves understanding their specific moisture needs throughout different stages of growth. During the initial establishment phase, newly planted cherry bushes require frequent watering to help develop a strong root system.

For the first few weeks, water the plants deeply every few days, ensuring the soil remains consistently moist but not waterlogged. As the plants become established, usually after the first growing season, they can tolerate less frequent watering. However, it's crucial to adjust watering based on weather conditions, as hot and dry periods will necessitate more frequent irrigation to prevent the soil from drying out.

Generally, mature cherry bushes in containers and raised beds should be watered deeply once or twice a week, depending on the climate and soil type. Deep watering encourages roots to grow deeper into the soil, making the plant more resilient during dry spells. The goal is to moisten the soil to a depth of at least 12-18 inches, ensuring the entire root zone receives adequate moisture.

To determine if your cherry bushes need watering, check the soil moisture level by sticking your finger about 2-3 inches into the soil; if it feels dry at this depth, it's time to water. In containers, make sure excess water can drain freely to prevent root rot, which can occur when water accumulates at the bottom.

During the fruiting period, consistent moisture is particularly important to support the development of high-quality cherries. Irregular watering during this time can lead to problems such as fruit splitting or underdeveloped fruit.

It's beneficial to mulch around the base of the plants with organic materials like straw or wood chips, which helps retain soil moisture and regulate soil temperature. This practice reduces the frequency of watering needed and protects the roots from extreme temperature fluctuations.

It's also important to adjust watering practices as the seasons change. In spring and fall, when temperatures are cooler, and rainfall is often more abundant, you may need to reduce the frequency of watering. Conversely, in summer, especially during heat waves, cherry bushes will need more frequent watering.

Always be mindful of the specific needs of your cherry bushes and the environmental conditions, adapting your watering schedule to ensure optimal plant health and fruit production. By understanding and responding to these needs, you can effectively manage water resources while promoting vibrant growth and bountiful harvests from your cherry bushes in containers and raised bed gardens.

Organic Fertilization For Container & Raised Bed Cherry Bushes

Organic fertilization is crucial for cherry bushes because it provides a balanced, slow-release source of essential nutrients while enhancing soil health and sustainability. Unlike synthetic fertilizers, organic fertilizers—such as compost, well-rotted manure, and organic plant-based fertilizers—release nutrients gradually, ensuring a steady supply that matches the plants' growth cycles without causing nutrient imbalances or runoff pollution.

This slow-release mechanism helps prevent the risk of over-fertilization, leading to issues like root burn and excessive foliage at the expense of fruit production. Additionally, organic fertilizers improve soil structure, increase microbial activity, and enhance the soil's ability to retain moisture and nutrients, creating a more favorable growing environment for cherry bushes.

The beneficial microorganisms promoted by organic fertilization also help protect plants from diseases and pests, further supporting the overall health of the cherry bushes. By using organic fertilizers, you can ensure that your cherry bushes receive the necessary nutrients for vigorous growth and abundant fruiting while maintaining a sustainable and eco-friendly gardening practice.

There are several types of organic fertilizers that are particularly beneficial for cherry bushes. One common choice is compost, rich in organic matter and nutrients such as nitrogen, phosphorus, and potassium. Compost improves soil structure, enhances microbial activity, and provides a steady release of nutrients.

Another excellent option is well-rotted manure, which supplies a balanced nutrient profile while also boosting soil fertility and moisture retention. Manure from herbivores like cows, horses, and chickens is particularly effective, provided it has been adequately aged to prevent plant burning. Additionally, organic plant-based fertilizers, such as alfalfa meal and kelp meal, can provide specific nutrients, including trace minerals, that support overall plant health and fruit production.

When fertilizing cherry bushes in containers and raised beds, timing and application methods are crucial to maximize the benefits. The best time to apply organic fertilizers is in early spring, just before the plants break dormancy and begin their active growth phase. This initial application helps stimulate root development and prepare the cherry bushes for the growing season.

To apply compost or well-rotted manure, spread a layer of 1 to 2 inches thick around the base of the plants, avoiding direct contact with the stems. Gently work the material into the top few inches of soil to ensure even distribution and incorporation into the root zone. For container-grown cherry bushes, a similar approach can be taken, but with careful attention to the limited soil volume to avoid over-application.

Throughout the growing season, additional fertilization may be necessary to support ongoing growth and fruit development. A mid-season boost can be provided using liquid organic fertilizers, such as fish emulsion or compost tea. These are easy to apply and quickly absorbed by the plants, offering an immediate nutrient boost.

Dilute the liquid fertilizer according to the manufacturer's instructions and apply it directly to the soil or as a foliar spray, ensuring thorough coverage. This supplemental feeding helps maintain nutrient levels during critical fruit set and maturation periods.

In late summer or early fall, a final light application of organic fertilizer can help cherry bushes store energy for the winter and promote strong root systems. However, it's important not to over-fertilize at this stage to avoid stimulating new growth that could be damaged by frost. It is key to monitor the health and growth of the cherry bushes regularly, adjusting the fertilization schedule based on the plant's appearance and performance. Organic fertilizers not only provide the necessary nutrients for vigorous growth and abundant fruiting but also contribute to a healthier, more resilient gardening ecosystem by fostering rich, fertile soil.

PROTECTING YOUR CONTAINER & RAISED BED CHERRY BUSHES

Extreme Temperatures

Protecting cherry bushes grown in containers and raised bed gardens from extreme temperatures is crucial for maintaining their health and productivity. Extreme heat can cause significant stress to the plants, leading to wilting, leaf scorch, and even fruit drop. To mitigate the effects of high temperatures, it's essential to provide adequate shading.

This can be achieved by placing shade cloths over the plants during the hottest part of the day or positioning containers in areas that receive filtered sunlight. Mulching around the base of the plants with organic materials such as straw, wood chips, or shredded leaves helps retain soil moisture and keeps the root zone cool. Regular watering is also vital during periods of intense heat, ensuring that the soil remains consistently moist but not waterlogged. Using a drip irrigation system can be particularly effective, delivering water directly to the roots while minimizing evaporation.

Protecting cherry bushes from cold temperatures and frost is equally important, especially during late spring frosts or early fall freezes. Frost can damage blossoms, young fruits, and new growth, significantly impacting the yield.

To protect against cold spells, consider using frost blankets, row covers, and insulating layers to trap heat and shield the plants from freezing temperatures. These covers should be applied in the evening and removed in the morning once the temperatures rise. For container-grown cherry bushes, you can move the containers to more sheltered locations, such as garages, sheds, or against south-facing walls that retain heat. Wrapping the containers with burlap or insulating materials can help protect the root systems from freezing.

Plants under temperature stress are more susceptible to diseases and pest infestations, which can further weaken the plant and reduce fruit quality. Extreme temperatures can also disrupt the physiological processes within the plant, such as photosynthesis and nutrient uptake, leading to stunted growth and poor fruit development.

Additionally, temperature fluctuations can impact the soil environment, affecting nutrient availability and microbial activity. In extreme heat, soil can dry out rapidly, making it difficult for roots to access the necessary moisture and nutrients. In contrast, freezing temperatures can slow down microbial processes essential for nutrient cycling, potentially leading to nutrient deficiencies.

In summary, protecting cherry bushes in containers and raised beds from extreme temperatures involves a combination of shading, mulching, watering, and using physical barriers like frost blankets and row covers.

These practices are essential not only for preventing immediate damage caused by heat or frost but also for ensuring the long-term health and productivity of the plants. By understanding and addressing the challenges posed by extreme temperatures, you can cultivate robust cherry bushes that thrive and produce abundant, high-quality fruit throughout the growing season.

Protecting Container & Raised Bed Cherry Bushes From Pests

Protecting cherry bushes grown in containers and raised bed gardens organically from pests is essential for several reasons. Organic pest control methods prioritize the health of the plant, the soil, and the surrounding ecosystem, avoiding the harmful chemicals found in synthetic pesticides that can lead to long-term soil degradation and harm beneficial insects like pollinators and natural predators.

Organic approaches such as using neem oil, insecticidal soaps, companion planting, and introducing beneficial insects help manage pest populations while maintaining a balanced ecosystem. This holistic strategy not only reduces the risk of chemical residues on the fruit, ensuring safer, healthier produce, but also supports the overall resilience of the garden.

By fostering a thriving, diverse environment, organic pest control enhances the health and productivity of cherry bushes, resulting in robust plants and high-quality fruit yields without compromising environmental sustainability.

Cherry bushes are susceptible to various pests, each capable of causing significant damage to the plants and reducing fruit yield. Common pests include aphids, tiny insects that feed on plant sap, causing distorted leaves and stunted growth. Spider mites, another sap-sucking pest, create fine webbing and can cause leaves to appear speckled or bronze.

Cherry fruit flies are particularly harmful as their larvae burrow into the fruit, making it unfit for consumption. Additionally, Japanese beetles and caterpillars can chew through leaves and flowers, severely impacting the plant's ability to photosynthesize and produce fruit. Scale insects can also be problematic, attaching themselves to stems and leaves and feeding on plant juices, leading to weakened plants and potentially spreading diseases.

Protecting cherry bushes from these pests organically involves a combination of preventive measures and direct control strategies. One effective preventive measure is maintaining plant health through proper watering, mulching, and fertilization, as healthy plants are more resistant to pest attacks. Introducing beneficial insects such as ladybugs, lacewings, and predatory wasps can naturally control pest populations.

These beneficial insects prey on common pests like aphids and caterpillars, reducing their numbers without chemical interventions. Planting companion plants like marigolds, nasturtiums, and garlic can also deter pests through their natural repellent properties.

For direct control, organic sprays such as neem oil, insecticidal soap, and horticultural oils can be applied to affected plants. Neem oil disrupts the life cycle of many pests, including aphids and spider mites, while insecticidal soap targets soft-bodied insects by breaking down their cell membranes. Horticultural oils smother pests and their eggs, providing an effective means of control. Applying these sprays in the early morning or late evening is essential to avoid harming beneficial insects and prevent leaf burn.

Physical barriers can also play a crucial role in protecting cherry bushes from pests. Using floating row covers or netting can prevent larger insects like Japanese beetles and cherry fruit flies from reaching the plants. Regularly inspecting and manually removing pests can be labor-intensive but effective, especially for small infestations. Removing fallen fruit and debris from around the plants reduces hiding places for pests and prevents the spread of disease.

In addition to these methods, practicing crop rotation and avoiding planting cherry bushes in the same spot every year can help prevent soil-borne pests and diseases. Implementing trap crops, which are plants more attractive to pests than cherry bushes, can also divert pests away from the main plants. For example, planting radishes nearby can attract flea beetles, sparing the cherry bushes from attack.

By combining these organic pest control methods, you can protect your container and raised bed-grown cherry bushes effectively. These practices not only minimize the use of harmful chemicals but also support a balanced and healthy garden ecosystem, leading to stronger plants and a safer, more abundant harvest of delicious cherries.

Protecting Container & Raised Bed Cherry Bushes From Diseases

Protecting cherry bushes from diseases organically is crucial, as it ensures the health and productivity of the plants while fostering a sustainable and eco-friendly gardening environment. Organic disease management practices, such as crop rotation, proper spacing, and effective sanitation, help prevent the spread of pathogens without relying on synthetic

201

chemicals that can harm beneficial microorganisms and cont-
aminate the soil and water.

By using organic fungicides like copper or sulfur sprays and
promoting natural disease resistance through the use of
compost teas and other biostimulants, you can maintain
vigorous plants and high-quality fruit. These methods safeguard the immediate crop and enhance soil health and biodiversity, which are essential for long-term garden vitality.

Avoiding chemical treatments protects pollinators and other
beneficial insects that play a critical role in maintaining
ecological balance and supporting plant reproduction, ultimately leading to healthier cherry bushes and a more robust,
resilient garden ecosystem.

Cherry bushes grown in containers and raised bed gardens
are susceptible to a variety of diseases that can significantly
impact their health and fruit production. Common diseases
include powdery mildew, cherry leaf spot, and bacterial
canker. Powdery mildew manifests as a white, powdery
coating on leaves, stems, and fruit, leading to reduced photosynthesis, stunted growth, and premature leaf drop.

Cherry leaf spot is caused by the fungus Blumeriella jaapii,
resulting in small purple or red spots on leaves, which eventually turn yellow and fall off, weakening the plant and
reducing fruit yield. Bacterial canker, caused by
Pseudomonas syringae, creates sunken, dark lesions on
branches and twigs, often accompanied by gum exudation,
leading to dieback and potentially fatal damage to the plant.

Organic protection against these diseases involves a combination of preventive measures, cultural practices, and targeted
treatments. One of the most effective strategies is selecting
disease-resistant cherry varieties when planting. These vari-

eties have been bred for increased resistance to common pathogens, significantly reducing the risk of infection.

Additionally, proper garden hygiene, such as regularly removing fallen leaves, pruning out diseased branches, and avoiding overhead watering, helps minimize the conditions that favor disease development and spread. Ensuring adequate air circulation around the plants by spacing them appropriately and thinning out dense foliage also reduces humidity levels, which can inhibit the proliferation of fungal spores.

Incorporating organic matter into the soil, such as compost, improves soil structure and fertility, promoting robust plant health and resilience against diseases. Compost tea, a liquid extract of compost, can be used as a foliar spray to intro-duce beneficial microorganisms that compete with pathogens and enhance the plant's immune responses. Mulching with organic materials like straw or wood chips helps regulate soil moisture and temperature, reducing plant stress and creating an unfavorable environment for many pathogens.

For direct control of existing infections, organic fungicides such as sulfur, copper-based sprays, and neem oil can be applied. Sulfur and copper are effective against various fungal diseases, including powdery mildew and cherry leaf spot, and should be used according to label instructions to avoid phytotoxicity.

Neem oil, derived from the neem tree, has antifungal proper-ties and can treat both fungal and bacterial diseases while acting as an insect repellent. It's important to apply these treatments early in the morning or late evening to avoid harming beneficial insects and ensure thorough plant surface coverage.

Regular monitoring and prompt action are essential in managing diseases organically. Inspecting the cherry bushes frequently for early signs of disease allows for timely intervention, preventing minor issues from escalating into severe outbreaks. Implementing crop rotation and alternating planting locations each season can also reduce the buildup of soil-borne pathogens that may affect cherry bushes.

By combining these organic methods—selecting disease-resistant varieties, maintaining proper garden hygiene, enhancing soil health, using organic fungicides, and practicing regular monitoring—you can effectively protect your cherry bushes from diseases in containers and raised beds. This holistic approach ensures the production of high-quality, chemical-free fruit and supports the overall health and sustainability of the garden ecosystem.

HARVESTING CONTAINER & RAISED BED CHERRY BUSHES

The time it takes for cherry bushes grown in containers and raised bed gardens to be ready for harvest can vary based on several factors, including the specific variety of cherry and the growing conditions.

Generally, cherry bushes will begin to produce fruit between 2 to 4 years after planting, with some dwarf or bush varieties potentially bearing fruit a bit earlier. The exact timing of fruit readiness depends on the climate and care provided. For example, if cherry bushes are grown in optimal conditions with adequate sunlight, water, and nutrients, they may reach maturity and begin producing fruit sooner than those grown in less ideal conditions.

Once the cherry bushes reach the appropriate age for fruiting, the actual harvest period typically occurs in late spring to early summer, depending on the local climate and the specific cherry variety. It is crucial to monitor the cherries closely as they ripen, as they do not continue to ripen once picked.

Signs that cherries are ready to be harvested include a deep, uniform color and a slight softness to the touch. The stems should still be green, and the fruit should easily detach from the stem when gently pulled. It is also helpful to taste a few cherries to ensure they have reached their maximum sweetness and flavor before proceeding with a full harvest.

When harvesting cherries from container-grown or raised bed cherry bushes, it is essential to handle the fruit carefully to avoid damaging the delicate skin and flesh. Ideally, cherries should be picked with their stems attached to prolong their shelf life and reduce the risk of post-harvest rotting.

To harvest, hold the stem close to where it attaches to the branch and gently pull or twist to detach the cherry. Using both hands, one to hold the branch and one to pick the cherries, can prevent unnecessary damage to the plant. If the cherries are being harvested for immediate use, such as fresh eating or making preserves, they can be picked without the stems, but this should be done carefully to avoid bruising.

Post-harvest handling is also important to maintain the quality and longevity of the cherries. Once picked, cherries should be placed in shallow containers to prevent crushing and stored in a cool, shaded area before being transferred to refrigeration.

Washing the cherries only before consumption or processing helps prevent mold and decay during storage. For those looking to extend the harvest season, cherries can be preserved through canning, freezing, or drying, all of which retain their delightful flavor and nutritional benefits.

Regular monitoring and timely harvesting ensure that the cherries are picked at their peak ripeness, providing the best flavor and texture. Each year, as the cherry bushes mature, their yield typically increases, rewarding gardeners with an increasingly abundant and delicious harvest.

By understanding the timeline and employing careful harvesting techniques, you can enjoy the fruits of your labor and maximize the productivity of your container-grown and raised bed cherry bushes.

CONTAINER & RAISED BEDS CHERRY BUSHES NOTES

Start: Seeds or Seedlings.

Germination: 30 – 90days, at temperatures between 70°F and 75°F (21°C to 24°C).

Seed Life: 2 Years.

Soil Type: Well-draining, loamy soil rich in organic matter - pH range of 6.0 to 7.0.

Seed Spacing: 1/2" depth.

Seedling Spacing:

Containers – Each cherry bush should be planted in an individual container that is at least 18-24 inches deep and 20-24 inches wide.

Raised Beds - Cherry bushes should be spaced about 3-4 feet apart within the raised bed. The raised bed should be at least 18 inches deep to accommodate the roots, ensuring enough space between rows—typically around 4-5 feet.

Sunlight: 6 – 8hrs full sunlight daily.

Growing Temperatures:

Cherry bushes thrive best in temperatures ranging from 60°F to 75°F (15°C to 24°C).

Duration Till Harvest:

Cherry bushes will begin to produce fruit between 2 to 4 years after planting, with some dwarf or bush varieties potentially bearing fruit a bit earlier.

The exact timing of fruit readiness depends on the climate and care provided. Once the cherry bushes reach the appropriate age for fruiting, the actual harvest period typically occurs in late spring to early summer, depending on the local climate and the specific cherry variety.

CHAPTER 7
STONE FRUIT BUSHES: CONTAINER & RAISED BED GARDENS – DWARF PEACHES

D warf peaches are an exceptional choice for fruit containers and raised bed gardening, offering a delightful combination of compact size and abundant fruit production. These miniature marvels are specifically bred to thrive in limited spaces, making them ideal for urban gardens, patios, and any area where maximizing space is essential. With their manageable height, typically reaching only three to six feet, dwarf peaches are easy to care for and harvest. They adapt well to the controlled environments of containers and raised beds, where gardeners can regulate soil quality, moisture, and exposure to pests more effectively.

Beyond their practicality, dwarf peaches add ornamental value with their beautiful blossoms in spring and vibrant foliage throughout the growing season. This makes them not only a productive addition but also an aesthetically pleasing one, ensuring that your garden remains both functional and visually appealing.

Planting dwarf peaches in containers and raised bed gardens offers numerous benefits that can significantly enhance your gardening experience. One of the primary advantages is space efficiency; these compact trees are ideal for small gardens, patios, balconies, or urban settings where traditional orchard space is unavailable. Containers and raised beds provide better control over soil quality, drainage, and root growth, allowing gardeners to create the optimal growing environment for the trees.

Additionally, the mobility of containers enables you to reposition the trees to maximize sunlight exposure or protect them from adverse weather conditions. Raised beds also offer improved soil temperature regulation and ease of maintenance, reducing back strain and facilitating closer monitoring of pests and diseases.

Furthermore, dwarf peaches produce high yields of delicious, full-sized fruit without requiring extensive pruning or ladder work, making them a practical and rewarding addition to any garden. This method of planting not only ensures a bountiful harvest but also adds aesthetic value with the tree's beautiful blossoms and lush foliage.

THE RIGHT SOIL TO GROW DWARF PEACHES IN CONTAINER & RAISED BEDS

Growing dwarf peaches in fruit containers and raised bed gardens requires careful attention to soil conditions to ensure the plants thrive and produce abundant, high-quality fruit. The ideal soil for dwarf peaches is well-draining, fertile, and slightly acidic to neutral, with a pH range of 6.0 to 7.0.

Soil that retains too much moisture can lead to root rot and other diseases, while overly dry soil can stress the tree and reduce fruit production. Therefore, a balanced soil mix that promotes good drainage while retaining adequate moisture is essential. A recommended mix for containers and raised beds includes equal parts of high-quality potting soil, compost, and sand or perlite. This combination ensures that the soil is both nutrient-rich and well-aerated, providing a suitable environment for the roots to develop and thrive.

In addition to drainage and pH balance, nutrient availability is crucial for the healthy growth of dwarf peaches. Incorporating organic matter such as compost or well-rotted manure into the soil not only improves its structure but also enriches it with essential nutrients.

These organic amendments help maintain a steady supply of nitrogen, phosphorus, potassium, and micronutrients vital for the tree's growth, fruit development, and overall health. For container gardening, it's important to use a high-quality potting mix specifically formulated for fruit trees, as garden soil alone may not provide the necessary drainage and aeration.

Raised beds, on the other hand, benefit from regular replenishment of organic matter to sustain soil fertility and structure over time.

Regular soil testing is an invaluable practice to monitor and adjust the soil conditions as needed. By testing the soil annually, you can determine nutrient levels and pH, allowing for precise adjustments through the application of fertilizers or soil amendments.

If the soil test indicates deficiencies, organic fertilizers such as blood meal, bone meal, or seaweed extract can be used to supplement nutrients without the risk of chemical buildup. Additionally, mulching around the base of the plants helps conserve soil moisture, regulate temperature, and suppress weeds, further contributing to optimal growing conditions.

Water management is another critical aspect of maintaining the right soil conditions for dwarf peaches. Both overwatering and underwatering can be detrimental, so it is essential to strike a balance. Using a drip irrigation system or soaker hoses can help deliver consistent moisture to the soil without causing saturation.

It's important to check the soil moisture regularly, especially during hot, dry periods, to ensure the tree receives adequate water without the risk of waterlogging. In containers, ensure that there are sufficient drainage holes to prevent excess water from accumulating at the bottom, which can lead to root rot.

By paying careful attention to these soil conditions and practices, you can create an optimal environment for growing dwarf peaches in containers and raised bed gardens. This ensures robust growth, disease resistance, and plentiful harvests, making the cultivation of these delightful fruit trees both rewarding and enjoyable.

HOW TO SOW DWARF PEACHES IN CONTAINERS & RAISED BEDS GARDENS

Correct Season To Sow Dwarf Peaches In Containers & Raised Beds Gardens

The correct season to sow dwarf peaches in fruit containers and raised bed gardens is during the late winter to early spring, before the onset of the growing season. This timing allows the young trees to establish their root systems and acclimate to their new environment before the warmer weather stimulates vigorous growth.

In regions with mild winters, late January to early March is ideal. For areas with harsher winter conditions, it may be necessary to wait until the threat of frost has passed, typically around March or April. Planting during this period ensures that the trees have the entire growing season to develop strong roots and foliage, which are critical for supporting future fruit production.

Additionally, early spring planting takes advantage of the naturally increasing daylight and rising temperatures, providing optimal conditions for the trees to thrive. Proper timing also helps avoid transplant shock, as the cool weather promotes gradual acclimatization. By planting dwarf peaches at the right time, you can set the stage for successful growth and a bountiful harvest.

Plant Needs & Requirements

Germinating dwarf peaches from seeds to seedlings correctly is vital when growing in containers and raised bed gardens because it establishes a strong, healthy foundation for the plants, ensuring optimal growth and productivity. Proper germination promotes the development of robust root systems, which are essential for efficient nutrient and water uptake, particularly in the confined spaces of containers and raised beds.

Healthy seedlings are better equipped to cope with transplanting stress and environmental fluctuations, reducing the risk of stunted growth and poor fruit production. Additionally, well-germinated seedlings are more resilient against pests and diseases, which can be more challenging to manage in limited growing environments.

By starting with vigorous, correctly germinated seedlings, you can maximize the potential of your dwarf peaches, ensuring they flourish and yield abundant, high-quality fruit even in restricted garden spaces.

Germinating dwarf peaches from seeds to seedlings involves several crucial steps that ensure successful growth and development. The first step is to select healthy, ripe peaches and extract the seeds (pits) from the fruit. It's essential to clean any remaining fruit flesh off the pits to prevent mold growth.

Next, the seeds need to undergo a process called stratification, mimicking the natural winter conditions that break seed dormancy. To stratify the seeds, place them in a moist paper towel or peat moss, seal them in a plastic bag, and store them in the refrigerator for 8 to 12 weeks. This cold treatment is critical for triggering germination once the seeds are planted.

Once the stratification period is complete, remove the seeds from the refrigerator and plant them in small pots filled with a well-draining seed-starting mix. Bury the seeds about an inch deep and water them thoroughly. It's essential to maintain consistent moisture without waterlogging the soil.

Place the pots in a warm, sunny location where the temperature remains between 60°F and 70°F (15°C to 21°C). This temperature range is ideal for the seeds to germinate and sprout. It typically takes a few weeks for germination to occur, and during this time, maintaining optimal moisture and temperature conditions is crucial for the successful emergence of seedlings.

As the seedlings grow, providing adequate light is essential. If natural sunlight is insufficient, supplement with grow lights to ensure the young plants receive at least 12-16 hours of light daily.

Once the seedlings have developed their first set of true leaves and are about 4-6 inches tall, they are ready to be transplanted into larger containers or raised bed gardens. Before transplanting, it's advisable to harden off the seedlings by gradually exposing them to outdoor conditions over a week.

This process involves placing the seedlings outside for a few hours each day, increasing the duration and intensity of exposure to sunlight, wind, and temperature fluctuations, which helps them acclimate to the new environment.

When transplanting into containers or raised beds, choose high-quality, well-draining soil mixed with organic matter such as compost. For containers, ensure they have adequate drainage holes to prevent waterlogging. Plant the seedlings at the same depth they were growing in their pots, and water them thoroughly after transplanting.

Mulching around the base of the plants can help retain soil moisture and suppress weeds. Consistent watering and monitoring for pests and diseases are essential for the continued health and growth of the dwarf peaches.

Spacing & Measurement

Spacing and measurements when transplanting dwarf peach seedlings into fruit containers and raised bed gardens are crucial for several reasons. Proper spacing ensures that each plant receives adequate sunlight, air circulation, and nutrients, which are essential for robust growth and high fruit yields.

Crowded plants can lead to competition for resources, resulting in stunted growth and poor fruit production. Additionally, good spacing helps reduce the risk of disease and pest infestations, as it allows for better airflow around the plants, minimizing the conditions that pathogens and pests thrive in.

In containers, appropriate spacing prevents root entanglement and ensures that each plant's roots have enough room to expand and access water and nutrients effectively.

For raised beds, maintaining the right distance between seedlings facilitates easier maintenance tasks like pruning, watering, and harvesting, making the gardening process more efficient and enjoyable. Ultimately, careful attention to spacing and measurements during transplantation sets the foundation for healthy, productive dwarf peaches.

When planting dwarf peach seedlings in fruit containers, the spacing and container size are critical for fostering healthy growth and maximizing fruit production. Containers should be at least 18-24 inches in diameter and 20-24 inches deep to accommodate the root system of the young tree. This size allows the roots ample space to spread out and access nutrients and water effectively. It's also important to ensure the container has adequate drainage holes to prevent waterlogging.

For larger dwarf varieties or if multiple trees are being planted in a single container, increasing the container size proportionally is essential to provide each tree with enough room to thrive.

In raised bed gardens, the desired spacing between dwarf peach seedlings is typically around 3 to 5 feet apart. This spacing ensures that each tree has sufficient room to grow both above and below ground.

The 3-foot distance is ideal for smaller dwarf varieties, while 5 feet is recommended for larger dwarf types that may have more extensive canopy and root systems. Adequate spacing promotes better air circulation, which helps reduce the risk of fungal diseases and pest infestations. It also allows sunlight to penetrate through the foliage, ensuring each tree receives the necessary light for photosynthesis and fruit development.

Proper spacing in raised beds also simplifies maintenance tasks such as pruning, watering, and harvesting, making it easier for gardeners to manage their plants effectively.

Considering the mature size of the trees when planning spacing is essential. Dwarf peaches, although smaller than standard varieties, still require adequate room to reach their full potential. Ensuring proper spacing from the start helps avoid the need for later adjustments, which can stress the trees and disrupt their growth.

Planning ahead and providing sufficient space for each tree to grow and expand will result in a more organized and visually appealing garden layout. This thoughtful approach to spacing and measurements not only enhances the health and productivity of the dwarf peaches but also contributes to a more enjoyable and manageable gardening experience.

Ideal Temperatures & Sun Requirements

The ideal temperatures and sun requirements are crucial for the successful growth of dwarf peaches in fruit containers and raised bed gardens, as they directly influence the plants' health, development, and fruit production.

Dwarf peaches thrive in temperatures ranging from 65°F to 75°F (18°C to 24°C) during the growing season, with cooler winter temperatures necessary for dormancy. They require a significant amount of sunlight—at least 6 to 8 hours of direct sunlight per day—to support photosynthesis, which fuels growth and fruiting. Insufficient sunlight can lead to weak, leggy plants and poor fruit yield.

Additionally, maintaining optimal temperatures helps prevent stress and diseases that can arise from extreme heat or cold. Ensuring these conditions also promotes vibrant blooms and enhances the quality and size of the fruit. By providing the appropriate temperature range and ample sunlight, you can create an environment conducive to the robust growth and high productivity of dwarf peaches, leading to a fruitful and healthy harvest.

MAINTAINING YOUR CONTAINER & RAISED BED DWARF PEACHES

Maintaining your dwarf peaches in fruit containers and raised bed gardens is essential for ensuring their health, productivity, and longevity. Regular maintenance practices, such as watering, pruning, fertilizing, and monitoring for pests and diseases, play a pivotal role in fostering robust growth and abundant fruit production.

Consistent watering ensures that the trees receive adequate moisture without becoming waterlogged, which can lead to root rot. Pruning helps shape the trees, encourages airflow, and enhances light penetration, all of which are critical for preventing fungal diseases and promoting healthy fruit set.

Fertilizing replenishes essential nutrients in the soil, supporting vigorous growth and high-quality fruit. Additionally, vigilant monitoring allows for early detection and management of pest infestations and diseases, reducing the risk of significant damage.

By maintaining your dwarf peaches meticulously, you create an optimal growing environment that supports their overall well-being and maximizes their yield, leading to a more successful and rewarding gardening experience.

Pruning & Thinning Your Dwarf Peaches

Pruning and thinning dwarf peaches are vital for several reasons, contributing significantly to the health, productivity, and overall management of the trees. Pruning involves removing dead, diseased, or overcrowded branches, which enhances air circulation and light penetration throughout the tree's canopy. This practice is crucial in preventing fungal diseases and promoting the healthy development of fruit buds.

Thinning, on the other hand, involves selectively removing some of the developing fruits, which helps to reduce the strain on the tree's resources. By doing so, the remaining fruits receive more nutrients and grow larger and higher in quality. Thinning prevents branch breakage due to the weight of excessive fruit load, thus maintaining the structural integrity of the tree.

Both pruning and thinning also encourage the growth of new, productive shoots and help maintain a manageable size for the trees, which is particularly important in the confined spaces of containers and raised beds. Overall, these practices are essential for fostering a robust and productive dwarf peaches, leading to an abundant and high-quality harvest.

Pruning and thinning dwarf peaches are crucial tasks that need to be carried out at specific times to optimize the health and productivity of the plants. Pruning is best performed during late winter to early spring, just before the buds begin to swell but after the risk of severe frost has passed. This timing allows the tree to heal rapidly from pruning cuts and encourages vigorous new growth in the coming season.

When pruning, start by removing any dead, diseased, or damaged branches to prevent the spread of pathogens. Next, thin out overcrowded and crossing branches to improve air circulation and light penetration within the canopy. Focus on creating an open, vase-shaped structure with evenly spaced branches to support healthy growth and fruit development.

Thinning is typically done in late spring to early summer, after the natural "June drop" when the tree naturally sheds some of its excess fruit. At this point, assess the remaining fruit load and carefully remove excess fruits to prevent the branches from becoming overloaded. Aim to leave about 6 to 8 inches between each fruit, allowing enough space for the remaining fruits to grow larger and ripen evenly.

Use clean, sharp pruning shears to snip off the fruits, making a clean cut close to the base of the fruit stem. Thinning not only improves the size and quality of the remaining fruits but also reduces the strain on the tree, which helps prevent branch breakage and promotes overall plant health.

Proper pruning and thinning techniques are essential for the longevity and productivity of dwarf peaches. In addition to improving fruit quality, they help maintain the tree's structural integrity and make other maintenance tasks more manageable.

For instance, an open and well-spaced canopy is easier to spray for pest and disease control, reducing the likelihood of infestations and infections. Additionally, well-pruned trees with fewer fruits are less prone to issues like fruit rot and can better withstand environmental stresses like strong winds or heavy rains. Regular pruning and thinning also encourage the formation of new growth and fruiting wood, ensuring that the tree remains productive year after year.

Understanding the appropriate timing and methods for pruning and thinning dwarf peaches is key to fostering a thriving and fruitful garden. By dedicating time to these practices, you can maximize your harvests, improve fruit quality, and ensure the long-term health and vitality of your peach trees.

Whether grown in containers or raised beds, well-maintained dwarf peaches will reward you with bountiful, delicious harvests season after season.

Watering Your Container & Raised Bed Dwarf Peaches

Watering your dwarf peaches in fruit containers and raised bed gardens is paramount for ensuring their overall health, vitality, and productivity. These plants rely on a consistent water supply to support essential physiological functions such as photosynthesis, nutrient absorption, and fruit development.

In the confined spaces of containers, soil moisture can deplete rapidly due to limited volume and increased exposure to air, making regular watering critical to prevent the plants from experiencing stress or dehydration. Similarly, raised beds offer enhanced drainage, which, while beneficial for preventing waterlogging, can lead to quicker soil drying, necessitating frequent and adequate irrigation.

Proper watering encourages robust root systems, improves nutrient uptake, and helps maintain turgor pressure within the plant cells, which is vital for growth and fruit formation. Insufficient watering can result in issues like leaf drop, poor fruit set, and reduced vigor, whereas overwatering can cause root rot and other complications. Therefore, maintaining an optimal watering regimen is essential to ensure that dwarf peaches remain healthy, resilient, and capable of producing abundant, high-quality fruit.

Watering dwarf peaches require a strategic approach to ensure the plants receive adequate moisture without becoming waterlogged. In general, these plants need to be watered deeply but infrequently, encouraging the development of a strong and extensive root system.

For young or newly planted dwarf peaches, aim to keep the soil consistently moist but not saturated by watering approximately 2 to 3 times per week, depending on weather conditions. As the plants mature and their root systems become more established, you can reduce the frequency of watering to once a week, ensuring that the top few inches of soil are allowed to dry out slightly between waterings to prevent root rot.

One of the best ways to determine when to water is by checking the soil moisture level. Insert your finger about 2 inches into the soil; if it feels dry at this depth, it's time to water.

Another effective method is using a soil moisture meter to provide a more precise reading. Early morning is the ideal time for watering, as it allows the plants to absorb moisture before the heat of the day, reducing evaporation losses and giving the foliage time to dry out, which can help prevent fungal diseases. During particularly hot or windy periods, you may need to increase the watering frequency to compensate for the faster evaporation rate.

For container-grown dwarf peaches, ensure that the containers have proper drainage holes to avoid water accumulation at the base. When watering containers, continue until water begins to drain out from the bottom, indicating that the entire root zone has been adequately moistened. This deep watering approach promotes healthy root growth and ensures that the plant can access water even during short dry spells. Mulching the surface of the soil with organic materials like straw or wood chips can also help retain moisture, reduce temperature fluctuations, and suppress weed growth.

In raised bed gardens, consistent watering practices are equally important. Due to the improved drainage properties of raised beds, the soil may dry out more quickly than ground-level gardens, especially during hot weather.

Installing a drip irrigation system or soaker hoses can provide an efficient and uniform way to water the plants without wetting the foliage, which helps reduce the risk of fungal issues. Monitor the soil moisture regularly and adjust the watering schedule based on weather conditions and plant needs, ensuring the soil remains evenly moist throughout the growing season.

By carefully managing the watering of dwarf peaches in containers and raised beds, you can create a conducive environment for sustained growth, robust health, and prolific fruit production. Adequate and timely watering supports essential physiological processes, enhances nutrient uptake, and helps the plants withstand environmental stress, ultimately leading to healthier trees and bountiful, high-quality harvests.

Organic Fertilization For Container & Raised Bed Dwarf Peaches

Organic fertilization is crucial for dwarf peaches because it provides a balanced, sustainable source of essential nutrients while promoting soil health and ecological balance. Unlike synthetic fertilizers, organic options such as compost, manure, and organic plant-based fertilizers release nutrients slowly, ensuring a steady supply that aligns with the plants' growth cycles.

This gradual nutrient release helps prevent nutrient leaching and reduces the risk of over-fertilization, which can harm both the plants and the surrounding environment. Additionally, organic fertilization enhances soil structure, water retention, and microbial activity, creating a thriving ecosystem that supports robust root development and overall plant health.

By enriching the soil with organic matter, you also foster beneficial organisms that can help suppress pests and diseases, reducing the need for chemical interventions. Ultimately, organic fertilization promotes healthier, more resilient dwarf peaches, leading to higher-quality fruit production and contributing to a more sustainable gardening practice.

Organic fertilizers come in various forms, each offering unique benefits for container and raised bed-grown dwarf peaches. Compost is one of the most versatile and beneficial organic fertilizers. It is rich in essential nutrients and improves soil structure by increasing its ability to retain moisture and fostering a healthy microbial ecosystem.

To use compost, apply a 1-2 inch layer on the soil surface around the base of the plant in early spring, allowing it to be gradually incorporated into the soil through watering and natural processes. Manure, another excellent organic fertilizer, is high in nitrogen and other vital nutrients. Well-aged or composted manure should be mixed into the soil before planting for best results and can also be applied as a top dressing during the growing season. Avoid using fresh manure, as it can burn the plants and introduce pathogens.

Bone meal and blood meal are also valuable organic fertilizers for dwarf peaches. Bone meal, rich in phosphorus, promotes strong root development and enhances flowering and fruiting. Apply bone meal by sprinkling it around the base of the plant in early spring and gently working it into the soil.

Blood meal, high in nitrogen, stimulates leafy growth and should be used sparingly. Incorporate blood meal into the soil in early spring or as needed throughout the growing season. Fish emulsion is another effective organic fertilizer, providing a balanced blend of nutrients and trace elements. It is typically used as a liquid feed, diluted according to package instructions, and applied every 2-4 weeks during the growth period.

Timing and application methods are crucial for the effectiveness of organic fertilizers. Begin fertilizing dwarf peaches in early spring, just as new growth starts to emerge. This timing ensures that the plants have access to the necessary nutrients to support vigorous growth and fruiting.

Continue to fertilize periodically throughout the growing season, with applications spaced approximately every 4-6 weeks, depending on the specific product and its nutrient release rate. Always follow the manufacturer's recommendations for application rates to avoid over-fertilization, which can lead to nutrient imbalances and potential harm to the plants.

For container-grown dwarf peaches, liquid or water-soluble organic fertilizers are particularly beneficial as they provide nutrients directly to the root zone in a form that is quickly available to the plants. These fertilizers should be applied more frequently, typically every 2-4 weeks, due to the limited soil volume and higher nutrient leaching rates in containers.

For raised bed gardens, granular organic fertilizers can be worked into the soil at the beginning of the growing season and supplemented with periodic top dressings or liquid feeds to maintain nutrient levels.

In addition to individual organic fertilizers, organic mulch such as straw, wood chips, or shredded leaves can be applied around the base of the plants to conserve moisture, regulate soil temperature, and slowly release nutrients as they decompose.

Mulching also helps suppress weeds, reducing competition for nutrients and water. By combining different types of organic fertilizers and mulches, you can create a nutrient-rich, healthy growing environment that supports the robust growth and prolific fruit production of dwarf peaches in both containers and raised beds.

PROTECTING YOUR CONTAINER & RAISED BED DWARF PEACHES

Extreme Temperatures

Protecting dwarf peaches from extreme temperatures is essential to ensure their health, productivity, and longevity. Extreme temperatures can cause significant stress to these plants, leading to reduced growth, poor fruit set, and increased susceptibility to diseases and pests.

During hot weather, container plants are particularly vulnerable because their limited soil volume heats up quickly, potentially leading to root damage. Similarly, raised beds, although offering better drainage, can also dry out faster and become excessively warm, stressing the plants. To mitigate these risks, it is crucial to implement protective measures such as mulch application, shading, and proper watering practices.

Mulching is a highly effective strategy for protecting dwarf peaches from extreme temperatures. Applying a thick layer of organic mulch, such as straw, wood chips, or compost, around the base of the plants helps insulate the soil, keeping it cooler in the summer and warmer in the winter.

Mulch also aids in retaining soil moisture, reducing the need for frequent watering during hot spells, and preventing the soil from drying out and cracking. By maintaining consistent soil temperatures and moisture levels, mulch helps create a stable environment that supports healthy root development and overall plant vigor.

Shading is another critical technique for safeguarding dwarf peaches from excessive heat. In particularly hot climates or during heatwaves, providing temporary shade can help reduce the direct impact of the sun on the plants.

This can be achieved using shade cloth, which can be draped over a simple frame constructed around the plants, or by placing containers in partially shaded locations during the hottest parts of the day. Shade cloths with a 30-50% shade rating are ideal, as they block enough sunlight to cool the plants without completely depriving them of the light needed for photosynthesis.

Proper watering practices are also vital for protecting dwarf peaches from both extreme heat and cold. During hot weather, it is essential to water deeply and regularly to ensure that the roots have access to sufficient moisture. Watering early in the morning allows the plants to absorb water before the temperature rises, reducing evaporation losses and helping the plants stay hydrated throughout the day.

During cold weather, especially in regions prone to frost, it is important to water the plants well before an expected freeze. Moist soil retains heat better than dry soil, providing some insulation to the roots and reducing the risk of frost damage.

In addition to these measures, protecting dwarf peaches from extreme cold may require additional precautions. For container-grown plants, moving the containers to a sheltered location, such as a garage, shed, or even indoors, can provide significant protection from freezing temperatures.

Raised bed plants can be insulated using frost blankets, burlap, or even old sheets, which can be draped over the plants and secured to the ground to trap heat and protect against frost. Ensuring that the plants are well-mulched and adequately watered before the onset of cold weather further enhances their resilience to low temperatures.

Overall, protecting container and raised bed-grown dwarf peaches from extreme temperatures is crucial for maintaining their health and productivity. By employing strategies such as mulching, shading, and proper watering, you can create a more stable and conducive environment for your plants. These efforts not only help the plants withstand temperature extremes but also promote robust growth, higher quality fruit production, and greater resilience to environmental stresses, ensuring a thriving and fruitful garden year after year.

Protecting Container & Raised Bed Dwarf Peaches From Pests

Protecting dwarf peaches organically from pests is crucial because it ensures the health and productivity of the plants while maintaining an eco-friendly garden environment. Organic pest control methods, such as introducing beneficial insects, using natural repellents, and implementing cultural practices like crop rotation and companion planting, help manage pest populations without resorting to chemical pesticides that can harm beneficial organisms and pollute the soil and water.

By avoiding synthetic chemicals, gardeners promote a balanced ecosystem where natural predators help keep pest levels in check, reducing the likelihood of pest outbreaks. This approach also minimizes the risk of pesticide residues on fruits, making them safer for consumption. Furthermore, organic pest management practices support overall plant health, leading to more resilient dwarf peaches that can better withstand environmental stresses and produce higher-quality fruit over time.

Dwarf peaches grown in containers and raised beds are susceptible to various pests that can significantly impact their health and fruit production. Common pests include aphids, which cluster on new growth and suck plant sap, leading to curled, yellowing leaves and stunted growth.

Spider mites are another frequent invader, particularly in hot, dry conditions, causing fine webbing and stippled, discolored foliage. Peach tree borers, which tunnel into the wood and can be particularly damaging, often go unnoticed until severe damage has been done.

Scale insects can also be problematic, forming hard, protective shells on stems and leaves while they sap the plant's strength. Additionally, caterpillars and other chewing insects may feed on leaves and young fruit, causing direct damage and creating entry points for diseases.

To protect dwarf peaches from these pests organically, you can employ a combination of beneficial insects, natural repellents, and cultural practices. Introducing beneficial insects such as ladybugs, lacewings, and predatory mites can effectively control pests like aphids and spider mites.

These natural predators help maintain a balanced ecosystem and reduce pest populations without harmful chemicals. Applying neem oil or insecticidal soap is another effective organic method for managing soft-bodied pests. Neem oil disrupts the life cycle of insects, preventing them from feeding and reproducing, while insecticidal soap physically removes and kills pests on contact. Regular applications, particularly during early infestations, can help keep pest numbers low.

Cultural practices play a vital role in organic pest management. Intercropping and companion planting can deter certain pests and attract beneficial insects. For example, planting marigolds around dwarf peaches can repel aphids and nematodes, while herbs like dill and fennel attract predatory insects.

Regularly inspecting the plants and maintaining good garden hygiene by removing debris, fallen leaves and pruning infested branches can prevent pests from establishing themselves. Crop rotation, even in raised beds, helps break pest life cycles by depriving them of continuous food sources.

Physical barriers and traps are additional organic strategies to protect dwarf peaches. Using floating row covers can prevent flying insects like moths and beetles from reaching the plants to lay eggs.

Sticky traps can capture adult flying pests, while pheromone traps specifically target peach tree borers and other specific pests by attracting them with synthetic sex hormones. Hand-picking larger pests, such as caterpillars, can also be an effective way to manage infestations on a small scale.

Maintaining optimal plant health through proper watering, fertilization, and mulching is fundamental for increasing the resilience of dwarf peaches against pests. Healthy plants are better equipped to withstand and recover from pest damage. Organic fertilizers such as compost and well-rotted manure provide essential nutrients that support robust growth and strengthen the plant's natural defenses.

Additionally, mulching with organic materials like straw or wood chips helps retain soil moisture, regulate temperature, and suppress weeds, reducing plant stress and making them less attractive to pests.

Overall, combining these organic methods creates a holistic approach to pest management that not only protects dwarf peaches from harmful insects but also fosters a balanced and sustainable garden ecosystem. By prioritizing organic practices, you can ensure the long-term health and productivity of your container and raised bed-grown dwarf peaches, producing high-quality fruit while maintaining an environmentally friendly and safe gardening space.

Protecting Container & Raised Bed Dwarf Peaches From Diseases

Protecting dwarf peaches from diseases organically is essential for maintaining the health and productivity of the plants while ensuring a safe and sustainable gardening environment. Organic disease management practices, such as improving soil health through composting, utilizing disease-resistant cultivars, practicing proper sanitation by removing infected plant debris, and employing natural treatments like copper-based fungicides, help prevent and control diseases without relying on synthetic chemicals.

These methods preserve the beneficial microorganisms in the soil, enhance biodiversity, and reduce the likelihood of chemical residues on the fruit, making them safer for consumption. By adopting organic disease prevention strategies, you can foster resilient plants that are better equipped to withstand disease pressures, ultimately leading to more vigorous growth and abundant harvests.

This holistic approach not only supports the well-being of the peach trees but also contributes to a more environmentally friendly and sustainable gardening practice.

Dwarf peaches grown in containers and raised beds are susceptible to several diseases that can impact their health and fruit production. One common disease is peach leaf curl, caused by the fungus Taphrina deformans. This disease leads to distorted, reddened leaves that eventually turn yellow and drop prematurely, weakening the plant and reducing its vigor.

Brown rot, caused by the fungus Monilinia fructicola, is another prevalent issue, affecting both blossoms and fruit.

Infected flowers wilt and turn brown, while developing fruits show brown, sunken spots and can decay rapidly.

Peach scab, caused by the fungus Cladosporium carpophilum, manifests as small, olive-green or black spots on the fruit and twigs, which can coalesce and crack, making the fruit unsightly and less marketable. Bacterial spot, caused by the bacterium Xanthomonas campestris pv. pruni, results in small, water-soaked lesions on leaves, fruit, and twigs, leading to defoliation, fruit blemishes, and potentially reduced yields.

To organically protect dwarf peaches from these diseases, cultural practices are paramount. For instance, selecting disease-resistant varieties is a proactive step in preventing many fungal and bacterial diseases.

Proper sanitation, including the removal of fallen leaves, diseased fruit, and pruning of infected branches, helps reduce the spread of pathogens. Pruning to improve air circulation and sunlight penetration within the canopy also creates an environment less conducive to fungal growth.

During the dormant season, applying organic fungicides such as copper-based sprays or lime sulfur can help control peach leaf curl and other fungal diseases by reducing overwintering spores.

Crop rotation and intercropping with non-host plants can disrupt the life cycles of soil-borne pathogens. For container-grown plants, using sterile, well-draining potting mix and avoiding reusing old soil without proper sterilization can prevent the introduction and spread of soil-borne diseases.

Additionally, maintaining optimal soil health through regular applications of compost and other organic amendments strengthens the plants' natural defenses, making them more resilient to disease pressures.

Biological control agents play a significant role in organic disease management. Beneficial microbes such as Bacillus subtilis and Trichoderma species can be introduced to the soil or applied as foliar sprays.

These beneficial organisms compete with and inhibit the growth of pathogenic fungi and bacteria, effectively reducing disease incidence. Neem oil, a natural fungicide, can be used to manage a variety of fungal diseases. It works by disrupting fungal growth and reproduction and can be applied as a preventive measure during the growing season.

Finally, consistent and appropriate watering practices are crucial in managing disease. Overhead watering can promote the spread of fungal spores and create a humid environment conducive to disease development. Instead, using drip irrigation or soaker hoses delivers water directly to the root zone, minimizing leaf wetness and reducing disease risk. Mulching with organic materials like straw or wood chips helps conserve soil moisture and prevent water splashing, which can spread soil-borne pathogens onto the foliage.

Overall, protecting dwarf peaches from diseases organically involves an integrated approach that combines cultural practices, biological controls, and precise watering techniques. By fostering a healthy, balanced garden ecosystem, you can reduce the incidence of diseases and enhance the overall vitality and productivity of your dwarf peaches. This holistic approach ensures high-quality, chemical-free fruit production while promoting environmental sustainability and biodiversity in the garden.

HARVESTING CONTAINER & RAISED BED DWARF PEACHES

Dwarf peaches grown in containers and raised bed gardens typically take about 2 to 4 years from planting to produce their first significant harvest, although this timeline can vary depending on the specific variety and growing conditions. Initially, these plants focus on establishing a robust root system and healthy vegetative growth.

By the second or third year, you may start to see some flowering and fruit set, but it is in the fourth year that the plants usually reach their full productive potential. Proper care during this period, including adequate watering, fertilization, and pest management, is crucial to ensure healthy growth and optimal fruit production.

When it comes to harvesting dwarf peaches, timing is key to ensure the best flavor and texture. Peaches are typically ready for harvest in mid to late summer, depending on the variety and local climate. The most reliable indicators of ripeness are the fruit's color and touch. A ripe peach will have a uniform color without any green undertones and yield slightly to gentle pressure.

Another method to check ripeness is to twist the peach gently; if it comes off the branch easily, it is likely ready to be picked. However, avoid pulling too hard, as this can damage both the fruit and the tree.

Harvesting should be done carefully to avoid bruising the delicate fruit. Hold the peach in your hand and twist it gently from the stem. If the fruit resists, it may need a few more days to ripen. It's best to harvest in the cooler parts of the day, such as early morning or late evening, to prevent the fruit from becoming too warm, which can affect its shelf life.

After picking, handle the peaches with care to prevent bruising and store them in a cool place. If immediate consumption is not planned, refrigerating the peaches can help prolong their freshness.

To maintain continuous production and plant health, it is important to practice proper post-harvest care. After harvesting, inspect the tree for any signs of disease or pest infestation and address these issues promptly. Prune the tree to remove any dead or diseased wood, which helps improve air circulation and reduces the risk of future problems.

Additionally, applying a balanced organic fertilizer after harvest can help replenish the nutrients in the soil, supporting the plant's recovery and preparation for the next growing season.

Harvesting dwarf peaches requires patience and careful attention to detail. By monitoring the ripeness indicators and handling the fruit gently, you can enjoy the delicious rewards of their efforts. With proper care and maintenance, these compact fruit trees can provide bountiful harvests for many years, adding beauty and productivity to any garden space.

CONTAINER & RAISED BEDS DWARF PEACH NOTES

Start: Seeds or Seedlings.

Germination: 3 weeks, at temperatures between 60°F and 70°F (15°C to 21°C).

Seed Life: 2 Years.

Soil Type: Well-draining, fertile, and slightly acidic to neutral, with a pH range of 6.0 to 7.0.

Seed Spacing: Plant seeds 1 to 2 inches deep.

Seedling Spacing:

Containers – One seedling per container.

Raised Beds - Space the seedlings approximately 8 to 10 feet apart.

Sunlight: 6 – 8hrs full sunlight daily.

Growing Temperatures:

Dwarf peach trees thrive in temperatures ranging from 65°F to 75°F (18°C to 24°C).

Duration Till Harvest:

Dwarf peaches usually require 2 to 4 years after planting to yield their first considerable harvest. Flowering and fruit set may begin in the second or third year, but the plants typically reach their peak productivity in the fourth year.

CHAPTER 8
CITRUS BUSHES: CONTAINER & RAISED BED GARDENS – CLEMENTINES

C lementine bushes, a cherished variety of mandarin oranges, are an exceptional choice for fruit container and raised bed gardening. Renowned for their sweet, tangy flavor and effortless peeling, these compact citrus bushes are perfect for gardeners seeking to cultivate fresh, homegrown fruit in limited spaces. Clementine bushes thrive in well-drained soil and can adapt well to container life, making them ideal for patios, balconies, and small garden plots. Their glossy green foliage, fragrant white blossoms, and vibrant orange fruits not only provide a visually pleasing display but also deliver abundant harvests throughout the growing season. Easy to maintain and highly productive, clementine bushes bring both beauty and functionality to container and raised bed gardens, offering a delightful and fruitful gardening experience.

Containers and raised beds provide superior control over soil quality, drainage, and nutrient levels, ensuring optimal growing conditions for clementine bushes. This method reduces the risk of soil-borne diseases and pests that can affect in-ground plantings, promoting healthier growth and higher fruit yields.

Additionally, the portability of containers allows gardeners to move plants to ideal locations for sunlight exposure and protection from adverse weather conditions, while raised beds improve root aeration and temperature regulation. These advantages make it easier to manage and care for clementine bushes, even in limited spaces such as patios, balconies, or small urban gardens.

The aesthetic appeal of lush foliage, fragrant blossoms, and vibrant fruits enhances the visual appeal of any garden, creating a productive and attractive outdoor space. Overall, growing clementine bushes in containers and raised beds combines practicality with beauty, making it an excellent choice for maximizing your garden's potential.

THE RIGHT SOIL TO GROW CLEMENTINES IN CONTAINER & RAISED BEDS

Growing clementine bushes requires careful attention to soil conditions to ensure the plants thrive and produce an abundant harvest. Clementines, like other citrus trees, prefer well-drained, loamy soil that is rich in organic matter. This type of soil provides the right balance of moisture retention and drainage, preventing waterlogged roots while ensuring the plants receive sufficient hydration.

A good starting mix for growing clementines in containers or raised beds includes a combination of high-quality potting soil, compost, and perlite or sand to improve aeration and drainage. The addition of organic matter, such as compost or well-rotted manure, enhances soil fertility, supplying essential nutrients and beneficial microorganisms that support healthy root development and vigorous growth.

Soil pH is another critical factor for successfully growing clementine bushes. These citrus plants thrive in slightly acidic to neutral soil with a pH range of 6.0 to 7.0. Testing the soil pH before planting is essential, as it allows you to make any necessary adjustments. If the soil is too acidic (below pH 6.0), adding agricultural lime can help raise the pH to the desired level.

Equally, if the soil is too alkaline (above pH 7.0), incorporating elemental sulfur or peat moss can lower the pH. Maintaining the correct pH balance ensures that clementine bushes can absorb essential nutrients efficiently, promoting optimal growth and fruit production.

In containers and raised beds, soil structure and consistency are paramount. Compacted soil can obstruct root growth and limit access to water and nutrients. Regular aeration is important to maintain a loose, friable soil texture. This can be achieved in containers by periodically loosening the soil with a small garden fork or by incorporating materials like coconut coir or vermiculite that help keep the soil airy.

Raised beds benefit from the same practices, along with occasional tilling or mixing to prevent compaction. Ensuring that the soil remains well-aerated and free of hard clumps allows clementine roots to expand and take up nutrients more effectively.

Nutrient management is also vital for growing healthy clementine bushes. Citrus plants have specific nutritional needs, particularly for nitrogen, potassium, and magnesium. Using a balanced, slow-release fertilizer formulated for citrus can provide a steady supply of essential nutrients over time.

Additionally, periodic applications of organic fertilizers such as fish emulsion or seaweed extract can give the plants a nutrient boost during crucial growth stages. Monitoring the plants for signs of nutrient deficiencies, such as yellowing leaves or poor fruit set, and adjusting the fertilization regimen accordingly can help maintain their health and productivity.

Watering practices need careful consideration to complement the soil conditions for clementine bushes. While these plants require consistent moisture, overwatering can lead to root rot and other issues. The well-drained soil in containers and raised beds helps mitigate this risk, but it's still crucial to monitor moisture levels regularly.

Water deeply and infrequently, allowing the top few inches of soil to dry out between watering sessions. Using mulch, such as straw or wood chips, on the soil surface can help retain moisture, reduce evaporation, and suppress weeds, creating a more stable growing environment.

By ensuring the right soil conditions, including proper drainage, pH balance, structure, and nutrient management, you can create an optimal environment for clementine bushes in containers and raised beds. These practices not only support healthy plant growth but also enhance the overall productivity and quality of the fruit, making the effort of maintaining suitable soil conditions well worth the investment.

HOW TO SOW CLEMENTINES IN CONTAINERS & RAISED BEDS GARDENS

Correct Season To Sow Clementines In Containers & Raised Beds Gardens

The correct season to sow clementine bushes in fruit containers and raised bed gardens is crucial for ensuring optimal growth and successful establishment. Clementine bushes are best planted in the spring after the last frost has passed and the soil has warmed up sufficiently. This timing allows young plants to take advantage of the longer daylight hours and milder temperatures, promoting vigorous root development and strong vegetative growth.

In regions with mild winters, planting can also be done in late winter or early spring, giving the bushes a head start before the heat of summer arrives. It's important to avoid planting during periods of extreme heat or cold, as these conditions can stress young plants and impede their development. For gardeners in colder climates, starting clementine bushes indoors in late winter can be beneficial.

Once the danger of frost has passed, the seedlings can be gradually acclimated to outdoor conditions through a process called hardening off before being transplanted into containers or raised beds. Ultimately choosing the right season to sow clementine bushes, you can provide an environment that supports healthy growth and enhances the chances of a bountiful citrus harvest.

Plant Needs & Requirements

Germinating clementine bushes from seeds to seedlings correctly is crucial when growing in containers and raised bed gardens because it sets the foundation for healthy, robust plants that can thrive in these controlled environments. Proper germination ensures that the seedlings develop a robust root system and sturdy stems, essential for supporting future growth and fruit production.

Starting with high-quality seeds and providing the right conditions—adequate warmth, moisture, and light—promotes successful germination and reduces the risk of seedling diseases such as damping-off.

Additionally, careful attention during the germination phase allows for early identification and removal of weaker or non-viable seedlings, ensuring that only the healthiest plants are transplanted into containers or raised beds. This meticulous start helps clementine bushes adapt better to their new growing environments.

Germinating clementine bushes from seeds to seedlings involves several key steps that ensure successful growth and development. The process begins with selecting fresh clementine seeds, ideally from a ripe fruit, and carefully cleaning them to remove any pulp or residue that can harbor mold or bacteria. After cleaning, the seeds should be soaked in warm water for about 24 hours to soften their outer shells and promote quicker germination. Following the soak, the seeds can be planted in small pots or seed trays filled with a sterile, well-draining seed starting mix. Plant the seeds about half an inch deep, covering them lightly with soil. It's important to keep the soil consistently moist but not waterlogged during this stage, as excessive moisture can cause rot.

The optimal temperature for germinating clementine seeds is between 70°F and 85°F (21°C to 29°C). Maintaining a warm environment is crucial, as clementine seeds require consistent warmth to sprout. Using a heat mat can help regulate the soil temperature, especially in cooler climates or during colder months.

Additionally, providing a clear plastic cover or placing the seed trays in a propagator can retain humidity and warmth, further encouraging germination. During this period, it's essential to ensure the seeds receive indirect sunlight or grow lights, as direct sunlight can create too much heat and dry out the soil.

Germination can take anywhere from 2 to 4 weeks. Once the seeds have sprouted and the seedlings have developed their first set of true leaves (the second set of leaves that appear after the initial seed leaves), they can be gradually acclimated to less humid conditions by removing the cover or lid for short periods each day.

This period of hardening off helps the seedlings adapt to the conditions they will face once transplanted. Care must be taken to continue providing adequate light, water, and warmth during this time to ensure strong growth.

Seedlings are generally ready to be transplanted into larger containers or raised beds when they have at least 3 to 4 sets of true leaves and are sturdy enough to handle the transition. This usually occurs around 8 to 12 weeks after germination. Before transplanting, it's advisable to prepare the planting area by ensuring it has the right soil mix—well-draining, fertile, and slightly acidic (pH 6.0 to 7.0).

Raised beds should be filled with a combination of high-quality garden soil, compost, and sand or perlite to ensure good drainage and aeration. Containers need to have sufficient drainage holes and be filled with a similar soil mix.

When transplanting, gently remove the seedlings from their original pots, being careful not to damage the roots, and plant them at the same depth they were growing in the seed trays. Water the seedlings thoroughly after planting to help settle the soil around the roots and reduce transplant shock.

It's also beneficial to place the newly transplanted seedlings in a shaded area or provide some form of protection from direct sunlight for a few days until they acclimate to their new environment. Proper care during this critical stage will set the foundation for vigorous growth and future fruit production in your container or raised bed garden.

Spacing & Measurement

Spacing and measurements when transplanting clementine bush seedlings into fruit containers and raised bed gardens are crucial for ensuring healthy growth and maximizing fruit production. Adequate spacing allows each plant to receive sufficient light, air circulation, and nutrients essential for photosynthesis, reducing the risk of diseases that thrive in crowded conditions.

In containers, ensuring that each seedling has enough room to grow helps prevent root crowding, which can lead to stunted growth and reduced fruit yield. Similarly, in raised beds, proper spacing ensures that the roots have ample space to expand and access soil resources without competing excessively with neighboring plants.

When planting clementine bush seedlings in fruit containers, selecting appropriately sized containers is important to accommodate their growth and ensure they have ample room for root development. For individual clementine bushes, a container with a minimum diameter of 18 to 24 inches and a similar depth is ideal, as this provides sufficient space for the roots to spread without becoming cramped.

The container should also have adequate drainage holes to prevent waterlogging. If you plan to grow multiple clementine bushes in containers, ensure each pot has enough space around it so that the plant's foliage does not overlap, allowing for sufficient air circulation and light penetration.

In raised bed gardens, the spacing between clementine seedlings is equally critical. Clementine bushes should be planted approximately 4 to 6 feet apart, depending on the variety and expected mature size of the plant. This spacing allows each bush to develop its canopy fully without competing for light and nutrients with neighboring plants.

Proper spacing also facilitates good air circulation, which helps reduce the risk of fungal diseases and pest infestations that can thrive in crowded conditions. Additionally, providing adequate room between the plants makes it easier to perform necessary maintenance tasks such as pruning, fertilizing, and harvesting.

The dimensions of the raised bed itself should be planned to accommodate the spacing requirements of clementine bushes. A typical raised bed for growing citrus might be around 4 feet wide, as this width allows for easy access from either side without stepping into the bed and compacting the soil. The length of the bed can vary based on available space and the number of plants you intend to grow. Ensuring that the bed is deep enough—at least 12 to 18 inches—is also crucial, as this provides ample soil volume for root growth and stability.

In both containers and raised beds, it's essential to monitor the growth of your clementine bushes and adjust spacing if necessary. As the plants mature, they may require additional room to accommodate their expanding root systems and canopies. If you notice that the plants are starting to encroach on each other, consider thinning them out or repositioning them to maintain optimal spacing.

Paying careful attention to spacing and measurements when transplanting clementine seedlings creates a conducive environment for healthy growth, robust fruit production, and easier garden management.

Ideal Temperatures & Sun Requirements

The importance of maintaining ideal temperatures and sun requirements when growing clementine bushes cannot be overstated, as these factors are crucial for ensuring vigorous growth, robust health, and abundant fruit production.

Clementine bushes thrive in warm conditions, with optimal daytime temperatures ranging between 70°F and 85°F (21°C to 29°C) and nighttime temperatures not falling below 50°F (10°C). Consistent exposure to these temperatures promotes strong vegetative growth and encourages the development of flowers and fruit.

Additionally, clementine bushes require full sun for at least 6 to 8 hours daily to perform photosynthesis effectively, which is essential for energy production and overall plant vitality. Sufficient sunlight also helps in the development of sweeter, juicier fruits. Inadequate light or fluctuating temperatures can stress the plants, leading to poor growth, reduced fruit set, and increased susceptibility to pests and diseases. Therefore, positioning containers and raised beds in locations where they receive ample sunlight and protecting them from extreme temperature fluctuations are key practices for successful clementine cultivation.

MAINTAINING YOUR CONTAINER & RAISED BED CLEMENTINE BUSHES

Maintaining clementine bushes in fruit containers and raised bed gardens is essential for ensuring sustained health, optimal growth, and maximum fruit production. Regular maintenance tasks such as pruning, watering, fertilizing, and monitoring for pests and diseases play a crucial role in fostering a thriving plant environment. Pruning helps shape the plant, remove dead or diseased branches, and improve air circulation, which reduces the risk of fungal infections.

Consistent watering ensures that the plants receive adequate moisture without becoming waterlogged, while timely fertilization provides the necessary nutrients to support vigorous growth and fruiting. Additionally, vigilant pest and disease management prevent infestations from compromising plant health and fruit quality.

By actively maintaining clementine bushes, you can create an ideal growing environment that promotes robust, productive plants, enhances the aesthetic appeal of your gardens, and ultimately leads to a more rewarding and fruitful gardening experience.

Pruning & Thinning Your Clementine Bushes

Pruning and thinning clementine bushes are vital horticultural practices that significantly impact the health, productivity, and longevity of the plants. Pruning involves selectively removing dead, diseased, or overcrowded branches, which enhances air circulation and light penetration throughout the bush. This improved airflow reduces the risk of fungal infections and pest infestations, creating a healthier growing environment.

Pruning also helps shape the plant, directing its energy towards developing robust branches and producing high-quality fruit. Thinning, on the other hand, involves removing some of the young fruits, which reduces the strain on the plant and allows it to allocate resources more effectively.

By thinning, each remaining fruit receives more nutrients and sunlight, resulting in larger, juicier, and more flavorful clementines. Both pruning and thinning are essential for preventing overburdened branches that could break under the weight of excessive fruit, ensuring the structural integrity of the bush.

Ultimately, these practices lead to a well-balanced, vigorous plant that consistently yields abundant and superior fruit harvests, making them indispensable for successful clementine cultivation in containers and raised beds.

Pruning and thinning clementine bushes are essential tasks that should be performed at specific times to maximize their benefits. For pruning, the ideal time is late winter to early spring, just before new growth begins. This timing allows the plant to recover quickly and encourages robust growth during the growing season. During this period, start by removing any dead, damaged, or diseased branches to prevent the spread of pathogens and enhance the overall health of the bush.

Next, focus on thinning out the dense areas of the canopy to improve air circulation and light penetration. Cut back any crossing or rubbing branches, as these can cause wounds that invite pests and diseases. Pruning should be done with clean, sharp pruning shears to make precise cuts and minimize damage to the plant.

Thinning of clementine bushes should occur during the fruit development stage, typically in late spring to early summer. Thinning involves selectively removing some of the developing fruits to prevent overcrowding, which ensures that the remaining fruits grow larger and healthier.

Begin by examining the clusters of small, green fruits and removing any that are misshapen, undersized, or damaged. Aim to leave about 4 to 6 inches between each fruit, allowing sufficient space for them to expand and receive adequate nutrients. When thinning, use a pair of small, sharp scissors or pruning shears to snip off the excess fruits carefully, avoiding any damage to the stems or remaining fruits.

Both pruning and thinning are ongoing processes that require regular attention throughout the year. Aside from the main pruning session in late winter or early spring, light pruning can be done in the summer to remove any suckers or water sprouts—vigorous shoots that drain energy from the main plant. These should be cut back to maintain the bush's shape and direct nutrients to the fruit-bearing branches.

Similarly, additional thinning may be necessary if you notice that the fruits are still too crowded as they grow. Regular monitoring and maintenance ensure that the clementine bush remains healthy and productive.

In addition to timing, the techniques used for pruning and thinning are crucial for the best results. Always make clean cuts close to the branch collar (the swollen area where the branch meets the stem) to promote proper healing. Avoid tearing or ripping the bark, as this can introduce disease.

When thinning the fruit, handle the branches gently to avoid breaking them, especially with young, tender branches. By adhering to these practices, you can ensure that your clementine bushes remain vigorous, aesthetically pleasing, and capable of producing a bountiful harvest of high-quality fruit.

Watering Your Container & Raised Bed Clementine Bushes

Watering clementine bushes in fruit containers and raised bed gardens is crucial for maintaining their overall health, ensuring robust growth, and maximizing fruit production. Clementine bushes have specific moisture needs, and consistent watering helps provide the necessary hydration that supports vital physiological processes such as photosynthesis, nutrient uptake, and fruit development.

In containers, soil tends to dry out more quickly than in-ground gardens, making it essential to monitor moisture levels frequently and water adequately to prevent drought stress, which can lead to wilting, leaf drop, and reduced fruit quality.

Similarly, raised beds, while offering excellent drainage, require regular watering to maintain optimal soil moisture levels, especially during hot and dry periods. Proper watering ensures that the plants receive a steady supply of water, keeping the root system healthy and promoting the development of juicy, flavorful clementines.

Watering clementine bushes requires careful attention to ensure that they receive the right amount of moisture at the correct times. The general recommendation is to water deeply and thoroughly, ensuring moisture reaches the root zone. For container-grown clementines, this typically means watering until you see water draining from the bottom of the pot.

In hot weather, containers may need watering as frequently as once a day, while cooler or humid conditions might require watering only two to three times per week. It's crucial to check the soil moisture regularly by inserting your finger about an inch into the soil; if it feels dry at this depth, it's time to water. Consistency is key, as fluctuations between overly dry and overly wet conditions can stress the plant and negatively affect fruit development.

For raised bed gardens, the watering frequency may differ slightly due to better soil drainage and larger soil volume compared to containers. In general, clementine bushes in raised beds should receive about 1 to 2 inches of water per week, either through rainfall or irrigation.

To determine when to water, monitor the top few inches of soil. If it starts to feel dry, it's time to water. Early morning is the best time for watering as it allows moisture to reach the roots before the day's heat causes evaporation. Watering in the morning also gives the foliage time to dry out, reducing the risk of fungal infections. During particularly hot or dry spells, you may need to increase the frequency of watering to keep the soil consistently moist but not waterlogged.

The method of watering is just as important as the timing and frequency. Employing a slow and steady approach, such as using drip irrigation or soaker hoses, ensures deep penetration of water into the soil, reaching the root zone effectively without causing runoff or soil erosion. This method also minimizes water wastage and ensures that it is delivered directly to the roots where it is needed most. Mulching around the base of the plants with organic materials like straw, wood chips, or compost can help retain soil moisture, regulate soil temperature, and reduce watering frequency by limiting evaporation.

In addition to regular watering schedules, it's important to adjust your watering practices based on the growth stage of the clementine bushes. Newly planted seedlings or young bushes require frequent watering to establish a robust root system. As the plants mature and enter the flowering and fruiting stages, maintaining consistent moisture levels becomes crucial to support healthy fruit set and development.

Conversely, reduce watering slightly during the dormancy period in winter to prevent root rot while still providing enough moisture to keep the plants alive. By tailoring your watering practices to the specific needs of clementine bushes in different growing conditions and developmental stages, you can ensure healthy, productive plants that yield a bountiful harvest.

Organic Fertilization For Container & Raised Bed Clementine Bushes

Organic fertilization is crucial for clementine bushes grown in containers and raised bed gardens as it provides a natural, sustainable source of essential nutrients that promote healthy growth and abundant fruit production.

Unlike synthetic fertilizers, organic fertilizers release nutrients slowly, ensuring a steady supply of vital elements like nitrogen, phosphorus, potassium, and trace minerals, which are critical for the plant's development over time. This slow-release mechanism also reduces the risk of nutrient runoff and leaching, protecting the surrounding environment and promoting a healthier soil ecosystem.

Organic fertilizers improve soil structure, enhance microbial activity, and increase water retention, which are particularly beneficial in the often limited and controlled environments of containers and raised beds. By enriching the soil with organic matter, you can create a more resilient and fertile growing medium that supports clementine bushes' long-term health and productivity, leading to stronger plants and higher-quality fruits without relying on harmful chemicals.

There are several types of organic fertilizers that are particularly beneficial for clementine bushes grown in containers and raised bed gardens.

Compost is one of the most versatile and readily available options. It enriches the soil with a broad spectrum of nutrients and improves soil structure, aeration, and moisture retention.

Manure, especially well-aged or composted manure from chickens, cows, or horses, is another excellent choice. It provides a rich source of nitrogen, phosphorus, and potassium, essential for vigorous growth and fruiting.

Bone meal, a byproduct of animal bones, is high in phosphorus, promoting strong root development and flowering. Fish emulsion from processed fish offers a balanced nutrient profile and is quickly absorbed by plants, making it ideal for foliar feeding. Additionally, kelp or seaweed extract supplies trace minerals and growth hormones that support overall plant health and resilience.

Incorporating these organic fertilizers can create a fertile growing environment tailored to the specific needs of clementine bushes.Timing is critical when it comes to fertilizing clementine bushes to ensure they receive nutrients when they need them most. The primary fertilization period should begin in early spring, just as new growth starts to appear, to give the plants a boost for the growing season.

This initial application helps jumpstart the growth processes, supporting the development of leaves, branches, and flower buds. A second round of fertilization is typically needed in late spring to early summer, during the fruit set and development phase. This timing ensures that the plants have sufficient nutrients to produce high-quality fruit.

A final, lighter application can be made in late summer to early fall to promote continued growth and prepare the plants for the winter dormant period. It's important to avoid fertilizing during the winter months when the plants are dormant, as this can lead to nutrient runoff and waste.

Applying organic fertilizers correctly is essential for maximizing their benefits and avoiding potential plant damage. For compost, spread a 1-2 inch layer on the soil surface around the base of the clementine bushes, mixing it gently into the top few inches of soil. This method improves soil fertility and structure over time.

With manure, ensure it is well-composted to prevent burning the roots. Apply it similarly to compost, taking care not to place it directly against the plant stems. For bone meal, sprinkle it lightly around the drip line of the plant where the feeder roots are located and gently work it into the soil.

Fish emulsion can be diluted according to package instructions and used as a foliar spray or soil drench, providing quick nutrient uptake. Kelp or seaweed extract can also be applied as a liquid feed, either directly to the soil or as a foliar spray.

Regular monitoring and adjusting fertilization practices based on plant performance and soil tests can further optimize nutrient management. Signs of nutrient deficiencies, such as yellowing leaves or poor fruit development, indicate the need for additional fertilization or adjustments in the type of organic materials used. Soil tests can provide detailed information on nutrient levels and pH, helping to tailor fertilization practices to the specific needs of your clementine bushes.

By carefully selecting and applying organic fertilizers, you can ensure your container and raised bed-grown clementine bushes receive the necessary nutrients for healthy growth and bountiful fruit production.

PROTECTING YOUR CONTAINER & RAISED BED CLEMENTINE BUSHES

Extreme Temperatures

Protecting clementine bushes from extreme temperatures is crucial for their health, productivity, and overall survival. Clementines, being subtropical plants, are particularly sensitive to temperature extremes, both hot and cold. In high temperatures, excessive heat can cause sunburn on the leaves and fruit, leading to reduced photosynthesis and impaired plant health. It can also exacerbate water loss through evaporation, causing dehydration and stress.

Conversely, freezing temperatures can damage or kill clementine bushes, with frost harming the blossoms and young fruit, resulting in reduced yield. Sustained cold can also harm the roots and bark, compromising the plant's structural integrity. By implementing protective measures, you can ensure that your clementine bushes maintain optimal growth conditions, thereby preserving the investment of time, effort, and resources put into cultivating these plants.

During the summer months, when temperatures soar, it's essential to keep clementine bushes cool to prevent heat stress. One effective method is to provide shade using shade cloths or garden umbrellas, which can significantly reduce the intensity of direct sunlight and mitigate the risk of leaf scorch and fruit sunburn. Positioning containers and raised beds in areas with partial shade, especially during the hottest part of the day, also helps.

Mulching around the base of the plants with organic materials like straw, wood chips, or compost can insulate the soil, retaining moisture and keeping the root zone cooler. Additionally, watering early in the morning ensures that the plants have sufficient moisture to withstand the day's heat. In extreme heat, misting the foliage lightly can help reduce temperature stress and improve humidity around the plants.

Protection from cold temperatures is equally important, especially in regions prone to frost and freezing weather. When frost is forecasted, covering clementine bushes with frost cloths, blankets, or burlap can provide a protective barrier against cold air.

For container-grown plants, a simple but effective strategy is to move them to a sheltered location, such as a garage, shed, or indoors, where temperatures are more stable. Raised bed plants can benefit from the addition of cold frames or cloches, which create a microenvironment that traps heat and protects against frost.

Applying a thick layer of mulch around the base of the plants helps insulate the roots from freezing temperatures. For more extended periods of cold, consider using string lights or heat lamps to provide gentle warmth, ensuring that the plants maintain a survivable temperature.

Beyond immediate protective measures, long-term strategies can enhance the resilience of clementine bushes to temperature extremes. Selecting appropriate varieties known for their hardiness and suitability to your climate can make a significant difference. Improving the soil structure with organic matter enhances its capacity to retain moisture and buffer temperature fluctuations.

Installing windbreaks, such as hedges or fences, can protect plants from cold winds that exacerbate temperature stress. Ensuring proper irrigation systems, like drip irrigation, maintains consistent soil moisture, which helps moderate soil temperatures. Lastly, regular monitoring and timely intervention based on weather forecasts allow for proactive management of temperature-related risks.

Effectively managing temperature extremes around clementine bushes results in numerous benefits, including healthier plants, higher yields, and better-quality fruit. By mitigating the adverse effects of heat and cold, plants experience less stress, leading to more robust growth and improved resistance to diseases and pests.

Consistent temperature management also supports optimal nutrient uptake and metabolic functions, promoting vigorous flowering and fruiting. Furthermore, protecting plants from temperature extremes extends their lifespan, ensuring that they remain productive for many years.

This proactive approach not only safeguards your gardening efforts but also contributes to a sustainable and resilient growing environment, allowing you to enjoy bountiful harvests of delicious clementines season after season.

Protecting Container & Raised Bed Clementine Bushes From Pests

Protecting clementine bushes grown in containers and raised bed gardens organically from pests is vital for several reasons, encompassing both plant health and environmental sustainability. Organic pest control methods, such as introducing beneficial insects, using natural repellents, and employing physical barriers, help maintain a balanced ecosystem that supports the health of the clementine bushes while avoiding the harmful effects of synthetic chemicals.

Chemical pesticides can lead to the development of pesticide-resistant pests and harm non-target organisms, including beneficial insects like pollinators and soil microbes essential for healthy soil. By opting for organic pest control, you can prevent the buildup of toxic residues in the soil and on the plants, ensuring that the clementines produced are safe for consumption.

Additionally, organic methods support long-term soil health by preserving the microbial activity and natural processes that contribute to nutrient cycling and soil structure. This holistic approach not only promotes robust growth and higher fruit quality but also fosters a healthier garden environment that can sustain productive plants season after season.

Clementine bushes are susceptible to a variety of pests that can cause significant damage if not managed properly. Aphids are one of the most common pests, clustering on the undersides of leaves and new growth, sucking sap, and secreting honeydew, which can lead to sooty mold.

Spider mites, particularly prevalent in hot, dry conditions, also feed on plant sap, causing stippling and bronzing of leaves. Citrus leafminers, whose larvae tunnel through leaf tissues creating serpentine trails, can severely weaken young plants. Scale insects, which attach themselves to stems and leaves, suck out nutrients and excrete honeydew, promoting fungal growth. Mealybugs, recognizable by their white, cottony appearance, feed on plant juices and can stunt growth.

Thrips, small slender insects, damage flowers and leaves by feeding on their cellular contents, often leading to distorted growth and reduced fruit quality. These pests not only weaken clementine bushes by draining essential nutrients but also potentially spread diseases.

Protecting clementine bushes organically involves a combination of cultural practices, biological controls, and organic treatments. Introducing beneficial insects like ladybugs, lacewings, and predatory mites can effectively control aphid and spider mite populations.

Encouraging birds and predatory insects by providing habitats such as birdhouses can also help maintain a balanced ecosystem. Companion planting with pest-repellent plants like marigolds, basil, and nasturtiums can deter various pests while attracting beneficial ones.

Regularly inspecting plants for early signs of pest infestations allows for prompt intervention. For instance, spraying neem oil or insecticidal soap solutions on affected areas can manage populations of aphids, mealybugs, and scale insects without harming beneficial organisms.

Neem oil, derived from the neem tree, disrupts the life cycle of pests by inhibiting feeding and growth. Insecticidal soaps break down the outer membranes of soft-bodied insects, leading to dehydration and death.

For citrus leafminers, removing and destroying infested leaves can reduce subsequent generations. Applying horticultural oils can smother eggs and larvae of leafminers and scales. Using sticky traps can monitor and reduce populations of flying pests like thrips. Additionally, ensuring good air circulation and proper watering practices reduces the likelihood of pest infestations by creating unfavorable conditions for their proliferation.

Implementing cultural practices that promote plant health is another critical aspect of organic pest management. Maintaining soil health through the addition of organic matter like compost improves plant vigor and resistance to pests.

Mulching helps regulate soil temperature and moisture, reducing stress on plants and creating a less favorable environment for pests. Pruning to improve air circulation and remove dead or diseased wood can prevent pest harborage and spread.

Rotating crops and avoiding planting the same family of plants in the same area year after year can break pest and disease cycles. Intercropping with diverse plant species can confuse pests and reduce their impact. Keeping garden tools clean and sanitized prevents the spread of pests and diseases from one plant to another.

Protecting Container & Raised Bed Clementine Bushes From Diseases

Protecting clementine bushes grown in containers and raised bed gardens from diseases organically is crucial for maintaining the health and productivity of the plants while ensuring environmental sustainability. Organic disease management practices, such as using disease-resistant varieties, implementing proper spacing for air circulation, applying compost teas, and practicing crop rotation, help mitigate the risk of infections without relying on synthetic fungicides that can disrupt soil ecology and harm beneficial organisms.

These natural methods promote a balanced garden ecosystem, enhancing the resilience of clementine bushes against pathogens. Additionally, organic disease control reduces the risk of chemical residues in fruits, making them safer to consume, and protects pollinators and other wildlife from harmful chemical exposure. By adopting organic practices, you can cultivate robust, disease-free clementine bushes that produce high-quality fruit, contributing to a healthier garden environment and promoting long-term sustainability.

Clementine bushes are susceptible to several diseases that can impact their health, vigor, and fruit production. One of the most common diseases is citrus canker, a bacterial infection that causes raised, corky lesions on leaves, stems, and fruit. This disease can spread rapidly through wind, rain, and contaminated tools, leading to significant defoliation and fruit drop.

Another prevalent issue is root rot, often caused by Phytophthora species, which thrives in poorly drained soils and attacks the roots, leading to wilting, yellowing leaves, and eventual plant death. Citrus greening (Huanglongbing) is a devastating disease transmitted by the Asian citrus psyllid, causing mottled leaves, stunted growth, and misshapen, bitter fruit.

Additionally, fungal diseases like powdery mildew and sooty mold can affect clementine bushes, covering leaves with white or black fungal growth that interferes with photosynthesis and overall plant health.

Organic protection against these diseases involves a combination of preventive measures, cultural practices, and natural treatments. Starting with disease-resistant varieties is the first line of defense; selecting clementine cultivars known for their tolerance to specific diseases can significantly reduce the risk of infection.

Ensuring proper air circulation around the plants is crucial, as many pathogens thrive in humid, stagnant conditions. Pruning to remove dense foliage and maintain an open canopy helps reduce humidity and promotes faster drying of leaves after rainfall or irrigation. Using well-draining soil mixes in containers and raised beds prevents waterlogging, reducing the risk of root rot and other waterborne diseases.

Sanitation and hygiene are critical components of organic disease management. Regularly inspecting plants for signs of disease and promptly removing and disposing of infected plant material helps prevent the spread of pathogens. Sterilizing pruning tools between uses with rubbing alcohol or a bleach solution reduces the risk of transferring diseases from one plant to another.

Mulching with organic materials not only conserves soil moisture but also creates a barrier that helps prevent soil-borne pathogens from splashing onto the plant foliage. Ensuring a balanced nutrient supply through organic fertilizers like compost and well-rotted manure supports robust plant growth and enhances the plants' natural defenses against diseases.

Natural treatments and biocontrol agents provide effective organic solutions for managing diseases in clementine bushes. Neem oil, with its antifungal and antibacterial properties, can be used as a foliar spray to prevent and control a range of diseases, including powdery mildew and citrus canker.

Copper-based fungicides, approved for organic use, are another option for controlling bacterial and fungal diseases. They should be applied as a preventative measure during periods of high disease pressure, such as wet weather.

Beneficial microbes, such as Trichoderma and Bacillus species, can be introduced into the soil or applied as foliar sprays to outcompete and inhibit harmful pathogens. Compost tea, made from steeping high-quality compost in water, contains beneficial microorganisms that enhance soil health and provide a protective microbial barrier against diseases.

Maintaining overall plant health through proper care practices is a cornerstone of organic disease prevention. Adequate watering, avoiding both drought stress and overwatering, supports strong root systems and reduces susceptibility to root diseases.

Regular feeding with organic fertilizers ensures that plants receive essential nutrients for vigorous growth and resilience against pathogens. Monitoring for pest infestations is also important, as pests like the Asian citrus psyllid can vector diseases such as citrus greening. By integrating these organic practices, you can effectively protect your container and raised bed-grown clementine bushes from diseases, fostering healthy plants and abundant, high-quality fruit production without relying on synthetic chemicals.

HARVESTING CONTAINER & RAISED BED CLEMENTINE BUSHES

Clementine bushes grown in containers and raised bed gardens generally take about two to three years to reach a stage where they can produce a significant harvest. The precise timeline can vary depending on several factors, including the variety of clementine, growing conditions, and care practices. When starting with young nursery plants or grafted saplings, it is essential to provide optimal growing conditions to encourage healthy growth and early fruiting.

During the first few years, the focus should be on establishing a robust root system, healthy foliage, and overall plant vigor. Proper watering, fertilization, pruning, and pest control are crucial during this period to ensure that the plants develop well and are capable of supporting fruit production as they mature.

Once the clementine bushes begin to bear fruit, typically around their third year, it's essential to monitor the maturation of the fruits closely. Clementine fruits usually take about 6-8 months to develop fully from flowering to ripening, depending on the specific variety and growing conditions.

Signs that the clementines are ready for harvest include a deep orange color, firm texture, and a slightly loose feel when gently twisted off the branch. It's vital to avoid picking the fruit too early, as premature harvesting can result in less flavorful and underdeveloped clementines. Equally, leaving the fruit on the tree too long can lead to over-ripening and reduced quality.

Harvesting clementines from container and raised bed-grown bushes should be done carefully to avoid damaging the fruit or the plant. The best way to harvest is by gently twisting the fruit until it detaches from the stem.

Alternatively, using sterilized pruning shears to cut the fruit from the branch can minimize any damage to the plant. It's important to handle the fruit gently and place it in a shallow basket or container to prevent bruising, which can affect the fruit's taste and shelf life. Harvesting should ideally be done in the morning when temperatures are cooler, as this helps preserve the fruit's quality.

Post-harvest, it's essential to continue caring for the clementine bushes to ensure they remain healthy and productive in subsequent seasons. After the main harvest, a light pruning can help shape the plant and remove any dead or diseased wood, promoting better air circulation and reducing the risk of pest and disease issues.

After harvesting, feeding the plants with a balanced organic fertilizer can replenish the nutrients used during fruit production, helping the bushes prepare for the next growth cycle. Maintaining regular watering schedules, especially in containers where soil can dry out more quickly, is also critical to support ongoing health and vigor.

In summary, clementine bushes grown in containers and raised beds can take a few years to reach full fruiting potential, but with proper care and attention, they can provide bountiful and high-quality harvests. Careful monitoring, timely harvesting, and post-harvest maintenance are key to ensuring that the plants remain healthy and productive over the long term.

CONTAINER & RAISED BEDS CLEMENTINE BUSHES NOTES

Start: Seeds or Seedlings.

Germination: 2 - 4weeks, at temperatures between 70°F and 85°F (21°C to 29°C).

Seed Life: 6 Months.

Soil Type: Well-drained, loamy soil that is rich in organic matter - slightly acidic with a pH range of 6.0 to 7.0.

Seed Spacing: Space the seeds about 4-6 inches apart.

Seedling Spacing:

Containers – If you're planting multiple seedlings in a single large container, space them at least 12-18 inches apart.

Raised Beds - Space the seedlings about 24-36 inches apart. This spacing allows each plant enough room to grow without competing for nutrients, water, and sunlight.

Sunlight: 6 – 8hrs full sunlight daily.

Growing Temperatures:

Clementine bushes thrive in warm conditions, with optimal daytime temperatures ranging between 70°F and 85°F (21°C to 29°C) and nighttime temperatures not falling below 50°F (10°C).

Duration Till Harvest:

Clementine bushes grown in containers and raised bed gardens generally take about two to three years to reach a stage where they can produce a significant harvest. During the first few years, the focus should be on establishing a robust root system, healthy foliage, and overall plant vigor.

Once the clementine bushes begin to bear fruit, typically around their third year, it's essential to monitor the maturation of the fruits closely. Clementine fruits usually take about 6-8 months to develop fully from flowering to ripening, depending on the specific variety and growing conditions.

CHAPTER 9

CITRUS BUSHES: CONTAINER & RAISED BED GARDENS – MEYER LEMONS

M eyer lemons, a delightful hybrid between a citron and a mandarin/pomelo, are a popular choice for fruit container and raised bed gardening due to their compact size, hardiness, and prolific fruit production. These versatile citrus plants are prized not only for their fragrant blossoms and glossy evergreen foliage but also for their thin-skinned, juicy, and slightly sweet lemons, which have a distinctive floral aroma and flavor. Ideal for small spaces, Meyer lemons thrive in containers and raised beds, making them accessible to urban gardeners and those with limited garden space. Their ability to produce fruit year-round, particularly during cooler months, adds to their appeal, providing a continuous supply of fresh lemons for culinary uses and beverages.

Planting Meyer lemons using containers and raised bed gardening offers numerous benefits that enhance your garden's productivity and aesthetic appeal. One of the key advantages is the ability to control soil quality and drainage, which is crucial for citrus plants that thrive in well-draining, nutrient-rich environments.

Containers and raised beds allow you to tailor the soil mix to meet the specific needs of Meyer lemons, reducing the risk of root rot and other soil-borne diseases. Additionally, these planting methods provide greater flexibility in managing environmental conditions; containers can be moved to optimize sunlight exposure or protect the plants from harsh weather, while raised beds offer improved temperature regulation and root aeration.

Meyer lemons are also naturally compact, making them ideal for small spaces, balconies, and patios, where traditional in-ground planting might not be feasible. Growing Meyer lemons in containers and raised beds simplifies maintenance tasks like pruning, watering, and pest control, ensuring your plants remain healthy and productive.

This approach not only yields an abundant supply of fragrant, flavorful lemons but also adds a touch of greenery and beauty to your outdoor living space, making it both functional and visually appealing.

THE RIGHT SOIL TO GROW MEYER LEMONS IN CONTAINER & RAISED BEDS

Creating the right soil conditions is essential for successfully growing Meyer lemons in containers and raised bed gardens. These citrus plants thrive in loamy, well-draining soil that retains moisture without becoming waterlogged. A mixture of organic compost, garden soil, and sand or perlite can create an ideal soil structure that supports healthy root development and prevents issues like root rot.

The addition of compost not only improves soil texture but also provides essential nutrients that Meyer lemons need to thrive and produce abundant fruit. It's important to ensure the soil pH remains slightly acidic, ideally between 5.5 and 6.5, as this range allows the plant to absorb nutrients effectively.

Proper drainage is a critical aspect of soil preparation for Meyer lemons. When planting in containers, choose pots with adequate drainage holes to allow excess water to escape, preventing waterlogging. You can add a layer of gravel or small stones at the bottom of the container to further enhance drainage.

In raised beds, incorporating coarse materials like sand or fine gravel into the soil mix can improve drainage and prevent compaction. Regularly checking the moisture level of the soil is also important; it should be kept consistently moist but not saturated. Using a well-draining potting mix specifically formulated for citrus or succulent plants can be particularly beneficial for container-grown Meyer lemons.

Besides good drainage, organic matter plays a crucial role in maintaining soil health and fertility. Incorporating well-rotted manure, compost, or leaf mold into the soil enriches it with vital organic nutrients and enhances its microbial activity. Organic matter helps retain moisture and promotes a healthy soil ecosystem, which is beneficial for root growth and overall plant health. Additionally, applying a layer of organic mulch around the base of the plants can conserve moisture, suppress weed growth, and regulate soil temperature. Mulching also contributes to the gradual decomposition of organic matter, further enriching the soil over time.

Fertilization is another key component of providing the right soil conditions for Meyer lemons. Citrus plants are heavy feeders and benefit from regular feeding with a balanced, slow-release fertilizer high in nitrogen, phosphorus, and potassium. Supplementing with micronutrients such as magnesium, iron, and zinc can address any deficiencies and promote lush foliage and fruit development. Using organic fertilizers, such as fish emulsion, seaweed extract, or citrus-specific granular fertilizers, ensures a steady supply of nutrients without the risk of chemical buildup in the soil.

In summary, creating optimal soil conditions for Meyer lemons in containers and raised bed gardens involves ensuring well-drained, nutrient-rich, and slightly acidic soil. A combination of organic compost, garden soil, and sand or perlite can provide the ideal growing medium while proper drainage techniques prevent waterlogging.

Incorporating organic matter and applying mulch supports soil health and moisture retention. Regular fertilization with balanced, slow-release nutrients tailored to citrus plants ensures vigorous growth and prolific fruit production. By paying careful attention to these soil conditions, you can cultivate thriving Meyer lemons that yield abundant, flavorful fruit in both containers and raised beds.

HOW TO SOW MEYER LEMONS IN CONTAINERS & RAISED BEDS GARDENS

Correct Season To Sow Meyer Lemons In Containers & Raised Beds Gardens

The optimal season to sow Meyer lemons in containers and raised bed gardens is during the spring after the last threat of frost has passed. This timing provides the young plants with the best possible conditions for growth, as the increasing daylight hours and warming temperatures support vigorous root and foliage development.

Spring planting allows Meyer lemons to establish themselves well before the onset of summer heat, reducing transplant shock and enabling them to build a strong root system capable of supporting future fruit production.

Additionally, by planting in spring, you can take advantage of the entire growing season, which is crucial for these evergreen citrus plants to acclimate and thrive. It's important to ensure that nighttime temperatures consistently stay above 50°F (10°C) to prevent cold stress on the young plants. Preparing the soil in advance by amending it with organic matter and ensuring proper drainage will further enhance the success of spring planting.

By carefully choosing the right season to sow your Meyer lemons, you can set the stage for healthy growth and bountiful harvests in your container and raised bed gardens.

Plant Needs & Requirements

Germinating Meyer lemons from seeds to seedlings correctly is vital when growing them in containers and raised bed gardens because it sets the foundation for the plant's overall health, vigor, and productivity. Proper germination ensures that the seedlings develop strong root systems and sturdy stems, essential for supporting robust growth and eventual fruit production. Starting with healthy, well-germinated seedlings reduces the risk of transplant shock, enhances the plants' resilience against pests and diseases, and improves their ability to adapt to their new environment.

Correct germination practices—such as using fresh, viable seeds, maintaining consistent moisture levels, providing adequate warmth, and ensuring sufficient light—lead to uniform seedling development, making it easier to manage and care for the young plants. This early attention to detail can significantly influence the long-term success of Meyer lemons, enabling them to flourish in the confined spaces of containers and raised beds, ultimately yielding abundant, high-quality lemons.

Germinating Meyer lemons from seeds involves several critical steps that must be carefully followed to ensure successful growth. The process begins with selecting fresh, ripe Meyer lemons to harvest the seeds. Once you've obtained the seeds, rinse them thoroughly to remove any remaining fruit pulp, as this can inhibit germination.

After cleaning, soak the seeds in warm water for about 24 hours to soften the seed coat and promote faster sprouting. It's important to use a high-quality seed-starting mix or a combination of peat moss and vermiculite to provide a light, well-draining medium that encourages healthy root development.

Next, plant the seeds approximately 1/2 inch deep in the seed-starting mix, ensuring that they are spaced adequately to allow room for growth. Cover the seeds lightly with the soil mix and water them gently to keep the medium consistently moist but not waterlogged. To create an optimal germination environment, cover the seed tray or pots with plastic wrap or a clear plastic lid to retain humidity and warmth. Place the covered trays in a warm location with indirect sunlight, such as on top of a refrigerator or near a sunny window. Meyer lemon seeds typically require temperatures between 70°F to 80°F (21°C to 27°C) to germinate successfully. Using a heat mat can also help maintain consistent warmth, particularly in cooler climates.

Germination can take anywhere from 2 to 4 weeks, during which it is essential to check the seeds regularly and ensure the soil remains moist. Once the seedlings emerge and develop their first true leaves (the second set of leaves after the initial seed leaves), it's time to gradually acclimate them to their future growing conditions.

Begin by removing the plastic cover for a few hours each day to reduce humidity levels and increase airflow. This hardening-off process helps the seedlings adapt to less protected environments and strengthens them for transplanting.

When the seedlings have grown to about 4 to 6 inches tall and have multiple sets of true leaves, they are ready to be transplanted into containers or raised bed gardens. Carefully loosen the soil around each seedling and gently lift them out, taking care not to damage the delicate roots. Plant the seedlings at the same depth they were growing in their seed-starting pots, firming the soil gently around the base to eliminate air pockets.

Spacing & Measurement

Proper spacing and measurements when transplanting Meyer lemons seedlings into fruit containers and raised bed gardens are crucial for ensuring their healthy growth and optimal fruit production. Adequate spacing allows each plant to access sufficient light, air circulation, and nutrients, which are essential for preventing overcrowding and promoting robust development.

In containers, choosing the right pot size ensures that the roots have ample room to spread out, reducing the risk of root-bound plants and facilitating better water and nutrient absorption. Proper measurements also make maintenance tasks such as watering, pruning, and harvesting more manageable, contributing to the overall health and productivity of your Meyer lemon plants.

When planting Meyer lemons seedlings in fruit containers, the size of the container plays a crucial role in ensuring healthy growth. Ideally, start with a container at least 12 inches in diameter and adequate depth to allow for root expansion.

As the plant grows, it may need to be transplanted into larger pots, such as those 18 to 24 inches in diameter. The depth of the container should also be sufficient, typically around 12 to 18 inches, to ensure the roots have ample space to grow vertically as well as horizontally. Proper container size helps prevent the roots from becoming root-bound, where they circle around the inside of the pot, which can stunt growth and reduce fruit production.

Additionally, containers should have multiple drainage holes to prevent waterlogging. Elevating the container slightly off the ground using pot feet or a plant stand can further improve drainage and air circulation around the root zone. Space the containers adequately if growing multiple Meyer lemons to ensure each plant receives enough sunlight and airflow.

Typically, placing containers about 3 to 5 feet apart is recommended. This spacing prevents the plants' canopies from overlapping, ensuring that every leaf gets the necessary light and reducing the risk of pest and disease spread.

In raised bed gardens, spacing Meyer lemon seedlings correctly is equally important for their development and productivity. When planning the layout, aim to plant the seedlings approximately 3 to 5 feet apart. This spacing allows enough room for each plant to expand without competing with its neighbors for water, nutrients, and sunlight.

The wider spacing also ensures good air circulation between plants, which helps to reduce the incidence of fungal diseases and pest infestations. Raised beds should be at least 12 to 18 inches deep to accommodate the root systems of the Meyer lemons, providing them with ample room to grow and access nutrients.

When planting, ensure that the seedlings are positioned at the same depth they were growing in their original pots. This consistency helps reduce transplant shock and supports continuous growth. It's also beneficial to mulch around the base of each seedling to retain soil moisture and suppress weeds, but leave a small gap around the stem to prevent moisture buildup and potential rot.

If the raised bed is located in an area with partial shade, position the Meyer lemons towards the sunniest side to maximize their exposure to direct sunlight, which is essential for their growth and fruiting.

By adhering to recommended spacing guidelines, you can create an environment where Meyer lemons thrive, ultimately leading to more consistent and bountiful harvests. Proper spacing thus not only optimizes plant health and productivity but also enhances the overall efficiency and enjoyment of gardening.

Ideal Temperatures & Sun Requirements

Ideal temperatures and sun requirements are crucial for successfully growing Meyer lemons as these factors directly influence their growth, health, and fruit production. Meyer lemons thrive in temperatures ranging from 70°F to 85°F (21°C to 29°C) during the day and prefer nighttime temperatures above 50°F (10°C). These temperature ranges support optimal metabolic activities and flowering processes.

Consistently warm temperatures help develop healthy leaves and robust roots, while cooler conditions can slow growth and even cause damage if they drop below freezing. Additionally, Meyer lemons require full sunlight to perform photosynthesis efficiently, necessitating at least 6 to 8 hours of direct sunlight daily.

Adequate sunlight exposure promotes vigorous growth, enhances flowering, and improves fruit quality by ensuring that the plant's energy requirements are met. Proper placement in sun-drenched areas or using grow lights when natural light is insufficient can greatly improve outcomes.

MAINTAINING YOUR CONTAINER & RAISED BED MEYER LEMONS

Maintaining your Meyer lemons in containers and raised bed gardens is essential for ensuring their long-term health, productivity, and resilience against environmental stressors. Regular maintenance activities such as watering, fertilizing, pruning, and monitoring for pests and diseases help create optimal growing conditions that support robust growth and abundant fruiting.

Consistent watering prevents drought stress and root rot, while appropriate fertilization provides the necessary nutrients for vigorous development and fruit production. Pruning helps shape the plant, improve airflow, and encourage the formation of fruit-bearing branches.

Monitoring for pests and diseases allows for early detection and intervention, minimizing damage and preventing the spread of infestations. Likewise, maintaining a clean growing environment by removing fallen leaves and debris reduces the risk of fungal infections and other issues.

By diligently caring for your Meyer lemons, you not only enhance their aesthetic appeal but also maximize their yield potential, ensuring a bountiful harvest of delicious, home-grown lemons.

Pruning & Thinning Your Meyer Lemons

Pruning and thinning Meyer lemons are vital horticultural practices that significantly impact the plants' health, productivity, and overall structure. Regular pruning helps maintain an open canopy, enhancing air circulation and sunlight penetration, which are crucial for reducing the risk of fungal diseases and promoting robust photosynthesis. By removing dead, damaged, or crossing branches, pruning also prevents pest infestations and encourages the growth of healthy, fruit-bearing wood.

Thinning, on the other hand, involves selectively removing some of the fruit when the tree is heavily laden. This ensures that the remaining fruits have enough space and resources to grow larger and more flavorful. This practice helps prevent limb breakage due to excessive weight and directs the plant's energy towards producing high-quality fruit rather than an overabundance of smaller, less desirable ones.

Together, pruning and thinning foster a balanced and vigorous growth habit, ultimately leading to a healthier plant and a more bountiful, high-quality harvest. Without these practices, Meyer lemons can become overgrown and stressed, resulting in poor fruit quality and increased susceptibility to diseases and pests.

Pruning and thinning Meyer lemons grown in containers and raised beds is a crucial aspect of their care, and knowing when and how to perform these tasks can make a significant difference in plant health and fruit production. Typically, the best time to prune Meyer lemons is in late winter or early spring, just before new growth begins. This timing allows the plants to recover quickly and promotes vigorous growth during the warmer months.

Additionally, light pruning can be done throughout the growing season to remove any dead or diseased branches or to maintain the desired shape of the bush. It's essential to use clean, sharp pruning shears to make precise cuts and minimize damage to the plant tissues.

The process of pruning involves several key steps. Start by removing any dead, damaged, or diseased wood, cutting back to healthy tissue to prevent the spread of pathogens. Next, focus on thinning out crowded branches to improve air circulation and light penetration within the canopy.

Aim to create an open, vase-like structure that allows sunlight to reach the inner branches and leaves. When thinning, remove any crossing or rubbing branches, as these can create wounds that are entry points for diseases. Additionally, cut back any excessively long or leggy stems to encourage bushier growth and maintain a manageable size, which is particularly important for container-grown plants.

Maintaining a balance between the plant's size and the container's capacity is critical for Meyer lemons in containers. Overgrown plants can become root-bound, leading to stress and reduced fruit production. Regularly thinning out the canopy helps to prevent this issue by limiting the overall biomass of the plant.

In raised bed gardens, where space might be less restricted, thinning still plays an essential role in preventing overcrowding and ensuring each plant has adequate room to grow and access nutrients. By removing excess branches and shoots, resources are directed towards developing stronger, more productive growth, ultimately leading to better fruit quality and yield.

In addition to structural pruning, consider performing rejuvenation pruning every few years for older Meyer lemon bushes. This involves cutting back about one-third of the oldest, unproductive branches to ground level to stimulate new growth from the base. Rejuvenation pruning can help revitalize the plant, promoting the development of vigorous, fruit-bearing stems.

After any pruning session, it is beneficial to apply a balanced citrus fertilizer to support the plant's recovery and encourage healthy new growth. Proper pruning and thinning practices not only enhance the overall appearance of Meyer lemon plants but also play a pivotal role in maintaining their health, productivity, and longevity in both containers and raised bed gardens.

Watering Your Container & Raised Bed Meyer Lemons

Determining how much to water Meyer lemons in containers and raised bed gardens depends on several factors, including the size of the plant, the type of soil, and the prevailing weather conditions. Generally, the soil should be kept consistently moist but not waterlogged. For container-grown Meyer lemons, this often means watering until water runs out of the drainage holes, ensuring all the roots have access to moisture.

The frequency may vary daily during hot, dry spells to every few days in cooler, more humid conditions. In raised beds, aim to provide enough water to moisten the soil to a depth of about 12 inches, which corresponds to the typical root zone of these plants. This usually translates to about one to two inches of water per week, applied through regular watering or rainfall.

The best time to water Meyer lemons is early in the morning or late in the afternoon. Watering in the morning allows the plants to absorb moisture before the day's heat, reducing evaporation and ensuring that the plants are well-hydrated to handle the day's temperatures.

Watering late in the afternoon or early evening can also be effective, provided there is enough time for the foliage to dry before nightfall, which helps prevent fungal diseases. Avoid watering during the hottest part of the day, as much of the water will evaporate before it can penetrate the soil effectively, and the rapid temperature change from cold water can stress the plants.

It's essential to regularly check the soil moisture to determine when to water your plants. For container plants, insert your finger about two inches into the soil; if it feels dry at that depth, it's time to water. You can also use a moisture meter for more precise readings.

In raised beds, a similar approach can be taken by checking the soil a few inches down. Mulching around the base of the plants in both containers and raised beds can help retain soil moisture, reduce evaporation, and keep the root zone cooler. Use organic mulches like straw, wood chips, or compost, but keep the mulch a few inches away from the trunk to prevent rot and pest issues.

It is important to adjust your watering practices to accommodate seasonal changes. During the growing season in spring and summer, your plants will typically require more frequent watering due to increased temperatures and active growth phases.

Equally, they will need less water in fall and winter, especially if the plants are moved indoors or experience cooler outdoor conditions. Be cautious not to overwater during these periods, as reduced light and lower temperatures slow down the plant's water uptake, increasing the risk of root rot. Always reduce watering if the plant is showing signs of overwatering, such as yellowing leaves, soggy soil, or a musty smell from the container or raised bed.

By understanding and implementing correct watering techniques, you can significantly enhance the vitality and yield of your home-grown Meyer lemons.

Organic Fertilization For Container & Raised Bed Meyer Lemons

Using organic fertilizers for container and raised bed grown Meyer lemons is an excellent way to provide balanced nutrition while promoting soil health. Organic options such as compost, well-rotted manure, and worm castings add essential nutrients and improve soil structure.

Compost provides a slow-release source of nutrients, including nitrogen, phosphorus, and potassium, as well as beneficial microorganisms that help break down organic matter and improve soil fertility.

Well-rotted manure from cows, horses, or chickens is rich in nitrogen and micronutrients necessary for vigorous growth. Worm castings are another superb organic fertilizer known for their high nutrient content and ability to enhance soil microbial activity.

In addition to these general organic fertilizers, specific products designed for citrus trees can be particularly beneficial. Organic citrus fertilizers often contain a balanced mix of macronutrients (N-P-K) tailored to the needs of citrus plants, along with micronutrients like magnesium, calcium, and iron, which are crucial for preventing deficiencies that can affect fruit quality and yield.

Examples include products made from fish emulsion, kelp meal, bone meal, and alfalfa meal. These fertilizers not only nourish the plant but also contribute to building healthy, resilient soil through the addition of organic matter and beneficial microbes.

Timing is critical when fertilizing Meyer lemons to ensure they receive nutrients during their crucial growth periods. The primary feeding times are in early spring, as new growth begins, and then again in late spring and late summer. This schedule supports the plant's active growth phases, flowering, and fruit development.

In early spring, a thorough application of a balanced organic fertilizer helps kick-start the growing season. A second application in late spring supports continued leaf and root development, while a final feeding in late summer prepares the plant for fruiting and sustains it through the fall.

Avoid fertilizing during the winter months when the plant is dormant, as this can lead to nutrient buildup in the soil and potentially harm the roots. Also, refrain from over-fertilizing, as too much nitrogen can encourage excessive foliage growth at the expense of fruit production and can also cause nutrient imbalances that may lead to deficiencies in other essential minerals.

Applying organic fertilizers properly ensures that Meyer lemons make the most of the nutrients provided. For container grown plants, start by lightly mixing a layer of compost or worm castings into the top inch of soil, being careful not to disturb the roots. Follow this with a dilute solution of fish emulsion or a citrus-specific organic fertilizer according to the product instructions. Water the plant thoroughly after application to help the nutrients penetrate the soil and reach the roots.

In raised beds, spread compost or well-rotted manure evenly over the soil surface at the recommended rate, usually about one to two inches thick. Lightly work the material into the top few inches of soil using a garden fork or cultivator. Then, apply an organic granular fertilizer around the drip line of the plant—the area directly beneath the outermost branches —where feeder roots are concentrated. Water the area well to dissolve the fertilizer and carry the nutrients down to the root zone.

PROTECTING YOUR CONTAINER & RAISED BED MEYER LEMONS

Extreme Temperatures

Providing protection against extreme temperatures is crucial for the health and productivity of Meyer lemon plants. These plants are native to subtropical climates and are not well-adapted to severe heat or cold. High temperatures can lead to water loss through faster transpiration than the roots can absorb, resulting in dehydration and stress. This reduces the plant's ability to photosynthesize efficiently, weakening its overall health and reducing fruit yield and quality. Consistently high temperatures can also cause sunscald on the fruits, making them less appealing and potentially affecting their taste.

Similarly, exposure to cold temperatures can be equally detrimental. Frost damage can destroy new growth, flowers, and developing fruits, significantly impacting the plant's productivity for the season. Prolonged cold exposure can lead to leaf drop and branch dieback, weakening the plant and making it more susceptible to diseases and pests. In extreme cases, freezing temperatures can kill the plant, especially if the roots are affected.

Whether grown in containers or raised bed gardens, Meyer lemons require protection from extreme temperatures to thrive and produce high-quality fruit. In regions with hot summers, excessive heat can stress these plants, leading to leaf burn, fruit drop, and inhibited growth.

To shield your lemon plants from high temperatures, consider placing your containers in locations that receive partial shade during the hottest part of the day. Using shade cloths or building temporary structures can also help filter intense sunlight and keep the ambient temperature around the plants cooler. In raised beds, applying a thick layer of organic mulch, such as straw or wood chips, helps retain soil moisture and regulate soil temperature, creating a more stable environment for the roots.

During cold weather, particularly in winter, Meyer lemons are susceptible to frost damage and freezing temperatures, which can harm leaves, branches, and even kill the plant. For container-grown plants, moving them indoors or into a green-house is the most effective way to protect them from cold snaps.

If indoor space is limited, wrapping the containers with insulating materials like burlap, bubble wrap, or frost blankets can help preserve root warmth. For raised bed plants, covering the plants with frost cloths or using outdoor heaters can provide additional warmth. Mulching the base of the plants heavily with organic material also insulates the soil, protecting the roots from freezing conditions.

In addition to shading and mulching, there are several other practical steps you can take to protect Meyer lemons from summer heat. Regularly watering your plants early in the morning helps them cope with daytime heat by ensuring they are well-hydrated. Using drip irrigation systems or soaker hoses can deliver water directly to the root zone, minimizing water loss through evaporation.

Grouping containers together can create a microclimate that retains humidity and reduces heat stress. Reflective mulch or white plastic can also be used on the soil surface in raised beds to reflect sunlight away from the plants, helping to keep the soil cooler.

For winter cold protection, it's essential to anticipate frost events and prepare accordingly. Monitoring local weather forecasts allows you to take timely action to protect your plants. As we previously mentioned moving container-grown Meyer lemons to a sheltered location such as a garage or enclosed porch can offer necessary protection.

However, if moving the containers is not feasible, using heat lamps or Christmas lights (non-LED) can provide gentle warmth when wrapped around the plants. Raised bed plants can benefit from windbreaks made of materials like plywood or heavy-duty plastic, which reduce wind chill and prevent frost damage. Applying anti-transpirant sprays can also help by reducing moisture loss from the leaves during cold spells.

Consistently managing the temperature around your Meyer lemon plants yields long-term benefits, including enhanced plant vigor, increased fruit production, and improved resistance to pests and diseases. By maintaining optimal growing conditions, you support the plant's natural defense mechanisms, reducing the likelihood of stress-related issues.

Healthy plants are more efficient at nutrient uptake, leading to better growth and more robust flowering and fruiting cycles. Investing in temperature protection measures helps ensure that your efforts in planting, fertilizing, and caring for your Meyer lemons are not undone by extreme weather events, ultimately leading to a more rewarding gardening experience.

Protecting Container & Raised Bed Meyer Lemons From Pests

Container and raised bed grown Meyer lemons can fall prey to a variety of pests that can compromise their health and productivity. One of the most common pests is the aphid, which feeds on the sap of young leaves and shoots, causing distortion and weakening the plant. Aphids also excrete honeydew, a sticky substance that can lead to sooty mold growth.

Another frequent pest is the citrus leaf miner, which tunnels through leaves, leaving serpentine trails and causing leaves to curl and distort. Spider mites, tiny web-spinning insects, thrive in hot, dry conditions and can cause stippling and severe defoliation. Whiteflies, scale insects, and mealybugs also pose significant threats by sucking sap and secreting honeydew. Finally, caterpillars and snails may chew on the leaves and fruits, causing direct damage and reducing the plant's aesthetic and productive value.

Protecting your plants from pests using organic methods involves a combination of preventive practices and targeted treatments. One of the most effective preventive measures is maintaining plant health through proper watering, fertilization, and pruning, as healthy plants are more resistant to pests.

Regularly inspecting the plants for early signs of pest infestation allows for timely intervention before the problem escalates. Encouraging natural predators, such as ladybugs, lacewings, and predatory mites, can help keep pest populations in check. These beneficial insects can be attracted by planting companion plants like dill, fennel, and marigolds or by purchasing them from garden centers.

For treating existing infestations, several organic options are available. Insecticidal soaps and neem oil sprays are effective against soft-bodied insects like aphids, whiteflies, and mealybugs. These products work by disrupting the pests cell membranes and interfering with their life cycles, while being safe for humans, pets, and beneficial insects when used as directed.

Horticultural oils can be used to smother scale insects and spider mites. Bacillus thuringiensis (Bt), a naturally occurring soil bacterium, is particularly effective against caterpillars, causing them to stop feeding and eventually die. Diatomaceous earth, a powder made from fossilized algae, can be sprinkled around the base of the plants to deter snails and other crawling insects by causing physical damage to their exoskeletons.

In addition to direct treatments, implementing cultural practices can significantly reduce pest problems. Crop rotation and interplanting with pest-repellent plants like garlic, onions, and nasturtiums can help disrupt pest life cycles and reduce their numbers. Maintaining good garden hygiene by removing fallen leaves, fruits, and other debris minimizes habitat for pests and reduces the risk of infection.

Using physical barriers like row covers can protect young plants from flying insects while still allowing light and air to penetrate. Ensuring proper spacing between plants improves air circulation, making the environment less favorable for pests and diseases.

Consistent monitoring is essential for effective pest control. Regularly inspecting the underside of leaves, stems, and fruit for signs of pests can help catch infestations early. Sticky traps can be used to monitor flying insect populations.

Integrated Pest Management (IPM) combines various control methods, focusing on long-term prevention and minimal environmental impact. IPM strategies include using resistant plant varieties, encouraging natural predators, applying organic treatments judiciously, and maintaining overall plant health. By adopting organic pest management strategies, you can cultivate healthy, productive Meyer lemons while contributing to ecological balance and sustainability.

Protecting Container & Raised Bed Meyer Lemons From Diseases

Container and raised bed grown Meyer lemons are susceptible to several diseases that can impact their health and fruit production. One prevalent issue is citrus canker, a bacterial disease that causes raised, corky lesions on leaves, stems, and fruit. It spreads rapidly in warm, wet conditions and can lead to premature leaf and fruit drop.

Another common problem is sooty mold, a fungal growth that develops on the honeydew excreted by sap-sucking insects like aphids and whiteflies. This black, sticky mold interferes with photosynthesis and reduces plant vigor.

Root rot, often caused by the water mold Phytophthora, affects plants grown in poorly draining soil or overwatered conditions, leading to wilting, yellowing leaves, and eventual death if untreated.

Greasy spot, another fungal disease, results in yellowish-brown blisters on the undersides of leaves, causing defoliation and weakening the plant. Lastly, citrus tristeza virus (CTV) is a devastating viral disease spread by aphids that can cause stem pitting, decline in vigor, and even tree death.

Preventing diseases in Meyer lemon plants requires a multi-faceted approach focused on maintaining plant health and environmental conditions that discourage pathogen development. Start by selecting disease-resistant varieties and healthy, certified disease-free plants from reputable nurseries.

Proper site selection is crucial; ensure containers and raised beds are positioned in areas with good air circulation and ample sunlight, as this helps keep foliage dry and less hospitable to fungal pathogens. Using well-draining potting soil or amending garden soil with organic matter improves drainage and reduces the risk of root diseases.

Regularly pruning to remove dead or diseased wood and thin out dense canopies enhances air flow through the plant, further reducing humidity levels that promote fungal growth. Sanitation practices, such as cleaning pruning tools with a 10% bleach solution between cuts and disposing of infected plant material away from the garden, help prevent the spread of pathogens. Mulching with organic materials can protect the soil surface and reduce splashing of soil-borne pathogens onto plant foliage during watering or rain.

When disease symptoms appear, early intervention with organic treatments is essential to manage and mitigate damage. For fungal diseases like sooty mold and greasy spot, spraying affected plants with organic fungicides such as neem oil, potassium bicarbonate, or copper-based products can help control the spread.

These treatments work by inhibiting fungal spores and are safer for the environment and beneficial insects when used according to label instructions. For bacterial diseases like citrus canker, removing and destroying infected plant parts can help limit spread, though severe infections may require more drastic measures.

Root rot prevention hinges on improving soil drainage and adjusting watering practices to avoid waterlogged conditions. If root rot is detected, removing affected plants and treating the soil with biofungicides containing beneficial microbes, such as Trichoderma or Bacillus subtilis, can suppress pathogenic fungi and promote healthy root growth.

For viral diseases like CTV, there is no cure once a plant is infected, so focus on preventive measures such as controlling aphid populations with insecticidal soap or neem oil and using virus-free planting material.

Implementing an integrated disease management (IDM) strategy is crucial for long-term health and productivity of Meyer lemons. IDM involves combining cultural, biological, and organic treatment methods to create a holistic approach to disease prevention and control. Regular monitoring for symptoms of disease allows for early detection and prompt action. Incorporating beneficial organisms, like mycorrhizal fungi and beneficial nematodes, into the soil can improve plant health and resilience against pathogens. Rotating citrus crops with non-host plants in raised beds can break disease cycles, reducing the incidence of recurring issues.

Maintaining balanced soil nutrition through regular applications of organic fertilizers ensures that plants are vigorous and better able to resist infections. Additionally, fostering biodiversity in the garden by planting a variety of species can create a balanced ecosystem where natural predators and beneficial organisms help keep disease-carrying pests under control.

By integrating these diverse strategies, you can effectively manage disease pressures while promoting a sustainable and healthy growing environment for your Meyer lemons.

HARVESTING CONTAINER & RAISED BED MEYER LEMONS

Meyer lemons, whether grown in containers or raised beds, typically take between one to three years to begin producing fruit if they are started from grafted nursery plants. This relatively short time frame compared to other citrus varieties is due to the fact that Meyer lemons are often grafted onto hardy rootstocks that promote vigorous growth and early fruiting.

If you start from seeds, the process can take much longer, often taking up to seven years before the plants are mature enough to bear fruit. The time to harvest also depends on factors such as plant health, growing conditions, and care practices, including proper watering, fertilization, and pruning.

Once the plants start flowering, it usually takes about six to nine months for the fruits to mature. The flowers bloom in clusters, and after pollination, small green fruits will begin to develop. These will gradually enlarge and change color as they ripen, transitioning from green to a yellow-orange hue. Optimizing growing conditions by ensuring adequate sunlight (at least 6-8 hours a day), maintaining consistent soil moisture, and providing balanced nutrition can accelerate the growth and fruiting process.

Harvesting Meyer lemons at the right time is crucial for obtaining the best flavor and juiciness. The fruits are ready to be picked when they reach their characteristic bright yellow color with a slight orange tint and are slightly soft to the touch when gently squeezed. Unlike other citrus fruits, Meyer lemons have a thinner skin, so they should be handled carefully to avoid bruising or puncturing the skin.

To harvest, use a pair of sharp pruning shears or scissors to cut the fruit from the tree, leaving a small part of the stem attached to the lemon. This helps prevent damage to the fruit and reduces the risk of introducing pathogens into the plant through torn tissue. While some gardeners prefer to twist and pull the fruit directly from the branches, this method can sometimes cause damage to the plant or the fruit itself, especially if not done gently.

After harvesting, Meyer lemons can be stored at room temperature for about a week or two. For longer storage, place them in the refrigerator where they can keep for several weeks. However, for the best flavor and nutritional value, it is advisable to consume or use the lemons shortly after harvest. Freshly picked Meyer lemons can be used in a variety of culinary applications, from juices and desserts to savory dishes and marinades, taking advantage of their unique sweetness and low acidity compared to regular lemons.

If you find yourself with an abundant harvest, consider preserving the lemons by making marmalade, lemon curd or even freezing the juice and zest for later use. Sharing excess produce with friends and neighbors is also a great way to enjoy the fruits of your labor and spread the joy of homegrown Meyer lemons.

Timely harvesting ensures that Meyer lemons remain on the tree long enough to develop their full flavor and nutritional profile without overripening and potentially falling off the plant. Overripe fruits left on the tree can attract pests and diseases, which may affect the overall health of the lemon bush. Regular harvesting also encourages the plant to continue producing flowers and fruits, extending the harvest period and increasing yield.

Furthermore, timely harvesting helps manage the size and shape of the plant. By removing mature fruits, you reduce the weight burden on branches, minimizing the risk of breakage or structural damage to the plant. This practice also improves air circulation within the canopy, reducing the likelihood of fungal infections and promoting overall plant vigor.

CONTAINER & RAISED BEDS MEYER LEMONS NOTES

Start: Seeds or Seedlings.

Germination: 2 - 4weeks, at temperatures between 70°F to 80°F (21°C to 27°C).

Seed Life: 3 - 6 Months.

Soil Type: Well-drained, loamy soil that is rich in organic matter - slightly acidic with a pH range between 5.5 and 6.5.

Seed Spacing: Space the seeds about 1-2 inches apart.

Seedling Spacing:

Containers – A single container 18 to 24 inches in diameter. With a depth of 12 to 18 inches.

Raised Beds - In raised bed gardens, space Meyer lemon seedlings about 3 to 5 feet apart. If planting in multiple rows, maintain a distance of about 5 to 6 feet between rows.

Sunlight: 6 – 8hrs full sunlight daily.

Growing Temperatures:

Meyer lemons thrive in temperatures ranging from 70°F to 85°F (21°C to 29°C) during the day and prefer nighttime temperatures above 50°F (10°C).

Duration Till Harvest:

Meyer lemons grown in containers and raised bed gardens generally take about 2 to 3 years to reach a stage where they can produce a significant harvest of lemons. The plants focus on establishing a strong root system and healthy foliage, with the first year primarily dedicated to growth rather than fruiting.

By the second or third year, assuming they have been given proper care including adequate watering, fertilization, and pest management, these citrus plants typically begin bearing fruit. Meyer lemons are known for their nearly year-round fruiting cycle, so once the plants start producing, you can expect multiple harvests annually.

The precise timeline can vary based on factors such as climate conditions and specific care practices, but with consistent attention, your Meyer lemon plants should yield a bountiful crop within this timeframe.

CHAPTER 10
VINE FRUITS: CONTAINER & RAISED BED GARDENS – DWARF GRAPES

D warf grapes are an excellent choice for gardeners looking to cultivate their own grapevines in containers and raised bed gardens. These compact varieties offer the same delicious fruit and vibrant foliage as their full-sized counterparts but in a more manageable form that fits well in limited spaces. Ideal for urban gardening, patios, and small backyard plots, dwarf grapes thrive in well-drained soil and require adequate support structures such as trellises or stakes to encourage vertical growth. They are not only prized for their sweet, juicy grapes, which can be enjoyed fresh or used in a variety of culinary applications, but also for their ornamental value, with lush leaves providing a beautiful backdrop throughout the growing season.

Planting dwarf grapes in containers and raised bed gardens can offer numerous benefits, making them an attractive option for gardeners of all experience levels. One significant advantage is the ability to control soil quality and drainage more effectively, providing an optimal growing environment that promotes healthy root development and vigorous plant growth.

Containers and raised beds also elevate the plants, improving air circulation and reducing the risk of diseases and pests commonly associated with ground-level gardening. Additionally, these planting methods facilitate easier maintenance tasks such as watering, pruning, and harvesting, minimizing physical strain and making it accessible for those with limited mobility.

Dwarf grapes compact size suits urban settings, patios, and small yards, allowing gardeners to enjoy fresh, homegrown grapes even in restricted spaces. Furthermore, growing grapes in containers or raised beds can extend the growing season by enabling early planting and easier protection from unexpected weather changes.

Overall, incorporating dwarf grapes into your container or raised bed garden can enhance productivity, aesthetic appeal, and convenience, creating a rewarding gardening experience.

THE RIGHT SOIL TO GROW DWARF GRAPES IN CONTAINER & RAISED BEDS

One of the significant benefits of using containers and raised beds for growing dwarf grapes is the ability to create and maintain optimal soil conditions. Unlike traditional in-ground planting, where soil quality and drainage can vary widely, containers and raised beds offer the opportunity to start with a perfect soil mix tailored to the needs of grapevines.

This controlled environment reduces the risk of common soil-borne pests and diseases, promoting healthier plants. Furthermore, adjusting soil composition, pH, and nutrient levels easily means that you can respond quickly to the plant's needs, ensuring consistent growth and productivity.

Growing dwarf grapes in containers necessitates careful selection and preparation of soil to ensure optimal plant health and productivity. The ideal soil for container-grown grapevines should be well-draining to prevent waterlogged roots, which can lead to root rot and other diseases.

A high-quality potting mix specifically designed for fruiting plants or a custom blend of equal parts garden soil, compost, and perlite or vermiculite works well. This mixture provides the necessary nutrients and aeration while ensuring excess water drains efficiently. Additionally, using containers with drainage holes is crucial to avoid water accumulation at the bottom, which could harm the roots.

Soil pH is another critical factor for growing dwarf grapes successfully. Grapevines prefer a slightly acidic to neutral pH range, ideally between 6.0 and 7.0. Testing the soil pH before planting and making adjustments with agricultural lime to raise pH or sulfur to lower it can help maintain the desired level. Regularly monitoring pH levels ensures that the soil remains conducive to nutrient uptake, promoting robust growth and fruit production.

Raised bed gardening offers several advantages for growing dwarf grapes, particularly when it comes to soil management. The elevated structure of raised beds allows for better control over soil composition and drainage, critical factors for thriving grapevines. Similar to container gardening, the soil in raised beds should be well-draining yet capable of retaining sufficient moisture.

A mix of garden soil, organic compost, and sand can create an ideal environment that balances aeration with moisture retention. Adding organic matter not only improves soil structure but also enhances its fertility, providing essential nutrients that support vigorous plant growth.

In raised beds, maintaining the appropriate soil pH is equally important. Before planting, test the soil pH and amend it as necessary to achieve a range of 6.0 to 7.0. Raised beds also benefit from periodic soil testing to monitor nutrient levels and pH, ensuring that any deficiencies or imbalances are promptly corrected.

Organic fertilizers, such as compost tea, fish emulsion, or well-rotted manure, can be added to maintain nutrient-rich soil throughout the growing season. These amendments support healthy root development and fruiting, contributing to the overall success of your dwarf grape plants.

By offering these controlled conditions, you can maximize the growth potential of your dwarf grapes, leading to higher yields of delicious, homegrown grapes.

HOW TO SOW DWARF GRAPES IN CONTAINERS & RAISED BEDS GARDENS

Correct Season To Sow Dwarf Grapes In Containers & Raised Beds Gardens

The correct season to sow dwarf grapes in containers and raised bed gardens is typically in the early spring, just as the last frost has passed and temperatures begin to rise consistently. This timing allows the young grapevines to establish their root systems and acclimate to their new environment before the intense heat of summer sets in.

Planting in early spring provides the vines an entire growing season to develop robust foliage and strong roots, which are crucial for their long-term health and productivity. In regions with milder climates, where winters are not severe, late winter planting can also be an option, giving the plants an even longer period to settle in.

For those growing in containers, the flexibility to move pots indoors or to a sheltered location can extend the planting window slightly earlier in the season, protecting young plants from unexpected cold snaps.

Starting your dwarf grapes during these seasons ensures they have the best conditions for a robust start, setting the stage for successful fruit production in the coming growing season. Additionally, it helps synchronize their growth cycle with natural seasonal changes, leading to healthier plants and more bountiful harvests.

Plant Needs & Requirements

Germinating dwarf grapes from seeds to seedlings correctly is crucial when growing in containers and raised bed gardens because it establishes a strong foundation for the plant's overall health and productivity.

Proper germination techniques ensure that the plants develop robust root systems and vigorous growth habits, vital for thriving in the confined spaces of containers and the controlled environments of raised beds. By meticulously managing factors such as temperature, moisture, and soil quality during germination, you can significantly reduce the risk of diseases and promote uniform growth among seedlings. This initial care sets the stage for successful transplantation, minimizing transplant shock and enabling the young plants to adapt quickly to their new surroundings.

Ultimately, correctly germinated seedlings are more resilient and capable of producing higher yields of quality grapes, making the effort invested in this early stage essential for long-term success in container and raised bed gardening.

Germinating dwarf grapes from seeds requires patience and careful attention to detail. Begin by selecting high-quality seeds from a reputable source to ensure the best chances of successful germination. Before sowing, soak the seeds in warm water for 24 hours to soften the seed coat and enhance germination rates.

Next, prepare a seed-starting mix composed of sterile potting soil, perlite, and peat moss to provide a well-draining and nutrient-rich environment for the seeds. Fill seed trays or small pots with this mix and moisten it thoroughly before planting.

Sow the seeds about 1/4 inch deep into the prepared soil and cover them lightly. Place the seed trays or pots in a location that receives indirect sunlight and maintain consistent moisture levels without waterlogging the soil. To create a humid environment conducive to germination, cover the trays with a plastic dome or plastic wrap. This helps retain moisture and warmth, crucial factors for seed sprouting. Regularly check the soil moisture and air out the trays briefly each day to prevent mold growth.

The temperature is a critical factor in the successful germination of dwarf grape seeds. The optimal temperature range for germinating grape seeds is between 70°F and 85°F (21°C to 29°C). Maintaining these temperatures consistently can be achieved using a heat mat specifically designed for seed starting.

This constant warmth stimulates the seeds to break dormancy and begin the germination process. Under these ideal conditions, grape seeds generally take about 2 to 8 weeks to germinate, though some variability in timing is normal.

It's important to monitor the temperature closely, as fluctuations can delay or inhibit germination. If you are starting your seeds indoors during cooler months, placing the seed trays in a warm spot, like on top of a refrigerator or near a heating vent, can help maintain the necessary temperature range. Once the seeds have germinated and seedlings begin to appear, gradually acclimate them to lower temperatures to prepare them for eventual transplanting.

As the seedlings grow, they will develop their first set of true leaves, distinct from the initial seed leaves. This stage indicates that they are beginning to establish a root system and are ready for the next phase of growth. Continue to provide adequate light, either through natural sunlight or a grow light, ensuring they receive about 12-16 hours of light daily. Maintain consistent soil moisture and introduce a weak liquid fertilizer to support healthy development.

When the seedlings reach about 4-6 inches in height and possess several sets of true leaves, they are typically ready to be transplanted into larger containers or raised bed gardens. However, it's essential to harden off the seedlings before transplanting.

This process involves gradually exposing them to outdoor conditions over a week or two. Start by placing them outside in a sheltered location for a few hours each day, gradually increasing the time and exposure to direct sunlight. This acclimation helps reduce transplant shock and prepares the seedlings for the more variable outdoor environment.

Once the seedlings are hardened off and the danger of frost has passed, they are ready to be transplanted into their permanent growing containers or raised beds.

Spacing & Measurement

Spacing and measurements when transplanting dwarf grape seedlings into containers and raised bed gardens are crucial for several reasons. Proper spacing ensures that each plant receives adequate sunlight, air circulation, and room to grow, which are all essential for healthy development and robust fruit production.

In containers, overcrowding can lead to competition for nutrients and water, resulting in stunted growth and lower yields. In raised beds, insufficient spacing can promote the spread of diseases and pests, as closely planted vines create a humid microenvironment conducive to mold and mildew.

Additionally, appropriate spacing simplifies maintenance tasks such as pruning, watering, and harvesting by providing easy access to each plant. By paying careful attention to spacing and measurements during transplantation, you can create an environment conducive to the thriving of dwarf grapes plants, ultimately enhancing the success and enjoyment of your container and raised bed gardens.

When planting dwarf grapes in containers, ensuring the right spacing and measurements is essential for the plant's health and productivity. Each grapevine should be provided with sufficient space to grow and spread its roots comfortably.

A container with a minimum diameter of 18-24 inches and a depth of at least 15-20 inches is recommended for each dwarf grape plant. This size allows ample room for root development and provides stability for the plant as it matures. If using larger containers, such as half-barrels, multiple vines can be planted, but they should still be spaced about 3 feet apart within the container to avoid overcrowding and ensure each plant receives adequate light, air, and nutrients.

In addition to container size, it is important to consider the placement of the containers. They should be positioned in an area that receives at least 6-8 hours of direct sunlight daily, as grapevines thrive in sunny conditions.

Adequate spacing between containers is also necessary to maintain good air circulation, which helps prevent fungal diseases and promotes healthy foliage. A gap of about 2-3 feet between containers is advisable to ensure that the vines have enough room to grow laterally without interfering with one another. This spacing will also make it easier to access the plants for routine maintenance tasks like watering, pruning, and harvesting.

In raised bed gardens, the desired spacing and measurements for planting dwarf grapes are equally crucial to ensure optimal growth and yield. Raised beds should be prepared with a soil depth of at least 12-18 inches to accommodate the deep root systems of grapevines.

When planting multiple dwarf grape plants, spacing them 3-4 feet apart within the raised bed is recommended. This distance allows each vine to develop its canopy fully and ensures that the roots have enough space to expand without competing excessively for nutrients and water. Rows of grapevines should be spaced about 6-8 feet apart to facilitate air circulation and provide ample room for the plants to receive uniform sunlight exposure throughout the day.

Proper spacing in raised beds also aids in managing the microclimate around the plants. By allowing sufficient distance between plants, you can reduce humidity levels around the foliage, decreasing the likelihood of mildew and other fungal infections.

Well-spaced plants are easier to manage during fertilization, irrigation, and pest control activities, contributing to overall plant health and productivity. Trellising systems, often used in raised beds, should be designed to complement the spacing of the grapevines, providing support and guidance for vertical growth while maintaining the necessary gaps for air and light penetration.

When planning the spacing and measurements for planting dwarf grapes, it's essential to consider the long-term growth and maintenance of the plants. Grape vines can live for many years and grow vigorously once established. Therefore, initial spacing should account for the mature size of the vines to avoid future overcrowding.

Regular pruning and training will help manage the growth and maintain the desired shape and size of the plants, but adequate initial spacing provides the foundation for these maintenance practices to be effective.

In both containers and raised bed gardens, incorporating a staking or trellising system can optimize space utilization and support the vines as they grow. Trellises allow the grapevines to climb and spread vertically, promoting better air circulation and sunlight exposure while making efficient use of limited space.

For containers, portable trellises or stakes can be used, allowing you to move the containers without disrupting the plant structure. In raised beds, more permanent trellising systems can be installed to guide the growth and provide sturdy support for the vines over the years.

By paying careful attention to the desired spacing and measurements when planting dwarf grape seedlings, you can create a thriving environment that supports healthy growth, maximizes fruit production, and simplifies ongoing care and maintenance. Whether in containers or raised bed gardens, thoughtful planning and execution of spacing strategies are key to the long-term success and enjoyment of growing dwarf grapes.

Ideal Temperatures & Sun Requirements

The ideal temperatures and sun requirements are crucial for successfully growing dwarf grapes in containers and raised bed gardens, as they directly impact the plant's growth, fruit production, and overall health. Grapevines thrive in warm, sunny conditions, requiring at least 6-8 hours of direct sunlight daily to photosynthesize effectively and produce abundant, high-quality fruit.

Temperatures should generally range between 60°F and 85°F (15°C to 29°C) during the growing season, with optimal growth occurring in the 70°F to 80°F (21°C to 27°C) range. Consistently warm temperatures support vigorous vine growth, flowering, and fruit setting, while cooler temperatures can slow down these processes.

Extreme heat above 90°F (32°C) may cause heat stress, leading to wilting or sunburn on the leaves and fruit. In containers, positioning the plants in a location that receives ample sunlight but is protected from excessive afternoon heat can help maintain the ideal temperature range.

Similarly, raised bed gardens should be situated in an area with full sun exposure and good air circulation to prevent overheating and mitigate the risk of fungal diseases. By providing the right balance of sunlight and temperature, you can ensure your dwarf grapes flourish, yielding vibrant and flavorful grapes season after season.

MAINTAINING YOUR CONTAINER & RAISED BED DWARF GRAPE VINES

Maintaining your dwarf grapes in containers and raised bed gardens is essential for ensuring their long-term health, productivity, and resilience against pests and diseases. Regular maintenance tasks such as watering, pruning, fertilizing, and monitoring for signs of stress or illness help create an optimal growing environment that supports vigorous vine growth and abundant fruit production.

In containers, consistent care is crucial because the limited soil volume can quickly deplete nutrients and moisture, leading to potential deficiencies and poor plant performance. Similarly, raised beds, while offering better soil control, still require diligent upkeep to prevent weed competition, maintain soil fertility, and manage water drainage.

Pruning helps in shaping the vines, improving air circulation, and reducing the risk of fungal infections, while timely fertilization ensures that the plants receive the necessary nutrients for robust growth. Maintaining a regular care routine can address issues promptly, promote healthy development, and ultimately enjoy higher yields of quality grapes from your well-tended dwarf grape vines.

Pruning & Thinning Your Dwarf Grape Vines

Proper pruning and thinning of dwarf grape vines in containers and raised bed gardens offer numerous benefits that contribute to the overall success of your grape-growing endeavors. Regular pruning helps shape the vines and directs their energy towards producing strong, fruit-bearing canes, ultimately leading to more abundant and higher-quality harvests.

Thinning, on the other hand, prevents overcrowding and ensures that each grape cluster has access to sufficient nutrients and sunlight, enhancing the size and flavor of the fruit. These practices improve air circulation and reduce the risk of fungal diseases, promoting healthier plants.

Pruning dwarf grapes is best conducted during their dormant season, typically late winter to early spring, just before new growth begins. This timing allows for the removal of dead, diseased, or damaged wood without interfering with the plant's energy reserves, which are still stored in the roots and main stems.

Additionally, pruning at this time helps shape the vine structure and encourages the development of strong, productive canes that will bear fruit in the upcoming growing season. Summer pruning may also be necessary to manage vigorous growth, improve airflow, and ensure that sunlight penetrates the canopy efficiently. However, extensive pruning should be avoided during this period to prevent stressing the plants.

To prune dwarf grape vines effectively, start by sterilizing your pruning shears to prevent the spread of diseases. Begin by removing any dead, damaged, or diseased canes, cutting them back to healthy wood.

Next, focus on thinning out overcrowded areas to improve air circulation and light penetration, which helps reduce the risk of fungal infections and promotes healthier growth. Select 1-3 of the strongest canes to become the primary framework of the plant, cutting back these canes to about 3-6 buds each, depending on the vine's vigor and desired size.

Remove any suckers or shoots that emerge from the base of the plant or below the graft union, as these can sap energy from the main fruiting canes. Ensure that the remaining canes are well-spaced and not crossing or rubbing against each other, which can cause wounds and increase disease susceptibility.

Thinning dwarf grape vines is another vital task that should be carried out during the growing season, particularly in late spring to early summer when the young grapes begin to develop. Thinning involves selectively removing some grape clusters to prevent overcrowding and ensure the remaining clusters receive adequate nutrients and sunlight.

This practice is essential for producing larger, higher-quality grapes and preventing overloading of the vines, which can lead to structural damage and reduced fruit quality. Thinning also helps maintain the health of the plant by reducing the risk of fungal diseases that thrive in dense, humid conditions.

When thinning your dwarf grapes, carefully inspect each vine and identify clusters that are closely packed together or those showing signs of poor development. Using sterilized scissors or pruning shears, remove the smaller or less vigorous clusters, leaving a balanced number of well-spaced, healthy clusters on each cane.

Aim to retain one cluster per shoot and ensure that there is sufficient space between clusters to allow for air circulation and sunlight exposure. By doing so, you enhance the overall quality and size of the grapes, as the vine can concentrate its resources on fewer, more robust clusters. Additionally, thinning prevents the plants from becoming overburdened, leading to weaker vines and reduced yields in subsequent years.

By maintaining a disciplined approach to pruning and thinning, you can ensure that their dwarf grape vines remain vigorous, productive, and capable of delivering bountiful harvests season after season.

Watering Your Container & Raised Bed Dwarf Grape Vines

Watering dwarf grape vines, whether grown in containers or raised bed gardens, is a critical aspect of their care that directly impacts their growth, fruit development, and overall health. Given that grapevines have deep-rooted systems, they require consistent moisture to thrive, particularly during the growing season.

While these plants are relatively drought-tolerant compared to other fruiting species, insufficient watering can lead to stress, reduced fruit quality, and lower yields. Equally, over-watering can cause root rot and other fungal diseases. There-fore, understanding the precise watering needs and timing is essential for maintaining healthy and productive grapevines.

The best time to water dwarf grapes is early in the morning or late in the afternoon, allowing the plants to absorb the moisture before the day's heat evaporates. During the active growing season, from spring through late summer, dwarf grapevines require regular watering to support their vigorous growth and fruit development.

Early spring is a crucial period as new shoots and buds form, while the summer months demand increased attention to watering due to higher temperatures and potential drought conditions. As the grapes begin to ripen, typically late summer to early fall, it's important to moderate watering to avoid diluting the flavor and causing the fruit to split.

For container-grown dwarf grapes, maintaining consistent soil moisture is key. Containers tend to dry out faster than garden beds due to their limited soil volume and exposure to air on all sides. Water deeply until water begins to drain out of the bottom holes of the container, ensuring the entire root system gets hydrated.

Generally, watering once or twice a week is sufficient, but this can vary depending on weather conditions, container size, and the grapevine's growth stage. During prolonged hot or windy periods, you may need to increase watering frequency. It's also beneficial to mulch the surface of the soil in containers to help retain moisture and regulate soil temperature.

Raised bed-grown dwarf grape vines benefit from a similar deep watering approach to ensure that moisture reaches the deeper roots. Water the plants thoroughly, aiming for at least 6-12 inches of soil penetration with each watering session. Typically, watering every 7-10 days is adequate, but this can fluctuate based on rainfall, temperature, and plant growth demands.

Mulching around the base of the grapevines with organic materials such as straw or wood chips can significantly aid in moisture retention and weed suppression. Additionally, installing a drip irrigation system or soaker hoses in raised beds provides a consistent and efficient method for delivering water directly to the root zone, minimizing water wastage and reducing the risk of foliar diseases.

Regardless of the growing medium, consistently monitoring soil moisture levels is crucial for determining the exact watering needs of your dwarf grape plants. Using a soil moisture meter can help gauge the moisture content at different soil depths, offering precise insights into when to water.

Alternatively, a simple method involves sticking your finger about 2-3 inches into the soil; if it feels dry at this depth, it's time to water. Observing the plants themselves can also provide clues—wilting leaves or reduced growth may indicate that the grapevines are under-watered while yellowing leaves and overly wet soil suggest over-watering.

Proper water management for container and raised bed-grown dwarf grapes ensures that the plants receive the right amount of moisture to foster healthy growth, robust fruit production, and disease resistance. Consistent watering helps maintain soil structure and nutrient availability, critical for developing strong root systems and vibrant foliage.

By carefully timing and adjusting your watering practices based on seasonal changes and plant needs, you create an optimal environment that supports the grapevines through their various growth stages, leading to higher-quality fruit and more bountiful harvests.

Organic Fertilization For Container & Raised Bed Dwarf Grape Vines

Using organic fertilizers for dwarf grapes offers numerous benefits that contribute to the overall health and productivity of the plants. Organic fertilizers release nutrients slowly, aligning with the natural growth cycles of the grapevines and reducing the risk of nutrient leaching and runoff.

They also improve soil structure, increase water retention, and promote a healthy soil ecosystem by encouraging beneficial microbial activity. This holistic approach to plant nutrition results in stronger, more resilient grapevines that are better equipped to resist pests and diseases, leading to higher-quality fruit. Additionally, organic fertilizers are environmentally friendly and sustainable, supporting long-term soil health and reducing the reliance on synthetic chemicals.

Choosing the right organic fertilizer for dwarf grapes grown in containers and raised bed gardens is crucial for promoting healthy growth and maximizing fruit production. Organic fertilizers improve soil health by adding essential nutrients and enhancing microbial activity.

Common types of organic fertilizers suitable for grapevines include compost, well-rotted manure, bone meal, blood meal, and fish emulsion. Compost provides a balanced mix of nutrients and improves soil structure, while well-rotted manure adds nitrogen and beneficial microbes. Bone meal is an excellent source of phosphorus, which supports root development and flowering, whereas blood meal is rich in nitrogen, promoting leafy growth. Fish emulsion, a liquid fertilizer, offers a quick nutrient boost and contains a balanced mix of nitrogen, phosphorus, and potassium.

The timing of fertilization is critical to ensure that dwarf grapes receive nutrients when they need them most. The primary fertilization period begins in early spring, just as new buds start to swell and the vines begin to grow. This initial application sets the stage for robust growth and development throughout the growing season.

A second round of fertilization can be applied in late spring to early summer to support the rapid vegetative growth phase and fruit set. It's important to avoid fertilizing late in the growing season, particularly after mid-summer, as this can encourage new growth that may not harden off before winter, making the plants susceptible to frost damage.

When fertilizing dwarf grapes in containers, it's essential to consider the confined root space and limited soil volume. Begin by mixing organic fertilizer into the potting soil before planting. During the growing season, apply a balanced organic liquid fertilizer, such as fish emulsion, every 2-4 weeks following the recommended dilution rates. This frequent but light feeding method ensures that nutrients are consistently available without overloading the container's soil.

Additionally, top-dressing the soil with compost or worm castings in early spring and mid-summer can provide a slow-release nutrient source and enhance soil fertility. Always water the plants thoroughly after applying fertilizers to help distribute the nutrients evenly through the soil.

Fertilizing dwarf grapes in raised beds follows a similar approach but can accommodate more substantial amendments due to the larger soil volume. Start by incorporating compost or well-rotted manure into the top 6-12 inches of soil in early spring. This base layer provides essential nutrients and improves soil structure.

Throughout the growing season, side-dress the grapevines with organic fertilizers such as bone meal or blood meal, applying them around the drip line of the plants and gently working them into the soil. Liquid fertilizers like fish emulsion can be used every 3-4 weeks during the active growth period, providing a quick nutrient boost. Mulching with organic materials, such as straw or wood chips, helps retain moisture, suppress weeds, and gradually adds nutrients as it decomposes.

Regularly monitoring the health and growth of your dwarf grape vines is essential for adjusting fertilization practices as needed. Observing signs of nutrient deficiencies—such as yellowing leaves (nitrogen deficiency), poor flowering (phosphorus deficiency), or weak stems (potassium deficiency)—can guide you in tweaking your fertilization strategy.

Soil testing is another valuable tool that provides insights into the nutrient levels and pH of your soil, helping you make informed decisions about what additional amendments may be necessary.

By staying attuned to the needs of your plants and making adjustments accordingly, you can ensure that your dwarf grape vines receive the optimal nutrition required for vigorous growth and abundant harvests.

PROTECTING YOUR CONTAINER & RAISED BED DWARF GRAPE VINES

Extreme Temperatures

Protecting dwarf grapes from extreme temperatures is vital for their health, productivity, and survival. Grapevines are sensitive to both excessive heat and severe cold, which can cause significant stress, damage, or even death if not managed properly. High temperatures above 90°F (32°C) can lead to heat stress, causing wilting, sunburn on the leaves and fruit, and interrupted photosynthesis.

Equally, freezing temperatures can damage the vine's tissues, disrupt water uptake, and kill unprotected buds and canes. Ensuring that grapevines are shielded from these extremes helps maintain their growth cycles, supports consistent fruit production, and preserves the long-term vitality of the plants.

To protect dwarf grapes from extreme heat, especially in container gardens where soil can heat up quickly, consider several strategies. First, position containers in areas that receive morning sunlight but are shaded during the hottest part of the afternoon. Using materials like shade cloths or umbrellas can provide temporary relief from intense heat.

Mulching the soil surface with organic materials such as straw or wood chips can help retain moisture and keep the root zone cool. Watering deeply and consistently ensures that the plants have adequate hydration to withstand high temperatures. In extreme cases, moving containers to a cooler location, such as under a pergola or near a shaded wall, can be an effective way to mitigate heat stress.

For raised bed gardens, protecting dwarf grapes from cold temperatures involves a combination of insulation and strategic placement. Applying a thick layer of mulch around the base of the plants helps insulate the roots and retain soil warmth. In regions with harsh winters, consider using row covers, frost blankets, or even burlap wraps to shield the vines from freezing temperatures and cold winds.

Raised beds should be positioned in locations that receive maximum sunlight during the winter months, ideally with some wind protection from structures or natural barriers. For container-grown grapevines, moving the containers to sheltered areas such as garages, basements, or enclosed patios during extreme cold spells can prevent freezing damage. If indoor space is limited, clustering containers together and wrapping them with insulating materials like bubble wrap or old blankets can offer additional protection.

Regularly monitoring weather forecasts and staying informed about temperature fluctuations allows you to implement protective measures proactively. During sudden temperature changes, having materials like shade cloths or frost blankets readily available ensures a swift response to protect the grapevines. Additionally, maintaining healthy plants through proper watering, fertilization, and pruning enhances their resilience against temperature stress. Strong, well-nourished plants are better equipped to recover from adverse conditions compared to those already stressed by other factors.

By diligently protecting dwarf grape plants from extreme temperatures, you can enjoy long-term benefits, including healthier plants, consistent yields, and extended vine lifespan.

Protecting Container & Raised Bed Dwarf Grape Vines From Pests

Dwarf grapes grown in containers and raised beds are susceptible to various pests that can damage leaves, stems, and fruit, potentially compromising the plant's health and productivity. Some of the most common pests include aphids, spider mites, grape mealybugs, Japanese beetles, and grapevine moths. Aphids are tiny sap-sucking insects that can cause curled leaves and stunted growth, often leaving behind a sticky residue called honeydew.

Spider mites, which thrive in hot and dry conditions, create webbing on the undersides of leaves and can lead to leaf stippling and premature leaf drop. Grape mealybugs hide in clusters around stems and fruit, producing a white, cottony mass and feeding on plant sap, which weakens the vines. Japanese beetles are voracious eaters that skeletonize leaves, while grapevine moth larvae feed on foliage and can damage fruit clusters.

Protecting your dwarf grapes from aphids and spider mites involves a combination of preventive measures and organic treatments. Introducing beneficial insects such as ladybugs, lacewings, and predatory mites can help control aphid and spider mite populations naturally, as these predators feed on the pests. Regularly inspecting plants and manually removing infestations can also be effective; use a strong spray of water to dislodge aphids or wipe off spider mite webs with a damp cloth.

Applying insecticidal soap or neem oil is another organic method that disrupts the pest's life cycle without harming beneficial insects. These treatments should be applied early in the morning or late in the afternoon to avoid burning the foliage.

Grape mealybugs and Japanese beetles can be managed through vigilant monitoring and targeted organic interventions. For mealybugs, regular pruning to improve air circulation and reduce humidity around the plants can deter infestations. Remove and destroy any heavily infested plant parts.

Applying neem oil or horticultural oil can suffocate mealybugs and disrupt their development. Additionally, introducing beneficial insects such as parasitic wasps can naturally reduce mealybug populations. To combat Japanese beetles, handpicking and placing them in soapy water can be surprisingly effective for small infestations.

Utilizing row covers during peak beetle activity periods can protect the plants, though this method may not be practical for large growing areas. Beneficial nematodes can also be introduced into the soil to target the larvae stage of Japanese beetles, reducing future generations.

Grapevine moths and their larvae can be particularly damaging to both foliage and fruit. Monitoring for adult moths using pheromone traps can help identify when they are active and allow for timely intervention. Bacillus thuringiensis (Bt), a naturally occurring bacterium, is an effective organic treatment against caterpillars and larvae.

Spraying Bt on the foliage targets the larvae while being safe for humans, pets, and beneficial insects. Additionally, maintaining garden hygiene by removing fallen leaves and debris can reduce overwintering sites for moths and interrupt their life cycle.

Implementing preventive measures and adopting an integrated pest management (IPM) approach is key to organically protecting your dwarf grape plants. Start by selecting disease-resistant grape varieties and planting them in well-draining soil with good air circulation. Regularly inspect your plants for signs of pests and stress, addressing issues promptly to prevent larger infestations.

Interplanting with companion plants like marigolds, garlic, and chives can deter pests through natural repellents. Maintaining a healthy ecosystem by encouraging biodiversity and avoiding the overuse of chemical pesticides supports the presence of beneficial insects that keep pest populations in check.

Using organic methods to protect your dwarf grape vines from pests offers numerous advantages, including maintaining the health and safety of the environment, preserving beneficial insect populations, and promoting sustainable gardening practices. Organic pest control methods minimize the risk of harmful chemical residues on your fruit, ensuring that your harvest is safe for consumption.

By fostering a balanced ecosystem and utilizing natural predators and organic treatments, you can effectively manage pest populations while supporting the overall health and resilience of your grapevines. This holistic approach not only protects your plants but also contributes to a thriving garden environment that benefits all its inhabitants.

Protecting Container & Raised Bed Dwarf Grape Vines From Diseases

Dwarf grapes grown in containers and raised beds are susceptible to various diseases that can hinder their growth, reduce fruit quality, and even lead to plant death if not managed properly. Some of the most common diseases include powdery mildew, downy mildew, black rot, and botrytis bunch rot. Powdery mildew manifests as a white, powdery coating on leaves, stems, and fruit, causing distorted growth and reduced photosynthesis.

Downy mildew appears as yellowish, oily spots on the upper leaf surfaces with a corresponding white, fuzzy growth on the undersides. Black rot presents as dark, sunken lesions on leaves, shoots, and berries, leading to fruit shriveling and significant yield loss. Botrytis bunch rot, also known as gray mold, affects the fruit clusters, causing them to rot and develop a grayish mold.

Preventing and managing powdery and downy mildew organically involves a combination of cultural practices and natural treatments. To prevent powdery mildew, ensure good air circulation by spacing plants appropriately and pruning regularly to remove overcrowded canes and foliage.

Applying a homemade spray consisting of baking soda (1 tablespoon) and water (1 gallon) with a few drops of liquid soap can effectively control powdery mildew when applied weekly. Neem oil, sulfur, and potassium bicarbonate are other organic options that help manage the disease. For downy mildew, avoid overhead watering to minimize leaf wetness and water early in the day so foliage dries quickly. Copper-based fungicides, applied preventatively, can help control downy mildew outbreaks. Remember to rotate treatments to prevent resistance buildup.

Black rot requires diligent monitoring and early intervention to prevent significant damage. Pruning and removing infected plant parts as soon as symptoms appear is crucial in reducing the spread of the disease. Dispose of all affected plant debris away from the garden to prevent re-infection.

Apply organic fungicides such as copper or sulfur-based products at the first sign of disease and continue treatment during humid conditions, which favor black rot development. Maintaining garden hygiene by clearing fallen leaves and pruning clippings can further minimize the presence of the fungus in the environment.

Botrytis bunch rot thrives in moist, humid conditions, making it essential to keep the grape clusters dry. Pruning the vines to improve air circulation and sunlight penetration reduces humidity around the fruit. Avoid overhead irrigation, especially during the fruiting stage; instead, use drip irrigation or soaker hoses to water directly at the soil level.

Regularly inspect clusters and remove any damaged or diseased grapes to prevent the spread of botrytis. Applying Bacillus subtilis, a beneficial bacterium, as a foliar spray can help control botrytis bunch rot naturally by outcompeting the pathogen on the plant surfaces.

Implementing preventive measures and an integrated disease management approach is essential for maintaining healthy dwarf grapes. Start by choosing disease-resistant grape varieties suitable for your local climate and growing conditions. Ensure proper planting techniques, such as well-draining soil and adequate spacing, to minimize stress and enhance plant vigor. Regularly monitor your plants for early signs of disease, allowing for prompt action to prevent severe outbreaks.

Crop rotation and diversifying plantings in raised beds can reduce disease pressure by interrupting pathogen life cycles. Additionally, applying compost and organic mulches boosts soil health and microbial activity, which can help suppress soil-borne diseases.

In summary organic disease management offers numerous benefits, including promoting environmental sustainability, enhancing soil health, and producing safer, chemical-free fruit. By relying on natural treatments and cultural practices, you minimize the risk of harmful chemical residues on your plants and the surrounding ecosystem.

Organic methods encourage biodiversity and support beneficial organisms that contribute to a balanced and resilient garden environment. Moreover, healthy, disease-free grapevines are better equipped to withstand other stresses, such as pests and adverse weather conditions, leading to more robust growth and higher-quality yields. Embracing organic disease management practices ensures that your dwarf grape vines remain productive and thriving, providing bountiful harvests season after season.

HARVESTING CONTAINER & RAISED BED DWARF GRAPE VINES

Growing dwarf grape vines is a rewarding endeavor, but it requires patience as the vines take time to mature and produce fruit. Typically, it takes about 2 to 3 years for newly planted dwarf grape plants to reach a stage where they can produce a significant harvest. The exact timeline can vary based on factors such as the grape variety, growing conditions, and care practices.

In the first year, the focus should be on establishing strong roots and healthy vine growth rather than expecting substantial fruit production. By the second year, some small clusters of grapes may appear, but it is often recommended to remove these early fruits to encourage the plant to focus on vegetative growth and root establishment.

By the third year, grapevines are usually mature enough to produce a full crop. During this period, the plants will have developed a robust framework of canes capable of supporting many grape clusters. Optimal growing conditions, including adequate sunlight, proper watering, and regular fertilization with organic materials, contribute significantly to the time it takes for the vines to reach maturity and the quality of the fruit produced. You should remain vigilant about pest and disease management during these formative years to ensure the vines grow without setbacks.

The readiness of grapes for harvest is determined by several indicators, including color, taste, and sugar content. Different grape varieties have distinct colors when ripe, ranging from green and yellow to red and purple. Visual assessment is a primary method to estimate ripeness, but it should be complemented by taste testing. Ripe grapes will have a rich, sweet flavor with the characteristic taste of the variety being grown. Berries should also feel firm but yield slightly under gentle pressure.

Another reliable method to determine ripeness is measuring the sugar content using a refractometer, an instrument that assesses the Brix level (a measure of sugar concentration). Most grape varieties are ready for harvest when they reach a Brix level of 18-24, depending on the type and intended use (e.g., table grapes or wine grapes). Regularly testing a few berries from different clusters ensures that the entire crop is uniformly ripe before harvesting.

Harvesting from container and raised bed grown dwarf grapes requires care to avoid damaging the fruit and the plant. Use clean, sharp pruning shears or grape scissors to cut the grape clusters from the vine. Make the cut above the cluster stem, leaving a small portion of the stem attached to the bunch to help preserve the fruit's freshness. Handle the clusters gently to prevent bruising or crushing the berries, which can accelerate spoilage.

For smaller-scale harvesting, such as in a home garden, picking individual clusters as they ripen is feasible. However, for a larger harvest, consider harvesting all the ripe clusters at once and storing them in a cool, shaded area. It's best to harvest grapes in the early morning when temperatures are cooler, as this helps maintain the fruit's firmness and prolongs its shelf life.

Proper post-harvest handling and storage of grapes are crucial to maintaining their quality and extending their usability. After harvesting, rinse the grapes gently in cool water to remove any dirt or residues.

Allow them to dry thoroughly before storage to prevent mold growth. Store fresh grapes in a refrigerator, ideally in perforated plastic bags or shallow containers covered with a damp cloth to maintain humidity. This storage method can keep the grapes fresh for up to two weeks.

For long-term storage, grapes can be processed into various products such as jams, jellies, and juices or dried into raisins. If you plan to make wine, ensure that the grapes are kept at optimal conditions to preserve their flavors and sugar content until they can be processed.

By following these harvesting and post-harvest techniques, you can enjoy the fruits of your labor and maximize the yield and quality of your container and raised bed grown dwarf grape vines.

CONTAINER & RAISED BEDS DWARF GRAPES NOTES

Start: Seeds or Seedlings.

Germination: 2 – 8 weeks, at temperatures between 70°F and 85°F (21°C to 29°C).

Seed Life: 1 - 5 Years.

Soil Type: Well-draining, fertile, loamy soil with a slightly acidic to neutral pH (6.0 to 7.0), enriched with organic matter such as compost, and light in texture to ensure proper aeration and root development.

Seed Spacing: Sow the seeds about 1/4 inch deep.

Seedling Spacing:

Containers – A container with a minimum diameter of 18-24 inches and a depth of at least 15-20 inches.

Raised Bed - Space seedlings 3-4 feet apart - Rows of grapevines should be spaced about 6-8 feet apart.

Sunlight: 6 – 8hrs full sunlight daily.

Growing Temperatures:

Dwarf Grapes thrive in temperatures ranging between 60°F and 85°F (15°C to 29°C) during the growing season, with optimal growth occurring in the 70°F to 80°F (21°C to 27°C) range.

Duration Till Harvest:

Dwarf grape plants takes about 2 to 3 years for newly planted dwarf grapes to reach a stage where they can produce a significant harvest. The exact timeline can vary based on factors such as the grape variety, growing conditions, and care practices.

In the first year, the focus should be on establishing strong roots and healthy vine growth rather than expecting substantial fruit production.

The second year, some small clusters of grapes may appear, but it is often recommended to remove these early fruits to encourage the plant to focus on vegetative growth and root establishment.

By the third year, grapevines are usually mature enough to produce a full crop.

CHAPTER 11
VINE FRUITS: CONTAINER & RAISED BED GARDENS – PASSION FRUIT

G rowing passion fruit in containers and raised beds offers an exciting and efficient way to enjoy this exotic and versatile fruit, even in limited spaces. This approach not only maximizes space but also simplifies maintenance, allowing gardeners to control soil quality, drainage, and other growing conditions more effectively. Passion fruit is highly prized for its unique, tropical flavor, making it a favorite ingredient in various culinary delights, from refreshing beverages to delectable desserts. Beyond its delicious fruit, the passion fruit bush enhances garden aesthetics with its lush green foliage and captivating, vibrant flowers.

One of the primary advantages of growing passion fruit in containers and raised beds is space efficiency. This method allows gardeners to cultivate these exotic plants even in small or non-traditional garden spaces like patios, balconies, or urban settings. Containers and raised beds provide superior control over soil quality, enabling the creation of an optimal growing medium that can be tailored to the specific needs of passion fruit plants.

This method also simplifies maintenance tasks such as watering and fertilization, as well as improves pest management by reducing the likelihood of soil-borne diseases and making it easier to apply organic treatments. Additionally, containers and raised beds facilitate better temperature regulation and mobility, allowing gardeners to move the plants to protected areas during extreme weather conditions.

Beyond practical benefits, these growing methods add aesthetic appeal, creating an attractive and functional garden space that showcases the vibrant foliage and striking fruits of the passion fruit.

THE RIGHT SOIL TO GROW PASSION FRUIT IN CONTAINER & RAISED BEDS

Growing passion fruit in containers and raised bed gardens requires careful attention to soil conditions to ensure healthy growth and prolific fruit production. One of the most critical factors is well-draining soil. Passion fruit plants are susceptible to root rot if their roots remain waterlogged, so the soil must allow excess water to drain away quickly.

A sandy loam or a well-draining potting mix is ideal. Incorporating materials like sand, perlite, or fine gravel into the soil can improve drainage. Raised beds naturally enhance drainage, making them an excellent choice for passion fruit cultivation.

The pH level of the soil is another essential consideration. Passion fruits thrive in slightly acidic to neutral soil, with an ideal pH range of 5.5 to 6.5. Soil that is too acidic or alkaline can inhibit nutrient uptake, leading to poor plant health. Soil testing kits are readily available and can help you determine the current pH level of your soil.

If the soil is too acidic, adding lime can help raise the pH. Equally, if the soil is too alkaline, incorporating sulfur or organic matter like peat moss can help lower the pH to the desired range.

Nutrient-rich soil is crucial for the vigorous growth of passion fruit plants. These plants are heavy feeders and require a steady supply of nutrients to support their rapid growth and fruit production. Adding compost or well-rotted manure to the soil can significantly enhance its fertility by providing essential nutrients and improving soil structure. Organic matter helps retain moisture and supports beneficial microbial activity, which is vital for nutrient cycling and overall soil health.

To further improve soil fertility, you can incorporate balanced organic fertilizers that provide a mix of nitrogen, phosphorus, and potassium. Nitrogen promotes leafy growth, phosphorus supports root development and flowering, and potassium enhances overall plant health and fruit quality. Regularly amending the soil with compost and organic fertilizers ensures that passion fruit plants receive a continuous supply of nutrients throughout the growing season.

Maintaining consistent moisture levels is essential for the health of passion fruits. Mulching is a highly effective practice that helps retain soil moisture, regulate soil temperature, and suppress weed growth. Organic mulches like straw, wood chips, or shredded leaves are excellent choices. Apply a layer of mulch around the base of the plants, but ensure it doesn't touch the stems to prevent stem rot.

While passion fruit plants require regular watering, it's important to avoid overwatering. Allow the top inch of soil to dry out between waterings to prevent waterlogged conditions that can lead to root rot. Containers and raised beds tend to dry out more quickly than in-ground gardens, so monitoring soil moisture levels is crucial. Self-watering containers or drip irrigation systems can help maintain consistent moisture levels and reduce the risk of water stress.

Regular soil testing is a valuable practice that helps gardeners understand the nutrient composition and pH of their soil. Soil tests can identify nutrient deficiencies or imbalances that may affect plant health. Based on the test results, you can make informed decisions about soil amendments and fertilization practices. For example, if the soil test indicates a deficiency in a specific nutrient, targeted organic fertilizers can be applied to address the deficiency.

Adjusting soil conditions based on test results helps create an optimal growing environment for passion fruit plants. By maintaining well-draining, nutrient-rich soil with the appropriate pH and consistent moisture levels, you can support the healthy growth and abundant fruiting of your passion fruit plants. This attention to soil conditions not only enhances the productivity of the plants but also contributes to a more sustainable and environmentally friendly gardening approach.

HOW TO SOW PASSION FRUIT IN CONTAINERS & RAISED BEDS GARDENS

Correct Season To Sow Passion Fruit In Containers & Raised Beds Gardens

The correct season to sow passion fruits in containers and raised bed gardens is typically during the spring, once the danger of frost has passed and temperatures consistently remain above 60°F (15°C). Passion fruit thrives in warm, sunny conditions, making spring the ideal time for sowing as the plants can benefit from the increasing daylight and warming soil temperatures, which are crucial for successful germination and vigorous growth.

For regions with mild winters, late winter sowing might also be feasible, but always consider the regional climate. In cooler areas, starting seeds indoors or using a greenhouse can help extend the growing season by providing a controlled, warm environment that mimics spring conditions.

Proper timing is essential to align the plant's lifecycle with the growing season, ensuring that it has enough time to establish, grow, and produce fruit before the onset of cooler temperatures in autumn. By sowing at the right time, you can maximize the health and productivity of passion fruit plants, leading to a more bountiful harvest.

Plant Needs & Requirements

Properly germinating passion fruits from seeds to seedlings is crucial when growing in containers and raised bed gardens due to its significant impact on overall plant health, growth, and fruit production. Correct germination practices ensure that the plants develop strong root systems, which are essential for nutrient uptake and stability in confined spaces.

Healthy seedlings are more resistant to diseases and pests, making them well-suited for the unique challenges of container and raised bed gardening. Starting with robust seedlings leads to better adaptability and resilience in their new environment, which translates to vigorous growth and higher fruit yields.

Additionally, well-germinated seedlings require less maintenance, reducing your workload while maximizing productivity. Establishing a solid foundation through proper germination ultimately supports successful gardening, even in limited spaces, ensuring a thriving and fruitful passion fruit garden.

Germinating passion fruit from seeds is a rewarding process that begins with proper seed preparation. Start by extracting seeds from a ripe passion fruit, cleaning off any pulp, and allowing them to dry for a day or two. Soaking the seeds in warm water for 24 hours can help soften the seed coat and enhance germination.

For the best results, plant the seeds in a well-draining seed-starting mix, spaced about an inch apart, and cover them lightly with soil. Water the seeds gently to moisten the soil evenly, being careful not to overwater.

Passion fruit seeds germinate best at temperatures between 70°F and 85°F (21°C to 29°C). Maintaining a consistent warm environment is crucial during this stage, so consider using a heat mat or placing the seed trays in a warm spot to ensure optimal conditions. Germination can take anywhere from 2 to

4 weeks, depending on the temperature and seed viability. During this period, keep the soil moist but not waterlogged and provide indirect light to encourage robust and healthy growth.

Seedlings are ready to be transplanted into containers or raised bed gardens when they have developed a strong root system and at least two sets of true leaves. Healthy seedlings will exhibit vibrant green foliage and sturdy stems. Gently check the root system by lifting a seedling from its container; if the roots hold the soil together and are not overly bound, the seedling is ready for transplanting. Before moving seedlings outdoors, it's essential to acclimate them to their new environment gradually.

To acclimate seedlings, begin by placing them outside in a sheltered, shaded area for a few hours each day, gradually increasing their exposure to sunlight and outdoor conditions over a week or two. This process, known as hardening off, helps prevent transplant shock and ensures the seedlings can withstand outdoor temperatures and conditions.

When transplanting, choose a well-draining soil mix enriched with compost to provide the necessary nutrients. Dig holes large enough to accommodate the root ball, place the seedlings in the holes, and gently firm the soil around them. Water thoroughly to help settle the soil and establish good root-to-soil contact.

After transplanting, continue to monitor the seedlings closely, especially during the first few weeks. Provide consistent moisture without overwatering, and consider using mulch to retain soil moisture and regulate temperature. If necessary, protect young plants from pests and extreme weather conditions by using row covers or other protective measures.

Spacing & Measurement

Proper spacing and measurements are essential when trans-planting passion fruit seedlings into fruit containers and raised bed gardens to ensure optimal plant health, growth, and fruit production. Adequate spacing allows each plant to receive sufficient sunlight, which is crucial for photosynthesis and healthy development. Proper air circulation around the plants reduces the likelihood of fungal diseases and pest infestations, promoting a healthier garden environment.

Additionally, correct measurements prevent overcrowding, minimizing competition for vital resources such as water and nutrients, which are especially limited in containers and raised beds. By ensuring each plant has enough room to grow, you can foster robust root systems and stronger plants, leading to increased fruit yields. Ultimately, proper spacing contributes to a more productive and low-maintenance garden, enhancing the overall success and sustainability of growing passion fruit in confined spaces.

For container gardening, each passion fruit seedling should be planted in a large container with a minimum diameter of 18 to 24 inches to provide sufficient space for root develop-ment. This ensures that the roots have enough room to spread out and absorb nutrients effectively.

The depth of the container should also be at least 12 inches to accommodate the deep root system of passion fruit plants. It's essential to use well-draining soil and place the containers in a location where they will receive at least six to eight hours of sunlight daily.

In raised bed gardens, spacing between passion fruit seedlings should be more generous to account for their vigorous growth and sprawling nature. Plant the seedlings approximately 8 to 10 feet apart within the raised beds. This spacing allows each plant ample room to grow and ensures that they do not compete for resources such as light, water, and nutrients.

Proper spacing also facilitates good air circulation, vital for preventing fungal diseases and promoting overall plant health. When arranging the plants, consider their climbing habit and the need for support structures like trellises or stakes.

Given passion fruit's climbing nature, incorporating trellises or stakes in your planting layout is essential. Position these supports close to the seedlings at the time of planting to guide their vertical growth. This not only saves space but also helps in managing the vines more efficiently, making it easier to prune and harvest the fruit. For container setups, place the container near a sturdy fence or install a trellis directly into the pot. In raised beds, ensure the trellis is firmly anchored into the ground and can support the weight of the mature vines laden with fruit.

Beyond the physical spacing, it's important to plan for the future growth of the passion fruit plant. By anticipating their mature size and providing adequate support structures, you can maintain a neat and productive garden. Regularly training the vines to climb the trellises and pruning any excess growth will help in maintaining the desired shape and prevent overcrowding.

These measures not only optimize space but also improve air circulation and sunlight penetration, contributing to healthier plants and higher yields. Proper planning and execution of spacing and measurements ensure that your passion fruit plants thrive, resulting in a bountiful and manageable garden.

Ideal Temperatures & Sun Requirements

Maintaining ideal temperatures and sun requirements is essential when growing passion fruits in containers and raised bed gardens, as these factors significantly influence plant health, growth, and fruit production. Passion fruit plants thrive best in temperatures between 64°F and 77°F, with optimal growth occurring at around 68°F to 75°F. Consistent exposure to full sunlight for at least 6 to 8 hours a day is crucial, as it drives photosynthesis, leading to vigorous growth and abundant fruiting.

Temperature fluctuations, especially prolonged exposure to temperatures below 50°F or above 90°F, can stress the plants, hindering their growth and reducing fruit yield. Inadequate sunlight can result in weak, leggy growth and poor fruit development.

Ensuring passion fruit plants receive the right temperature and sunlight conditions, you can promote robust, healthy plants that are capable of producing generous harvests, ultimately achieving a more successful and rewarding gardening experience.

MAINTAINING YOUR CONTAINER & RAISED BED PASSION FRUIT GARDENS

Maintaining passion fruits in fruit containers and raised bed gardens is crucial for ensuring their health, growth, and prolific fruit production. Regular maintenance tasks, such as consistent watering, proper pruning, fertilizing, and vigilant pest control, play a significant role in promoting vigorous plant development and bountiful yields.

Watering ensures the plants receive adequate moisture, preventing stress and supporting robust growth. Pruning helps manage the plant's shape, removing dead or over-crowded branches to encourage better air circulation and light penetration. Fertilizing replenishes essential nutrients in the soil, fostering optimal growth and fruiting. Pest control protects the plants from harmful insects and diseases that can stifle development and reduce fruit quality. Neglecting these maintenance practices can lead to stunted growth, lower fruit yields, and increased vulnerability to pests and diseases.

Dedicating time and effort to regular care, you can enjoy the long-term benefits of healthy, productive passion fruits, resulting in a more successful and fulfilling gardening experience.

Pruning & Thinning Your Passion Fruits

Pruning and thinning passion fruit plants grown in containers and raised bed gardens are essential for maintaining optimal plant health, promoting vigorous growth, and maximizing fruit production. These practices significantly enhance air circulation and sunlight penetration, which is critical for preventing fungal infections and supporting photosynthesis. By removing dead, damaged, or overcrowded branches, pruning helps manage the size and shape of the plants, making them easier to care for and harvest.

Thinning out dense foliage also redirects the plant's energy toward producing high-quality fruit instead of maintaining excessive leaves and vines. Regular pruning and thinning reduce competition for nutrients and water, leading to more robust and productive plants.

In the long term, these practices contribute to a healthier, more manageable garden that continually yields abundant and high-quality passion fruit, ensuring the sustainability and success of your gardening efforts.

Pruning and thinning passion plants are essential tasks that should be carefully timed and executed to promote optimal plant health and fruit production. The best time to prune passion fruits is during late winter or early spring before new growth begins. This timing allows the plant to recover quickly and encourages strong new growth as the growing season starts. Light pruning can also be done mid-season to manage growth and remove any damaged or diseased branches.

When pruning and thinning, it is important to use clean, sharp tools such as pruning shears or loppers to make precise cuts and minimize damage to the plant. Begin by removing any dead, diseased, or damaged branches, cutting back to healthy wood or the main stem.

Next, thin out overcrowded areas by selectively removing branches that are crossing or competing for space. Aim to create an open structure that allows light to penetrate and air to circulate freely through the plant canopy, which can reduce the risk of fungal diseases and help the plant thrive.

Identifying branches that need to be removed involves looking for signs of poor health or structural issues. For example, branches that are weak, spindly, or growing at awkward angles should be pruned to improve the overall shape and strength of the plant.

Additionally, any shoots growing from the base of the plant, known as suckers, should be removed to prevent them from sapping energy from the main vine. By focusing on shaping the plant and removing unnecessary growth, you can direct the plant's energy towards producing more and higher-quality fruit.

To maintain plant health and maximize fruit production through effective pruning and thinning, it is important to follow best practices and monitor the plant's response. After pruning, keep an eye on the plant for any signs of stress or disease, and provide adequate water and nutrients to support its recovery and growth. Regularly inspecting and main-taining the plant will help ensure that it remains healthy and productive throughout the growing season.

Watering Your Container & Raised Bed Passion Fruit Gardens

Watering passion fruit plants grown in containers and raised bed gardens is vital for maintaining optimal plant health, ensuring vigorous growth, and achieving high fruit production. Proper watering facilitates nutrient absorption, which is essential for robust plant development and the production of sweet, juicy fruits.

Water also plays a critical role in photosynthesis, the process by which plants convert sunlight into energy, and helps maintain the plant's structure by keeping cells turgid. Inconsistent watering can lead to severe consequences; underwatering causes stress, leading to wilted leaves and poor fruit set, while overwatering can result in root rot and fungal diseases.

Consistent and adequate watering ensures that the plant's roots can access the necessary moisture without drowning, promoting a balanced growth environment. Long-term, proper watering practices contribute to a thriving, productive garden, ensuring that the passion fruit plant remain healthy and continues to produce bountiful harvests season after season.

Watering passion fruits grown in containers and raised bed gardens requires careful attention to ensure optimal plant health and fruit production. The frequency and quantity of watering depend on various factors, including climate, soil type, and plant size. In general, passion fruits prefer consistently moist, well-drained soil.

During the growing season, which is typically spring through fall, it's important to water the plants deeply and regularly. Aim to provide about 1-2 inches of water per week, either from rainfall or supplemental watering. In hotter climates or during periods of drought, this amount may need to be increased to prevent the soil from drying out completely.

Monitoring soil moisture levels is essential to avoid the pitfalls of both overwatering and underwatering. Overwatering can lead to root rot and other fungal diseases, while underwatering can stress the plant, causing wilting and reduced fruit production.

To check soil moisture, insert your finger about an inch into the soil; if it feels dry, it's time to water. Using a moisture meter can also help provide more accurate readings. Watering should be done in the early morning or late afternoon to reduce evaporation and allow water to penetrate the soil effectively.

Mulching is a beneficial practice for retaining soil moisture and regulating soil temperature. Apply a layer of organic mulch, such as straw or wood chips, around the base of the plant, being careful not to let it touch the stem. Mulch helps prevent water loss through evaporation and can reduce the frequency of watering, especially during hot summer months. It also suppresses weeds, which can compete with passion fruit plants for water and nutrients.

Different growth stages and seasonal changes require adjustments in watering practices. Young fruit plants need more frequent watering to establish their root systems, while mature plants may require less frequent but deeper watering. During flowering and fruiting stages, consistent moisture is crucial to support the development of high-quality fruits. In winter, when the plants are less active, reduce the watering frequency but ensure the soil does not dry out completely.

By following these guidelines and paying close attention to the specific needs of your plants you can create an environment that supports vigorous growth and bountiful fruit production. Regularly monitoring soil moisture, adjusting watering practices based on plant and environmental conditions, and employing techniques like mulching will help ensure your passion fruits thrive in containers and raised bed gardens.

Organic Fertilization For Container & Raised Bed Passion Fruit Gardens

Organic fertilization is crucial for passion fruits grown in containers and raised bed gardens due to its numerous benefits for both soil and plant health. Organic fertilizers, derived from natural sources such as compost, manure, and bone meal, enrich the soil with essential nutrients slowly and steadily, promoting robust plant growth and enhanced fruit production.

The application of organic materials improves soil structure by increasing its ability to retain moisture and nutrients, which is particularly beneficial in the confined spaces of containers and raised beds. Additionally, organic fertilizers boost microbial activity in the soil, fostering a thriving ecosystem that supports healthy root development and nutrient uptake. Unlike chemical fertilizers, organic options minimize the risk of harmful chemical runoff, ensuring a safer and more sustainable gardening practice.

The use of organic fertilizers not only contributes to the long-term health and productivity of passion fruit plants but also enhances the nutritional quality of the fruit, offering a more wholesome and eco-friendly approach to gardening.

Passion fruit plants benefit significantly from the use of organic fertilizers, which provide essential nutrients in a sustainable and eco-friendly manner. Some of the most effective organic fertilizers include compost, manure, bone meal, and fish emulsion. Compost is an excellent all-purpose fertilizer that enhances soil structure, increases microbial activity, and provides a balanced supply of nutrients.

Manure, particularly well-aged composted manure, is rich in nitrogen and helps promote vigorous growth. Bone meal is a great source of phosphorus, essential for strong root development and flowering. Fish emulsion, a liquid fertilizer, offers a quick nutrient boost and is particularly useful during the growing season.

The timing and method of applying organic fertilizers are crucial for maximizing their benefits. During the early stages of growth, passion fruits require a higher nitrogen content to support leafy growth. Compost and manure should be incorporated into the soil at planting time and can be top-dressed throughout the growing season.

As the plants begin to flower and set fruit, switching to fertilizers high in phosphorus and potassium, such as bone meal and fish emulsion, promotes healthy blooms and fruit development. Applying bone meal at the base of the plant and fish emulsion as a foliar spray ensures that the nutrients are readily available.

Frequency and quantity of application are also important to avoid over-fertilization, which can harm the plants. Generally, compost and manure can be applied once or twice a year, while bone meal and fish emulsion can be used more frequently, around every 4-6 weeks during the growing season. It is essential to follow the recommended application rates on the fertilizer packaging and to monitor the plants for any signs of nutrient imbalances, such as yellowing leaves or stunted growth.

Balancing nutrients is vital for the health of passion fruit plants. Organic fertilizers contribute to a sustainable gardening practice by slowly releasing nutrients, reducing the risk of nutrient runoff, and improving the overall soil health. This balanced approach ensures that the plants receive a steady supply of essential nutrients, promoting long-term growth and productivity.

Using organic fertilizers not only supports the immediate health and yield of passion fruits but also enhances the soil ecosystem, leading to healthier plants and more bountiful harvests in the future.

The use of organic fertilizers is a sustainable way to maintain healthy and productive fruits and by understanding the types of organic fertilizers available and knowing when and how to apply them, you can ensure your plants receive the necessary nutrients throughout their growth stages. This approach not only benefits the plants but also promotes a healthier garden environment that can sustain fruitful harvests for years to come.

PROTECTING YOUR CONTAINER & RAISED BED PASSION FRUIT GARDENS

Extreme Temperatures

Protecting passion fruits grown in containers and raised bed gardens from extreme temperatures is crucial for ensuring their health, growth, and fruit production. Extreme heat can cause significant stress to passion fruit, leading to leaf scorch, flower drop, and reduced fruit set. Equally, cold temperatures can damage the plant tissues, impede growth, and even kill young or tender plants. Therefore, implementing strategies to shield your passion fruit plants from temperature extremes is vital for maintaining their vigor and productivity.

To protect your plants from high temperatures, consider using shade cloths or other shading materials to reduce the intensity of direct sunlight. This is especially important during the peak of summer when temperatures can soar. Shade cloths can be draped over the plants or installed as temporary structures around your garden.

Additionally, mulching around the base of the plants helps to regulate soil temperature and retain moisture, which can alleviate heat stress. Organic mulches like straw, wood chips, or grass clippings are effective options. For container-grown plants, relocating them to a shaded or partially shaded area during the hottest part of the day can also prevent heat damage.

Cold temperatures, particularly frost, pose a significant risk to passion fruit plants. To protect your plants during cold snaps, cover them with frost cloths, blankets, or burlap sacks during the night when temperatures are lowest. These coverings provide insulation and help retain heat around the plant.

For containers, consider moving the plants to a sheltered location, such as a greenhouse, garage, or indoors, where they can be shielded from freezing temperatures. Another effective strategy is to group containers together in a protected area, which can create a microclimate that is slightly warmer than the surrounding environment.

Maintaining optimal temperature conditions is essential to prevent plant stress and damage. Stress from extreme temperatures can weaken passion fruit plants, making them more susceptible to pests and diseases. It can also disrupt the plant's physiological processes, leading to poor growth and decreased fruit yields.

Monitoring and adjusting environmental conditions are key to the well-being of your passion fruit plants. Use a thermometer to track temperature changes in your garden and take action when necessary. For instance, during a heatwave, increase watering frequency to help plants cope with the additional stress.

In contrast, during cold spells, reduce watering to prevent excess moisture from freezing and damaging the roots. Regularly check weather forecasts to anticipate extreme temperatures and prepare your protective measures in advance.

By proactively protecting your plants from extreme temperatures, you can create a stable and supportive environment that promotes vigorous growth and abundant fruiting. These efforts will not only enhance the immediate health and productivity of your plants but also contribute to their long-term resilience and success in your container and raised bed gardens.

Protecting Container & Raised Bed Passion Fruits From Pests

Protecting passion fruits from pests organically is crucial for several reasons. Organic pest control methods help preserve beneficial insects like ladybugs and predatory mites, which naturally keep harmful pest populations in check. These practices also maintain soil health by avoiding the introduction of synthetic chemicals that can disrupt the soil ecosystem and leave harmful residues.

By using organic methods, you contribute to a sustainable and eco-friendly approach, ensuring that the garden remains a safe and healthy environment for both plants and wildlife. Long-term, organic pest control enhances plant health and fruit quality, promoting vigorous growth and bountiful harvests without the adverse effects associated with chemical treatments. Aligning with the principles of sustainable agriculture, organic pest management supports a balanced garden ecosystem and fosters a more resilient and productive garden overall.

Passion fruits grown in containers and raised bed gardens are vulnerable to various pests that can severely impact their health and productivity. Among the common pests are aphids, fruit flies, and spider mites. Aphids are tiny, sap-sucking insects that typically gather on new growth and the undersides of leaves. They cause leaves to curl, yellow, and stunt the plant's growth.

A telltale sign of aphid infestation is the presence of a sticky substance called honeydew and the subsequent growth of sooty mold. Fruit flies, particularly the Queensland fruit fly, pose another significant threat. These flies lay their eggs in ripening fruit, leading to internal rot.

Signs of fruit fly activity include small puncture marks on the fruit surface and premature fruit drop. Spider mites are another concern, as these minuscule pests feed on plant sap, leading to speckled, discolored leaves and overall plant stress. The presence of fine webbing on leaves and leaf drop are common indicators of spider mite infestation.

To protect passion fruits from pests organically, several effective strategies can be employed. Introducing beneficial insects such as ladybugs, lacewings, and predatory mites can naturally control pest populations. Ladybugs and lacewings are excellent predators of aphids, while predatory mites can help manage spider mite infestations.

These beneficial insects are available for purchase from garden supply stores and can be released into the garden as needed. Another effective method is using natural repellents like neem oil, insecticidal soap, and garlic spray. Neem oil disrupts the life cycle of many pests, including aphids and spider mites, preventing them from feeding and reproducing.

Insecticidal soap is particularly effective against soft-bodied insects like aphids, while garlic spray repels a variety of pests with its strong odor.

Maintaining garden hygiene is crucial for preventing pest infestations. Regularly removing weeds, fallen leaves and other debris from the garden eliminates hiding spots and breeding grounds for pests. Pruning and disposing of infested plant parts can also help limit the spread of pests.

Additionally, practicing crop rotation and planting pest-resistant varieties can reduce the likelihood of severe infestations. Ensuring that plants are well-watered and fertilized supports their overall health, making them less vulnerable to pest attacks.

Regular monitoring and early intervention are essential for managing pests organically. Inspecting plants frequently for signs of pest activity allows you to take action before infestations become severe. Yellow sticky traps can help monitor and reduce populations of flying insects like fruit flies, while hand-picking larger pests and washing plants with a strong jet of water can physically remove pests from the plants.

Protecting Container & Raised Bed Passion Fruits From Diseases

Protecting passion fruits from diseases organically is vital for several reasons. Organic disease control methods help preserve beneficial soil organisms, such as mycorrhizal fungi and earthworms, which play a crucial role in nutrient cycling and soil health. These practices also avoid the introduction of chemical residues that can harm both the plants and the surrounding environment.

By fostering a resilient plant immune system through organic methods, you can enhance the plant's natural defenses against diseases. This approach contributes to a sustainable and eco-friendly gardening practice, ensuring that the garden remains a safe haven for both flora and fauna.

Long-term, organic disease control supports healthier plants and higher fruit quality, reducing the need for repeated chemical treatments. Aligning with the principles of sustainable agriculture, organic disease management fosters a balanced garden ecosystem and encourages a more resilient and productive garden overall.

Passion fruits, whether grown in containers or raised bed gardens, can fall victim to several diseases that threaten their health and productivity. One common disease is Fusarium wilt, caused by the soil-borne fungus Fusarium oxysporum. This disease manifests as yellowing and wilting of leaves, stem rot, and ultimately, plant death. The fungus clogs the plant's vascular system, preventing water and nutrients from reaching essential parts.

Another prevalent disease is anthracnose, caused by the fungus Colletotrichum, leading to dark, sunken lesions on leaves, stems, and fruits. These lesions can cause significant fruit drop and reduce overall yield. Root rot, often caused by various fungal pathogens, including Phytophthora and Pythium species, leads to the decay of the root system, causing stunted growth, yellowing leaves, and plant collapse.

To manage these diseases organically, several strategies can be implemented. Crop rotation is a fundamental practice in preventing the build-up of soil-borne pathogens like Fusarium. By rotating passion fruit with non-host crops, the pathogen's life cycle can be disrupted, reducing disease pressure.

Using disease-resistant passion fruit varieties can also mitigate the risk of Fusarium wilt and other diseases. Selecting cultivars known for their resistance to specific pathogens provides a proactive approach to disease management.

Natural fungicides, such as neem oil and copper-based sprays, can be effective in controlling fungal pathogens like anthracnose. Neem oil has antifungal properties that inhibit fungal growth and can be applied as a preventative measure or at the first sign of infection.

Copper-based sprays work by disrupting the enzyme systems of fungi, thereby preventing their proliferation. These organic fungicides provide a safer alternative to synthetic chemicals, reducing environmental impact while protecting plant health.

Sustainable gardening practices are essential in maintaining overall plant health and preventing disease outbreaks. Proper plant spacing ensures adequate air circulation, reducing the humidity levels that favor fungal growth.

Mulching with organic materials like straw or wood chips helps retain soil moisture and suppresses weeds, but it also acts as a barrier against soil-borne pathogens splashing onto plant foliage. Maintaining soil health through the addition of organic matter and compost enhances the natural microbial balance, promoting a robust root system less susceptible to disease.

Regular monitoring and early detection of disease symptoms are crucial for effective management. Inspecting plants frequently allows for prompt removal of infected plant parts, preventing the spread of pathogens. Ensuring good garden hygiene by cleaning tools and equipment minimizes the risk of cross-contamination. Encouraging beneficial soil microbes through the use of compost teas and mycorrhizal inoculants can further bolster plant defenses against pathogens.

Implementing a holistic approach to disease management involves combining multiple practices to create a resilient garden ecosystem. Watering at the base of the plants rather than overhead reduces leaf wetness, which can deter fungal infections. Intercropping with plants that have known disease-preventative properties, such as marigolds, can create a less favorable environment for pathogens while ensuring proper drainage in containers and raised beds prevents waterlogging conditions that promote root rot.

Focusing on these organic and sustainable methods can protect your passion fruit plants from diseases and foster a healthy and productive garden environment. These practices not only improve immediate plant health and yield but also contribute to the long-term sustainability and ecological balance of the garden.

HARVESTING CONTAINER & RAISED BED PASSION FRUITS

Passion fruits grown in containers and raised bed gardens typically take about 12 to 18 months from planting to reach the stage where they are ready for harvest. The growth stages of the fruit plants begin with the initial planting and establishment phase, which takes about 3 to 4 months. During this time, the plant focuses on developing a strong root system and producing vigorous vine growth.

Following this, the plant enter the flowering stage, usually occurring around 5 to 7 months after planting. The flowers are striking and fragrant, attracting pollinators necessary for fruit set. After successful pollination, the fruit begins to develop and mature, a process that can take another 3 to 6 months depending on the variety and growing conditions.

Determining when passion fruit is ready for harvest involves observing several key indicators. One of the primary signs is a change in the fruit's color. For many varieties, the fruit will transition from green to a deep purple, yellow, or orange shade, depending on the specific type of passion fruit.

Another indicator is the slight wrinkling of the fruit's skin, which suggests that it is ripe and ready to be picked. Additionally, ripe passion fruits often detach naturally from the vine and may drop to the ground. This natural fruit drop is a reliable sign that the fruit has reached optimal ripeness. However, it is essential to pick up these fallen fruits promptly to avoid damage from pests or decay.

Proper harvesting techniques are crucial to ensure that the passion fruit vines remain healthy and continue to produce fruit. When harvesting passion fruit, gently twist or cut the fruit from the vine using a clean pair of pruning shears or scissors. It is important to avoid pulling or yanking the fruit, as this can damage the vine and reduce future yields. Handling the fruit carefully minimizes bruising and maintains its quality. Harvesting should be done regularly, as leaving ripe fruit on the vine for too long can attract pests and diseases.

After harvesting, handling and storage practices are vital to preserve the quality of the passion fruit. Once picked, the fruit should be washed gently to remove any dirt or debris. It is best to store the fruit in a cool, dry place. If the fruit is not immediately consumed, it can be refrigerated to extend its shelf life. Passion fruit can also be frozen or processed into juices, jams, or other products for longer-term storage. To freeze passion fruit, simply scoop out the pulp and place it in airtight containers or freezer bags. Proper post-harvest handling ensures that the fruit retains its flavor, aroma, and nutritional value.

The timing and technique of harvesting passion fruit are critical to achieving a successful and bountiful harvest. Harvesting at the right time ensures that the fruit is at its peak flavor and nutritional content. Using the correct techniques protects the plant from damage, allowing it to continue producing fruit for many seasons.

By following these guidelines, you can enjoy a steady supply of delicious passion fruit while maintaining the health and productivity of their container and raised bed gardens.

CONTAINER & RAISED BEDS PASSION FRUITS NOTES

Start: Seeds or Seedlings.

Germination: 2 – 4 weeks, at temperatures between 70°F and 85°F (21°C to 29°C).

Seed Life: 1– 2 Years.

Soil Type: Well-draining, loamy soil rich in organic matter, with a slightly acidic to neutral pH (around 6.0 to 7.0), amended with compost or well-rotted manure to enhance fertility and moisture retention.

Seed Spacing: Space the seeds an inch apart.

Seedling Spacing:

Containers – In a single large container with a minimum diameter of 18 to 24 inches. Depth of the container should also be at least 12 inches.

Raised Beds – Space the seedlings 8 to 10 feet apart.

Sunlight: 6 – 8hrs full sunlight daily.

Growing Temperatures:

Passion fruit plants thrive best in temperatures between 64°F and 77°F, with optimal growth occurring at around 68°F to 75°F.

Duration Till Harvest:

Passion fruits grown in containers and raised bed gardens typically take about 12 to 18 months from planting to reach the stage where they are ready for harvest.

CHAPTER 12
ACKNOWLEDGEMENTS

We are deeply grateful to the remarkable team at Green Roots. Your vast knowledge, extensive experience, unwavering commitment, and tireless dedication have been instrumental in bringing this book to life. Your collective efforts have not only made this project possible but have also enriched it with unparalleled understanding and practical wisdom.

A special debt of gratitude goes to Charles Craig, Annie Hayford, Jessica Reid, Adam Spencer, Nicole Robinson and Ricardo Costa. Each of you has made invaluable contributions that have significantly shaped the quality and substance of this book. Your expertise, creativity, and diligence have added layers of depth, making it a rich and comprehensive resource for all readers.

The ethos of the Green Roots team is exemplified by your strong desire to make a positive impact in people's lives. Your dedication to developing the community through gardening is truly unmatched. Your passion shines through in every page, reflecting your commitment to sharing your love for gardening with a wider audience.

This book represents the culmination of over 20 years of collective expertise, experience, insight, and passion in the field of gardening. It is a testament to your unwavering dedication to creating a comprehensive resource that caters to gardeners of all levels of experience, from novices to seasoned veterans.

We are extremely proud to have created this book, which stands as a beacon of knowledge and a guide for gardeners worldwide. Our hope is that it will inspire, educate, and empower readers, enhancing their gardening journey and enriching their experiences now and for many years to come.

AFTERWORD

As we reach the conclusion of our journey through the world of fruit containers and raised bed gardening, it is important to reflect on the key takeaways that you will have gained. First and foremost, you will have developed a solid understanding of soil health and its critical role in successful gardening.

Knowledge of soil types, pH levels, and the importance of organic matter will enable you to create the ideal growing conditions for your fruit plants. This foundational knowledge is essential for anyone looking to cultivate a thriving garden, as healthy soil leads to healthy plants.

Another essential skill you will have acquired is the ability to select the right fruit varieties for container and raised bed gardening. Understanding which plants are best suited for these methods and how to properly space and support them will significantly impact the success of your garden.

You will also have learned effective maintenance techniques, such as watering schedules, pruning, and pest management, ensuring your plants remain healthy and productive throughout the growing season. These practical skills are invaluable for gardeners at any level of experience.

We have also highlighted the numerous benefits of fruit container and raised bed gardening, which you can now fully appreciate. Increased accessibility means that whether you have a small balcony, a modest backyard, or a larger outdoor space, you can successfully grow your own fruit.

This flexibility makes gardening more inclusive, enabling people in various living situations to enjoy the rewards of homegrown produce. Additionally, the sustainability aspect of these gardening methods cannot be overstated. By growing your own fruit, you can reduce your carbon footprint, minimize waste, and contribute to a healthier environment.

The personal satisfaction that comes from gardening is another significant takeaway. You will have discovered the joy and fulfillment that comes from nurturing plants and watching them grow. The physical and mental health benefits, such as reduced stress and increased physical activity, add another layer of value to this rewarding hobby. Gardening encourages a closer connection to nature and provides a sense of accomplishment that can be deeply enriching.

Finally, we encourage you to apply the knowledge and skills you have gained to create your own successful fruit container and raised bed gardens. Regardless of your experience level, the insights provided in this book will serve as a valuable guide, inspiring you to explore and experiment with new gardening ideas.

The journey of gardening is one of continuous learning and discovery, and we hope that this book has ignited a passion for growing fruits that will last a lifetime. With the right tools and knowledge, anyone can create a beautiful and productive garden, reaping the benefits for years to come.

"Gardening is not just a hobby, but a way of life" - Green Roots.

ALSO BY GREEN ROOTS

Fruit and Veggies 101 - Container & Raised Beds Vegetable Garden: Gardening Guide On How To Grow Vegetables Using Organic Strategies For Containers & Raised Beds Gardens

Fruit and Veggies 101 - Vegetable Companion Planting : Companion Guide On How To Grow Vegetables Using Essential, Organic & Sustainable Gardening Strategies

Fruit and Veggies 101

VEGETABLE COMPANION PLANTING

Companion Guide On How To Grow Vegetables Using Essential Organic & Sustainable Gardening Strategies

(Perfect For Beginners)

GREEN ROOTS

Fruit and Veggies 101 - Salad Vegetables : Gardening Guide On How To Grow The Freshest & Ripest Salad Vegetables

Fruit and Veggies 101 - Summer Fruits: Gardening Guide On How To Grow The Freshest & Ripest Summer Fruits

Includes - Fruit Salad, Smoothies & Fruit Juices Recipes

Fruit and Veggies 101 - The Winter Harvest: Gardening Guide On How To Grow The Freshest & Ripest Winter Vegetables

GLOSSARY

Anthracnose

A term used to describe a group of fungal diseases that affect a wide variety of plants.

Acidic

Something that forms or becomes acid and has a pH of less than 7.

Allelopathic

Refers to the biological phenomenon where one plant inhibits the growth of another by releasing certain biochemicals into the environment.

Aeration

The act of circulating air through a garden, soil, and plants.

Aged manure

Old manure that has matured through a long period by letting it sit in a container.

Alkaline

Something that contains alkali and has a pH above 7.

Aphids

Tiny insects which consume the liquid plants produce, such as sap.

Aerate

The process of introducing air into the soil to improve its structure and promote root growth.

Alliums

A family of plants that includes onions, garlic, leeks, and chives. They are known for their strong scent, which can deter many pests.

Apiaceae

Also known as the carrot or parsley family, this group includes vegetables like carrots, celery, parsley, and fennel. They are often used in companion planting for their ability to attract beneficial insects.

Bacteria

A microorganism that causes disease and, at other times, improves the well-being of an organism.

Buttoning

A condition affecting certain vegetables, especially those in the cabbage family, like broccoli and cauliflower. Buttoning occurs when these plants form small, button-like heads prematurely instead of developing a single large one.

Botrytis cinerea

A type of fungus that is known for causing a plant disease called "gray mold."

Bacillus subtilis

A species of Gram-positive, rod-shaped bacteria commonly found in soil and the gastrointestinal tract of humans and other animals.

Biostimulants

Substances or microorganisms applied to plants or soils to enhance plant growth, health, and productivity.

Biodegradable

Something that can decompose into the soil and not harm the soil or other living organisms in it.

Bolting

When vegetable crops prematurely run to seed, usually making them unusable

Blunt

Something that is not sharp but softer around its edges and unable to penetrate through something.

Blanch

A method for growing vegetables. A condition in which a plant's young shoots are covered to block light, preventing photosynthesis and the production of chlorophyll, leaving them pale in color.

Bulb

A plant's fruit or organ grows in soil right above its roots and is typically edible when it's a vegetable plant.

Bushy

Something that is overgrown or grows to be dense, big, and has lots of leaves.

Beneficial Insects

Insects that help control pest populations by preying on them or acting as pollinators. Examples include ladybugs, lacewings, and bees.

Brassica

A plant family that includes cabbage, broccoli, kale, and Brussels sprouts. These plants are often companion planted with aromatic herbs or Alliums to deter pests.

Cabbage loopers

An insect or moth tends to be found crawling and laying eggs on cabbages. This insect is a cabbage pest that destroys crops.

Calcium carbonate

Insoluble chalk is natural and white. This is also called ground limestone.

Collar

A round object is used to cuff the base of a plant to protect it from pests such as worms and maggots.

Compaction

The compression of soil particles removes air pockets and hardens the soil. It is considered harmful when gardening and if you want to achieve successful results.

Companion planting

Planting two or more plants next to each other and is protective of each other to avoid disease and pests. It can improve harvest results and improve growth.

Cotyledon

A part of a plant embryo within the seed

Compost

A combination of biodegradable plants, objects, or waste that has been mixed to rot and build up nutrients necessary to soil health and fertility.

Container garden

A garden of plants grown in a pot that holds soil.

Crop rotation

Planting various crops in succession on the same piece of land helps to improve soil health, maximize nutrients, and reduce pest and weed pressure. This practice is known as crop rotation.

Cutworms

A damaging and destructive moth larva is a vegetable pest found in soil and on plants.

Crop Rotation

The practice of growing different types of crops in the same area in sequential seasons to improve soil health and reduce pest and disease problems.

Cucurbitaceae

A plant family that includes squash, cucumber, and melon. These plants often benefit from being planted with corn and beans, a combination known as "Three Sisters."

Debris

Remains or objects in the soil, such as rocks and previously dead crops, need to be removed to maintain the health of your garden.

Drainage

The process by which liquids or water is expelled from something, such as soil.

Drilling tractor

A gardening sowing machine that drills holes into the ground and helps a gardener avoid manual soil drilling to plant his plants.

Exudation

Refers to the process by which a substance is discharged or released from cells or tissues, often through pores or small openings.

Ecosystem

Different biological organisms interact with each other to maintain an environment.

Evaporation

Water that turns into vapor.

Floricanes

The second-year canes of certain types of bramble plants, such as raspberries and blackberries

Fertile soil

Soil that is healthy enough to give plants all nutrients they need to grow successfully until harvest.

Fertilization

Making soil fertile through the use of fertilizers.

Frost

Ice crystals can form on plants when temperatures are freezing or too cold.

Frost Cloth

A covering made of insulation that is positioned over plants, shrubs, trees, and crops to shield them from frost, wind, and chilly weather.

Fungus

Living organisms feed on other living organisms and create mold or discolored plants when present. They can destroy plants and cause disease.

Germinate

When a plant starts to grow out of a shell and form shoots or leaves.

Harvest

A collection of mature and ripe plants and their fruit. It's when your plants have matured, and you collect them from their stems.

Heart rate

How fast or slow are your heartbeats? It's a number or calculation which determines the heart's speed.

Humus

Decomposed organic matter consists of soil and compost.

Hybrid seed

Seeds have been altered and are offspring of two different types of seed varieties of the same plant.

Interplanting

Growing two or more types of plants together in the same space to maximize the use of garden space and enhance productivity.

Leguminosae

Also known as Fabaceae or the legume family, this group includes peas, beans, and lentils. These plants can fix nitrogen from the air into the soil, benefiting other plants grown with them.

Microbiota

The community of microorganisms, including bacteria, viruses, fungi, and archaea, that inhabit a particular environment.

Monilinia fructicola

A species of fungus that is a major plant pathogen, particularly affecting stone fruits like peaches, plums, cherries, and nectarines.

Mesh

A material you lace over your garden plants that protects them from insects and pests.

Minerals

Substances are naturally occurring and are needed to produce fertile soil and healthy plants.

Moisture

Dampness is caused by diffused water or liquid.

Mulch

Decayed matter, such as compost, is placed on the soil's surface to lock moisture in or protect the soil from harsh weather conditions.

Mycorrhizal

A type of symbiotic relationship between fungi and the roots of plants.

Nitrogen

A nutrient is needed to give plants their green color and healthy leaves.

Nutrients

Elements that feed plants the necessary food they need to grow.

Organic matter

Decomposed humus is in the soil and is essential in growing healthy vegetables.

Organic produce

Food that has been made or grown without the use of chemical alterations.

Pathogens

Organisms that cause disease in plants. These can include fungi, bacteria, viruses, nematodes (tiny worm-like creatures), and even certain types of insects.

Pesticides

Organic or chemical substances kill or repel insects and other pests from a garden.

Pests

Living organisms are destructive to a garden and need to be repelled or prevented from reaching plants.

Proliferation

Refers to the rapid increase or spread of something.

Primocanes

The first-year canes or shoots of certain types of perennial plants, particularly brambles like raspberries and blackberries

pH

A chemistry figure which communicates a scale of alkalinity or acidity. It helps you know how alkaline or acidic soil is.

Phosphate

Phosphoric acid is a salt needed for the soil's health.

Potassium

It is a nutrient that helps plants grow and is essential in their life cycle.

Pruning

Maintain a garden by cutting or trimming dead or potentially unwanted parts of a plant.

Pest Control

Methods used to manage and reduce damage from pests, which can include cultural practices, biological control, and organic or synthetic pesticides.

Pseudomonas syringae

A species of bacteria that is known for its role as a plant pathogen

Raised Bed Gardening

A method of gardening where the soil level is raised above the existing ground level, usually enclosed by a frame.

Roots

The bottom stingy and firm bits of a plant grow and stretch into the soil. They absorb the nutrients and water for a plant's needs.

Seedling

A small and recently germinated plant that is ready to be planted.

Soggy

A mushy, soft, and overly damp area such as soil.

Soilless

Matter which seeds can be grown in and is an alternative to soil.

Sowing

The act of planting, drilling, or scattering a seed onto or into the soil to grow.

Sprout

When a plant produces its first shoots or leaves.

Stem

The structure of a plant that supports all its branches, leaves, and fruit.

Suckers

Plant suckers are vigorous vertical growth originating from a plant's root system or lower main stem.

Solanaceae

A plant family that includes tomatoes, peppers, and eggplants. These plants often benefit from being planted with basil or marigold, which can deter certain pests.

Succession Planting

The practice of planting crops in a staggered manner so that as one crop is harvested, another one is ready to take its place.

Taphrina deformans

A fungal pathogen that causes a disease known as peach leaf curl.

Thinning

Separating seedlings clumped together or removing some overcrowded plants from the soil to space out your garden to give others the chance of growing properly.

Transplanting

When you take a plant from one soil, area, or tray into another area or garden, this is also known as replanting it into another space.

Trap Crop

A plant that is used to attract pests away from the main crop. The pests are then easier to control on the trap crop.

Trichoderma harzianum

A species of fungus known for its beneficial properties in agriculture and horticulture

Weed Control

Methods used to manage and reduce the growth of weeds, which can compete with crops for light, water, and nutrients. This can include mulching, hand weeding, and using weed-suppressing plants.

BIBLIOGRAPHY

Admin, W. (2023a, October 27). *Biodiversity helps Control Pests — Deep Roots Project*. Deep Roots Project. https://www.deep-roots-project.org/grow-your-own-food-all/biodiversity-is-an-important-drp-focus

Admin, W. (2023b, October 27). *Optimizing Sunlight — Deep Roots Project*. Deep Roots Project. https://www.deep-roots-project.org/grow-your-own-food-all/optimizing-sunlight

Administrator. (2024, July 5). *How often to water Vegetable Garden: The Ultimate guide | WATER*. WATER. https://www.watermedia.org/how-often-to-water-vegetable-garden

AgTec White Vinyl Raised Garden Bed - 4ft x 4ft. (n.d.). Agriculture Solutions LLC. https://www.agriculturesolutions.com/agtec-white-vinyl-raised-garden-bed-4ft-x-4ft/

Alabama Cooperative Extension System. (2023a, July 26). *Garden Bugs: Insect pest management in home Vegetable Gardens - Alabama Cooperative Extension System*. https://www.aces.edu/blog/topics/lawn-garden/garden-bugs-insect-pest-management-in-home-vegetable-gardens/

Alabama Cooperative Extension System. (2023b, July 26). *Garden Bugs: Insect pest management in home Vegetable Gardens - Alabama Cooperative Extension System*. https://www.aces.edu/blog/topics/lawn-garden/garden-bugs-insect-pest-management-in-home-vegetable-gardens/

Amazon.com: PASAMIC Durable Vinyl Raised Garden Bed, 4x4x1ft Raised Bed for Gardening, Planter Box with Open Bottom, Raised Garden Bed Outdoor, DIY Above Ground Garden Bed for Fruit, Vegetables, Herbs : Patio, Lawn & Garden. (n.d.-a). My Book

Amazon.com: PASAMIC Durable Vinyl Raised Garden Bed, 4x4x1ft Raised Bed for Gardening, Planter Box with Open Bottom, Raised Garden Bed Outdoor, DIY Above Ground Garden Bed for Fruit, Vegetables, Herbs : Patio, Lawn & Garden. (n.d.-b). My Book

An Interview with a Home Grower Using Hydroponic Systems. (2023, July 24). *Mister Duda*. https://misterduda.com/25676-an-interview-with-a-home-grower-using-hydroponic-systems-41/

Attracting birds to your landscape | Gardener's Supply. (2024a, March 11). www.gardeners.com. https://www.gardeners.com/how-to/raised-beds-benefits/5029.html

Attracting birds to your landscape | Gardener's Supply. (2024b, March 11).

www.gardeners.com. https://www.gardeners.com/how-to/raised-beds-benefits/5029.html

Attracting birds to your landscape | Gardener's Supply. (2024c, March 11). www.gardeners.com. https://www.gardeners.com/how-to/raised-beds-benefits/5029.html

Bahr, S. (2022, June 16). *What is Soilless Potting Mix?* Lawn Care Blog | Lawn Love. https://lawnlove.com/blog/soilless-potting-mix/

Beaulieu, D. (2022, September 12). *What are loamy soils?* The Spruce. https://www.thespruce.com/loamy-soils-why-gardeners-love-them-2131083

Be.Green. (n.d.). *Find out what light and water requirements your fruit tree. . .* https://be.green/en/blog/find-out-what-light-and-water-requirements-your-fruit-tree

Berry bushes for sale | Strawberries, blueberries & more - PlantingTree. (2020, January 2). PlantingTree. https://www.plantingtree.com/collections/berries

Building raised beds – gardening solutions. (n.d.). https://gardeningsolutions.ifas.ufl.edu/design/types-of-gardens/building-raised-beds.html

Bulletin #2761, Container Gardening Series: Gardening in Small Spaces - Cooperative Extension Publications - University of Maine Cooperative Extension. (2024a, May 23). Cooperative Extension Publications. https://extension.umaine.edu/publications/2761e/

Bulletin #2761, Container Gardening Series: Gardening in Small Spaces - Cooperative Extension Publications - University of Maine Cooperative Extension. (2024b, May 23). Cooperative Extension Publications. https://extension.umaine.edu/publications/2761e/

Burgard, D. (2022, April 7). *Stylish raised bed ideas - Fine Gardening.* Fine Gardening. https://www.finegardening.com/project-guides/fruits-and-vegetables/stylish-raised-beds

Butterfield, M. (2021, March 19). *Raised garden beds – Wood or stone? Help me decide.* One Hundred Dollars a Month. https://www.onehundreddollarsamonth.com/raised-garden-beds-wood-or-stone-help-me-decide/

Citrus Trees for sale | BrighterBlooms.com. (n.d.-a). BrighterBlooms.com. https://www.brighterblooms.com/collections/citrus-trees

Citrus Trees for sale | BrighterBlooms.com. (n.d.-b). BrighterBlooms.com. https://www.brighterblooms.com/collections/citrus-trees

Citrus trees for sale | Semi-Dwarf citrus trees for sale. (n.d.-a). Four Winds Growers. https://www.fourwindsgrowers.com/collections/citrus-trees

Citrus trees for sale | Semi-Dwarf citrus trees for sale. (n.d.-b). Four Winds Growers. https://www.fourwindsgrowers.com/collections/citrus-trees

CLASSIC 4x4x11 Garden bed. (n.d.-a). Vita. https://wearevita.com/products/4x4x11-classic-garden-bed

CLASSIC 4x4x11 Garden bed. (n.d.-b). Vita. https://wearevita.com/products/4x4x11-classic-garden-bed

Composting. (n.d.). USDA. https://www.usda.gov/peoples-garden/food-access-food-waste/composting

Composting 101. (2024a, March 26). https://www.nrdc.org/stories/composting-101

Composting 101. (2024b, March 26). https://www.nrdc.org/stories/composting-101

Composting at home | US EPA. (2024, September 27). US EPA. https://www.epa.gov/recycle/composting-home

County, G. SM. V. O. B. (2016a, August 27). *Integrated Pest Management Encourages Vegetable Gardening without Pesticides, Part Two.* NC State Extension Master Gardener Volunteers of Buncombe County. https://www.buncombemastergardener.org/vegetable-gardening-pesticides-integrated-pest-management-practice-part/

County, G. SM. V. O. B. (2016b, August 27). *Integrated Pest Management Encourages Vegetable Gardening without Pesticides, Part Two.* NC State Extension Master Gardener Volunteers of Buncombe County. https://www.buncombemastergardener.org/vegetable-gardening-pesticides-integrated-pest-management-practice-part/

David, David, & David. (2023, February 14). *Vertical gardening for plant cultivation in South Africa.* Agrolearner.com - Farming With Precision! https://agrolearner.com/vertical-gardening-for-plant-cultivation-in-south-africa/

Design from Patterns to Details: Decode Nature's Blueprints! – Permaculture Solutions. (n.d.). https://permaculturesolutions.uk/principles-ethics/design-from-patterns-to-details-decode-natures-blueprints/

Diffenderfer, D. (n.d.). *Steps to controlling insect pests in the garden.* https://extension.psu.edu/steps-to-controlling-insect-pests-in-the-garden

Direct or indirect sunlight, which one is better for fruit plants? (n.d.). Quora. https://www.quora.com/Direct-or-indirect-sunlight-which-one-is-better-for-fruit-plants

Do indoor plants need drainage? (2024a, January 29). uBloomd. https://ubloomd.com/blogs/news/do-indoor-plants-need-drainage

Do indoor plants need drainage? (2024b, January 29). uBloomd. https://ubloomd.com/blogs/news/do-indoor-plants-need-drainage

Double digging / RHS. (n.d.). Royal Horticultural Society. https://www.rhs.org.uk/advice/profile?PID=133

Eartheasy. (n.d.-a). *Control pests naturally in your raised garden beds – Eartheasy.* https://learn.eartheasy.com/guides/control-pests-naturally-in-your-raised-garden-beds/

Eartheasy. (n.d.-b). *Control pests naturally in your raised garden beds – Eartheasy.*

https://learn.eartheasy.com/guides/control-pests-naturally-in-your-raised-garden-beds/

Everglades Farm. (n.d.). *How to keep your plants Hydrated.* https://everglades.farm/pages/hydration

Explore Cornell - Home Gardening - Introduction. (n.d.-a). http://www.gardening.cornell.edu/homegardening/

Explore Cornell - Home Gardening - Introduction. (n.d.-b). http://www.gardening.cornell.edu/homegardening/

Fabric raised bed sizes 4x4, 4x8, 4x16 and 6x16. (n.d.-a). https://greenerhydroponics.com/Fabric-Raised-Beds_c_1089.html

Fabric raised bed sizes 4x4, 4x8, 4x16 and 6x16. (n.d.-b). https://greenerhydroponics.com/Fabric-Raised-Beds_c_1089.html

Fabric raised garden Bed FAQ. (n.d.-a). Back to the Roots. https://backtotheroots.com/pages/fabric-raised-garden-bed-faq

Fabric raised garden Bed FAQ. (n.d.-b). Back to the Roots. https://backtotheroots.com/pages/fabric-raised-garden-bed-faq

Farr, J. (2023, May 31). *It's Hot! Your Plants Are Thirsty.* Wasson Nursery. https://wassonnursery.com/2023/05/31/its-hot-your-plants-are-thirsty/

Fast-Growing-Trees.com. (n.d.). *Lemon-Lime Citrus Bush.* https://www.fast-growing-trees.com/products/lemon-lime-citrus-bush

Fast-Growing-Trees.com. (2024, September 27). *Citrus Trees for sale | Fast-GrowingTrees.com.* https://www.fast-growing-trees.com/collections/citrus-trees

Ferry-Morse. (n.d.). *Ferry-Morse Raised White Garden Bed 4ft. x 4ft.* https://ferrymorse.com/products/ferry-morse-raised-white-garden-bed-4ft-x-4ft

Francis, Francis, & Francis. (2023, April 28). *Gardening hobby: Cultivating health and happiness.* Greatsenioryears - Greatsenioryears. https://greatsenioryears.com/gardening-hobby-cultivating-health-and-happiness/

Freudenrich, C., PhD, & Hall-Geisler, K. (2023, November 9). *What is compost? How to start composting at home.* HowStuffWorks. https://home.howstuffworks.com/composting.htm

Gail. (2023a, April 6). *7 Benefits of raised bed gardening.* National Garden Bureau. https://ngb.org/raised-bed-gardening-benefits/

Gail. (2023b, April 6). *7 Benefits of raised bed gardening.* National Garden Bureau. https://ngb.org/raised-bed-gardening-benefits/

Gail. (2023c, April 6). *7 Benefits of raised bed gardening.* National Garden Bureau. https://ngb.org/raised-bed-gardening-benefits/

Gail. (2023d, April 6). *7 Benefits of raised bed gardening.* National Garden Bureau. https://ngb.org/raised-bed-gardening-benefits/

Gardener, E. (2023a, August 28). *Benefits of container gardening.* ECOgardener. https://ecogardener.com/blogs/news/benefits-of-container-gardening

Gardener, E. (2023b, August 28). *Benefits of container gardening.* ECOgardener.

https://ecogardener.com/blogs/news/benefits-of-container-gardening

Gardening tasks & How tos. (2023, June 6). The Spruce. https://www.thes pruce.com/tips-for-raised-bed-gardening-1402180

Gardens_Nursery. (2023, May 13). How to plant fruit trees in containers | GARDENS NURSERY. *GARDENS NURSERY.* https://gardensnursery. com/how-to-plant-fruit-trees-in-containers/

Geopot. (n.d.-a). *GeoPlanter fabric raised beds.* https://geopot.com/products/ geoplanter-fabric-raised-bed

Geopot. (n.d.-b). *GeoPlanter fabric raised beds.* https://geopot.com/products/ geoplanter-fabric-raised-bed

Grant, A. (2021, November 23). *Stone fruit varieties: Growing stone fruit in the garden.* Gardeningknowhow. https://www.gardeningknowhow.com/ edible/fruits/fegen/what-is-stone-fruit.htm

Grant, G. (2023, December 21). *Growing blackberries in East Texas.* The Arbor Gate. https://arborgate.com/blog/gregs-ramblings/growing-blackber ries-in-east-texas/

Green manures | RHS. (n.d.-a). Royal Horticultural Society. https://www.rhs. org.uk/advice/profile?pid=373

Green manures | RHS. (n.d.-b). Royal Horticultural Society. https://www.rhs. org.uk/advice/profile?pid=373

Greenlivingguy. (2023, May 14). *How Companion Planting works Better than Pesticides.* Green Guy, Green Living, Electric Vehicle Consultants, Compa nies, Car Expert, Electric Car News, New York, California, Florida, Missouri, Texas, Nevada. https://greenlivingguy.com/2017/09/how-companion-planting-works-better-than-pesticides/

Grow, S. (2023, January 29). *What is Potting Soil? The Ultimate Guide to Growing Healthy Plants.* Simple Grow. https://www.simplegrow.com/pages/ what-is-potting-soil

Growing fruit in raised beds. (2015, March 3). Growing Fruit. https://grow ingfruit.org/t/growing-fruit-in-raised-beds/353

Growing in a raised Garden bed versus In-Ground Gardening • Gardenary. (n.d.-a). https://www.gardenary.com/blog/growing-in-a-raised-garden-bed-versus-in-ground-gardening

Growing in a raised Garden bed versus In-Ground Gardening • Gardenary. (n.d.-b). https://www.gardenary.com/blog/growing-in-a-raised-garden-bed-versus-in-ground-gardening

Growing stone fruits in the home garden. (n.d.). UMN Extension. https://exten sion.umn.edu/fruit/growing-stone-fruits-home-garden

Hassani, N. (2024a, May 2). *The difference between potting soil and potting mix.* The Spruce. https://www.thespruce.com/difference-between-potting-soil-potting-mix-847812

Hassani, N. (2024b, May 2). *The difference between potting soil and potting mix.*

The Spruce. https://www.thespruce.com/difference-between-potting-soil-potting-mix-847812

Hayden, L. (2023, October 16). *How to take care of banana Tree: A Step-by-Step Guide*. Kansas City Tree Care. https://kansas-city-tree.com/how-to-take-care-of-banana-tree/

Hayes, V. E. (2023, August 23). Most delicious and best tomatoes for containers to grow. *Gardenings A to Z*. https://gardeningsaz.com/best-tomatoes-for-containers-to-grow/

Heft, T. (2024a, May 30). *What is Soilless Potting Mix?* Big Blog of Gardening. https://www.bigblogofgardening.com/what-is-soilless-potting-mix/

Heft, T. (2024b, May 30). *What is Soilless Potting Mix?* Big Blog of Gardening. https://www.bigblogofgardening.com/what-is-soilless-potting-mix/

Home Composting - Turn Your Spoils into Soil. (n.d.). CT.gov - Connecticut's Official State Website. https://portal.ct.gov/DEEP/Waste-Management-and-Disposal/Organics-Recycling/Home-Composting---Turn-Your-Spoils-into-Soil

Home Vegetable Garden Insect Pest Control - Oklahoma State University. (2016a, October 1). https://extension.okstate.edu/fact-sheets/home-vegetable-garden-insect-pest-control.html

Home Vegetable Garden Insect Pest Control - Oklahoma State University. (2016b, October 1). https://extension.okstate.edu/fact-sheets/home-vegetable-garden-insect-pest-control.html

Homemade weed Killer. (2023, August 8). *Recipe & Instructions*. https://www.fertilizewithalm.com/blog/homemade-weed-killer

Iannotti, M. (2024a, August 13). *What is Loam soil?* The Spruce. https://www.thespruce.com/what-is-loam-1401908

Iannotti, M. (2024b, August 13). *What is Loam soil?* The Spruce. https://www.thespruce.com/what-is-loam-1401908

Ideas, T. (2024a, July 22). DIY Wattle raised garden Bed: 5 easy steps. *DIY projects for everyone!* https://diyprojects.ideas2live4.com/2016/01/13/how-to-make-a-wattle-raised-garden-bed/

Ideas, T. (2024b, July 22). DIY Wattle raised garden Bed: 5 easy steps. *DIY projects for everyone!* https://diyprojects.ideas2live4.com/2016/01/13/how-to-make-a-wattle-raised-garden-bed/

Jackson, L. K., Williamson, J. G., & Horticultural Sciences Department, UF/IFAS Extension. (n.d.). *Growing fruit crops in containers*. https://www.lsuagcenter.com/~/media/system/5/5/6/4/55646c0e-f9404ad2073c46b006e13b51/growing%20fruit%20crops%20in%20contain-ers%20-%20uflpdf.pdf

Johnston, P. (2024, August 13). *Best square Foot Garden Layouts: Ideas for Maximum yield*. The Herb Prof. https://theherbprof.com/best-square-foot-garden-layouts-ideas-for-maximum-yield/

jp-rose-spacing. (n.d.). Jackson & Perkins. https://www.jacksonandperkins. com/how-to-choose-the-right-container-for-your-plants/a/513/

Judy, Judy, & Judy. (2023, December 27). *How to choose the right pergola materials for your Seattle home.* Seattle Pergola Company - Seattle Pergola Company. https://pergolaseattle.com/how-to-choose-the-right-pergola-materials-for-your-seattle-home/

Kellogggarden. (2022a, May 1). Raised bed garden tips for growing large fruits and vegetables. *Kellogg Garden Organics^{TM}.* https://kellogggarden. com/blog/gardening/raised-bed-garden-tips-for-growing-large-fruits-and-vegetables/

Kellogggarden. (2022b, May 1). Raised bed garden tips for growing large fruits and vegetables. *Kellogg Garden Organics^{TM}.* https://kellogggarden. com/blog/gardening/raised-bed-garden-tips-for-growing-large-fruits-and-vegetables/

Lemon-Lime Citrus Bush. (n.d.). BrighterBlooms.com. https://www. brighterblooms.com/products/lemon-lime-citrus-bush

Lerner, R. (2017, March 1). *What is Loam?* Indiana Yard and Garden - Purdue Consumer Horticulture. https://www.purdue.edu/hla/sites/ yardandgarden/what-is-loam/

oam. (2024). In *Merriam-Webster Dictionary.* https://www.merriam-webster. com/dictionary/loam

Lohmiller, G. a. B. (2024, February 21). *Stone Fruit: How to grow your own.* Almanac.com. https://www.almanac.com/stone-fruit-how-grow-your-own

McInerney, B. (2024, September 4). *Identifying the warning signs of overwatering trees.* GoTreeQuotes. https://www.gotreequotes.com/identifying-the-warning-signs-of-overwatering-trees/

Megan, E. (2022, December 24). *30 Best "Raised Garden Bed" ideas that won't break the budget.* https://craftydaily.com/raised-garden-bed/

My tiered wattle garden beds (projects forum at permies). (n.d.). https://permies. com/t/202212/permaculture/tiered-wattle-garden-beds

Nick. (2023, August 8). *Why do apple trees have to be grafted.* Tree Fluent. https://treefluent.com/why-do-apple-trees-have-to-be-grafted/

Nolan, T. (2019, November 13). *Fabric raised beds: The perks of growing fruit and vegetables in these versatile containers.* Savvy Gardening. https://savvygar dening.com/fabric-raised-beds/

Nolan, T. (2023a, December 18). *Benefits of raised garden beds: Grow a healthy vegetable garden anywhere.* Savvy Gardening. https://savvygardening. com/benefits-of-raised-garden-beds/

Nolan, T. (2023b, December 18). *Benefits of raised garden beds: Grow a healthy vegetable garden anywhere.* Savvy Gardening. https://savvygardening. com/benefits-of-raised-garden-beds/

Oak, M. (2023a, May 27). How long does it take for garden peas to grow - Tiny home ideas. *Tiny Home Ideas.* https://tinyhomesideas.com/how-long-does-it-take-for-garden-peas-to-grow/

Oak, M. (2023b, May 27). How to build container Garden - tiny home ideas. *Tiny Home Ideas.* https://tinyhomesideas.com/how-to-build-container-garden/

One Green World. (n.d.). *Fruiting Shrubs - One Green world.* https://onegreen world.com/product-category/fruiting-shrubs/

Pacheco, E. (2023, June 26). *Transplanting Raspberry Bushes: A Step-by-Step Guide.* ShunCy. https://shuncy.com/article/how-transplant-raspberry-bushes

Patricia. (2023, July 6). *Small yard, Big Potential: Ways to maximize Outdoor space.* 9HowTo.com - Guides for Home Devices, Family Life Hacks, Discoveries and More. https://9howto.com/small-yard-big-potential-ways-to-maximize-4145.html

Photographer, J. L. G. W. &. (2022, September 15). *Potting Soil 101: How to choose the right potting mix for your plants.* GardenDesign.com. https://www.gardendesign.com/how-to/potting-soil.html

Planet Natural. (2023, August 7). *What is Compost?* | *Planet Natural.* https://www.planetnatural.com/composting-101/soil-science/what-is-compost/

Planet Natural. (2024, July 16). *Organic Gardening since 1991* | *Planet Natural Garden Supply.* https://www.planetnatural.com/composting-101/making/compost-pests/

Plantsadmin, & Plantsadmin. (2023, August 23). *Determining the right amount of water* | *Tropical Office Plant Rental DC MD VA.* Plants Alive! | Helping Plants and People Get Along. https://plants-alive.com/determining-the-right-amount-of-water-2/

Pots, S. (2022a, March 4). *Raised bed gardening made easy.* Smart Pot®. https://smartpots.com/raised-bed-gardening-made-easy/

Pots, S. (2022b, March 4). *Raised bed gardening made easy.* Smart Pot®. https://smartpots.com/raised-bed-gardening-made-easy/

PP-221/PP145: *Petiole (Rachis) Blight of palm.* (n.d.). Ask IFAS - Powered by EDIS. https://edis.ifas.ufl.edu/pp145

Preventing pests in your yard and garden. (n.d.). UMN Extension. https://exten sion.umn.edu/how/preventing-pests-your-yard-and-garden

Raised bed gardening. (n.d.). Extension | West Virginia University. https://extension.wvu.edu/lawn-gardening-pests/gardening/creative-garden ing/raised-bed-gardening

Raised bed gardening | *UGA Extension – Madison County.* (2021, April 12). https://site.extension.uga.edu/madison/2021/04/raised-bed-garden ing/

Raised Garden Bed/Hugel Between Fruit Trees--Is It a Good Idea? (forest garden

forum at permies). (n.d.-a). https://www.permies.com/t/50364/Raised-Garden-Bed-Hugel-Fruit

Raised Garden Bed/Hugel Between Fruit Trees--Is It a Good Idea? (forest garden forum at permies). (n.d.-b). https://www.permies.com/t/50364/Raised-Garden-Bed-Hugel-Fruit

Richards, S. (2023, August 2). How to compost for your garden? - WormsKill-Waste. *WormsKillWaste.* https://wormskillwaste.com/how-to-compost-for-your-garden/

Robinson, A. (2023, April 25). *Gardening has always been a popular hobby for people all over the world : Garden Street.* Garden Street. https://www.garden street.eu/gardening-has-always-been-a-popular-hobby-for-people-all-over-the-world/

Ron. (2023, July 30). *How to grow in a raised bed Garden: a comprehensive guide.* Garden Fresh to Table. https://gardenfreshtotable.com/how-to-grow-in-a-raised-bed-garden-a-comprehensive-guide/

Santoni, S., & Santoni, S. (2021a, January 13). *my kitchen garden, wattle fencing and a happy dog.* MY FRENCH COUNTRY HOME. https://sharonsantoni.com/2020/06/my-kitchen-garden-wattle-fencing-and-a-happy-dog/

Santoni, S., & Santoni, S. (2021b, January 13). *my kitchen garden, wattle fencing and a happy dog.* MY FRENCH COUNTRY HOME. https://sharonsantoni.com/2020/06/my-kitchen-garden-wattle-fencing-and-a-happy-dog/

Seven Habits for Organic Gardening | Gardener's Supply. (2024, March 13). www.gardeners.com. https://www.gardeners.com/how-to/managing-garden-pests-diseases/5064.html

Smart Gardening: Integrated pest management in vegetable gardens - Gardening in Michigan. (n.d.). Gardening in Michigan. https://www.canr.msu.edu/news/ipm_smart_pest_management_for_the_vegetable_garden

Storey, A. (2018, December 26). *How to use and mix your own Soilless potting mix for hydroponics - Upstart University.* Upstart University. https://university.upstartfarmers.com/blog/mix-your-own-soilless-potting-mix-hydroponics

Sweetser, R. (2024, May 13). *Vegetable container gardening for beginners.* Almanac.com. https://www.almanac.com/content/container-gardening-vegetables

Taste, J. A. (2024, September 2). 10 Best vegetables for raised beds (2024 Update) - Just a taste. *Just A Taste.* https://www.just-a-taste.com/best-vegetables-for-raised-beds/

Taste.com.au. (2019, October 16). *Vine fruits.* www.taste.com.au. https://www.taste.com.au/quick-easy/articles/vine-fruits/qqby6jqp

Taylor, L. H. (2022, April 25). *Where to find cheap plants—12 places to look.* The Spruce. https://www.thespruce.com/benefits-of-growing-your-own-berries-1388590

The Editors of Encyclopaedia Britannica. (2024, August 9). *Loam ǀ soil*. Encyclopedia Britannica. https://www.britannica.com/science/loam

The most common grow room bugs and diseases. (2024, February 28). *Canada Grow Supplies*. https://canadagrowsupplies.com/blogs/main/the-most-common-grow-room-pests-and-diseases

Tilley, N. (2022, February 19). *Dwarf Fruit Trees - a planting guide for fruit trees in containers*. Gardeningknowhow. https://www.gardeningknowhow.com/edible/fruits/fegen/dwarf-fruit-trees-a-planting-guide-for-fruit-trees-in-containers.htm

Tilley, N., & Barnett, T. (2024a, March 1). *Soilless Potting mix: What is it and how to make your own*. Gardeningknowhow. https://www.gardeningknowhow.com/garden-how-to/soil-fertilizers/soilless-growing-mediums.htm

Tilley, N., & Barnett, T. (2024b, March 1). *Soilless Potting mix: What is it and how to make your own*. Gardeningknowhow. https://www.gardeningknowhow.com/garden-how-to/soil-fertilizers/soilless-growing-mediums.htm

Topsoil ǀ geology. (n.d.). Encyclopedia Britannica. https://www.britannica.com/science/topsoil

Triangle Gardener LLC. (2020, September 1). *Making Woven Wattle Edging ǀ Triangle Gardener Magazine*. Triangle Gardener Magazine. https://www.trianglegardener.com/making-woven-wattle-edging/

Understanding soil types for vegetable gardens. (2010, November 5). GrowVeg. https://www.growveg.com/guides/understanding-soil-types-for-vegetable-gardens/

Université de Montréal & Département de Biochimie et Médecine Moléculaire, Faculté de Médecine. (2023). Microbial endophytes and their interactions with cranberry plants. In *Université De Montréal* [Thesis]. https://papyrus.bib.umontreal.ca/xmlui/bitstream/1866/28567/2/Bustaman te_Villalobos_Peniel_2023_memoire.pdf

Using compost ǀ StopWaste - Home, work, school. (n.d.). https://www.stopwaste.org/at-work/landscape-design/compost-mulch-for-healthier-soil/using-compost

Waddington, E. (2022, October 12). *20 fruit canes or bushes to plant in fall*. Rural Sprout. https://www.ruralsprout.com/fruit-canes-bushes/

Walliser, J. (2019a, January 23). *Preventing pests in your garden: 5 strategies for success*. Savvy Gardening. https://savvygardening.com/preventing-pests-in-your-garden/

Walliser, J. (2019b, January 23). *Preventing pests in your garden: 5 strategies for success*. Savvy Gardening. https://savvygardening.com/preventing-pests-in-your-garden/

Wayside Gardens. (2023, June 22). *Citrus Trees Plants ǀ Grow Orange, Lemon, and more*. Main Website. https://www.waysidegardens.com/edibles/citrus-trees.html

Weidner, C. (2024, August 29). *How much sun do fruit trees need?* Nature Hills Nursery. https://www.naturehills.com/blog/post/how-much-sun-do-fruit-trees-need

What are some fruits that grow on trees and shrubs but not on vines? (n.d.). Quora. https://www.quora.com/What-are-some-fruits-that-grow-on-trees-and-shrubs-but-not-on-vines

What are the differences between potting soil, topsoil, and garden soil? (n.d.). Quora. https://www.quora.com/What-are-the-differences-between-potting-soil-topsoil-and-garden-soil

What is a soilless potting mix? (n.d.-a). Quora. https://www.quora.com/What-is-a-soilless-potting-mix

What is a soilless potting mix? (n.d.-b). Quora. https://www.quora.com/What-is-a-soilless-potting-mix

Wikipedia contributors. (2024a, May 10). *Loam*. Wikipedia. https://en.wikipedia.org/wiki/Loam

Wikipedia contributors. (2024b, June 17). *Potting soil*. Wikipedia. https://en.wikipedia.org/wiki/Potting_soil

Wikipedia contributors. (2024c, August 31). *Grape*. Wikipedia. https://en.wikipedia.org/wiki/Grape

Winter Care Guide – Jeffrey Younggren. (2023, August 25). https://jeffreyyounggren.com/category/bearded-dragon/health-care/winter-care-guide/

Writers, S. F. (n.d.). *Greenhouse Coverings- What are the Differences?* https://www.solawrapfilms.com/greenhouse-plastic-blog/greenhouse-coverings-what-are-the-differences

Yarden.com. (2024, September 27). *Citrus Trees for sale | Dwarf citrus trees for sale | Yarden.com*. Yarden. https://www.yarden.com/

Zheng, L. (2023, November 22). 5 Surprising ways to use aluminum foil around the house - Yongsheng Aluminum Industry Co., Ltd. *Aluminum Stock Supplier*. https://aluminumstock.com/5-surprising-ways-to-use-aluminum-foil-around-the-house/

virginijavaidakaviciene via Canva

Yuliia Bilousova from Getty Images Signature via Canva

huePhotography from Getty Images Signature via Canva

hmproudlove from Getty Images Signature via Canva

lzf from Getty Images via Canva

Taras_Bulba from Getty Images via Canva

PavelRodimov from Getty Images via Canva

lesichkadesign via Canva

nitrub from Getty Images via Canva

Yuliya Ivanova from Getty Images via Canva

BIBLIOGRAPHY

Irina Vodneva from Getty Images via Canva
Nuture from Getty Images via Canva
fiota from Getty Images via Canva
OLEKSANDR KOZACHOK from Getty Images via Canva
konstantinks from Getty Images via Canva
Mafphoto from Getty Images via Canva
MariuszBlach from Getty Images via Canva
srdjan111 from Getty Images Signature via Canva
CaroleGomez from Getty Images Signature via Canva
pixelshot via Canva
flockine from pixabay via Canva
nelic from Getty Images via Canva
NinaMalyna from Getty Images Pro via Canva
Zdeno_Kajzr from Getty Images via Canva
filo from Getty Images Signature via Canva
Tatiana Terekhina from Getty Images via Canva
DVrcan from Getty Images via Canva
Stopboxstudio from Getty Images via Canva
Tonelson from Getty Images via Canva
Heidi Patricola from Getty Images via Canva
P Hans from pixabay via Canva
Leung Cho Pan via Canva
bluegame from Getty Images via Canva
FunTravelGal from Getty Images via Canva
matteodestefano from Getty Images Signature via Canva
Irfanmnur from Getty Images via Canva
Jobrestful from Getty Images via Canva
asiandelight from Getty Images via Canva
slpu9945 from Getty Images via Canva

Cover Design by Freepix